EDUCATION
Understanding the Learner

EDUCATION

Understanding the Learner

Editors

Sarita Kumari

D.S. Srivastava

ISHA BOOKS

DELHI-110 033

Education: Understanding the Learner

ISBN: 81-8205-156-8

Reprinted in 2012 in India by
Isha Publications
B-69, New Gupta Colony
Near DDA Market
Delhi-110009

Printed at: G. Print Process, Delhi

PREFACE

Just as there are differences in personality, there are differences in the ways that students learn and use information. Some students are quiet and tend to be reflective in the way they process information. Others are "take charge" kinds of people who need to put information to immediate use and to solve problems. Just as they have different preferences and ways of learning, they also change and adjust their learning strategies based on their own development and on the different learning situations in which they find themselves.

The role of the teacher is to facilitate deep learning by setting a positive climate for learning, clarifying the purposes of the learners, organising and making available learning resources, balancing intellectual and emotional components of learning and sharing feelings and thoughts with learners. Learning is facilitated when the student participates and directly confronts problems and discover things for themselves with the teacher only providing guidance and help when mistakes are made. Significant learning can take place when the subject matter is relevant to the personal interests of the student.

The insights into how students learn, their conception of learning, differences in learning styles and backgrounds of students and the factors associated with the approaches they take can assist the teacher in planning teaching strategies. The teacher must ensure that he/she is providing variety and enthusiasm. As such, strategies such as case studies, role playing, simulations and self-evaluation are useful. Students need to be less burdened with detail and given the ability to see the overview and linkages. All in all, a positive learning environment needs to be created with some degree of freedom for the students.

The present book is a study of the major psychological variables that influence learning in schools, and their applications to teaching. Theories and systems of learning and major developmental processes are addressed. Group and individual differences are examined, including cultural aspects of learning and learners with special needs. Practices associated with effective teaching, including classroom management and valid assessment of student learning, are also major topics of this work. Particular emphasis is placed on principles of learning and those conditions within classrooms that influence learning.

Editor

Contents

	Preface	*v*
1.	Introduction	1
2.	Understanding the Learner in the Light of Interest	27
3.	Under Standing the Learner in the Light of Needs	100
4.	Understanding the Learner in the light of Individual	150
5.	Understanding the Learner in the Light of Differences	186
6.	Personality Development with a Special Reference of Freud's Theory	221
7.	Learning in a New Era	248
	Index	302

1

INTRODUCTION

The power of self-understanding is central to overcoming difficulties in learning. Listen to the thoughts of students who are willing to meet the challenges of learning because they have begun to develop an understanding of themselves and how their minds work.

BETTER UNDERSTANDING OF LEARNER NEEDS

A major goal of the institutional planning process is to gain an understanding of the needs of the learners. Understanding the learner involves:

- identifying features of the learner's past and present experience and respecting the influence of these features on the learner's personal development;
- recognising factors-such as location, gender, ethnicity, ability, disability, and socioeconomic and political circumstances - that place the learner within power relationships in the learning context as well as in society;
- recognising and supporting each learner's motivation and capacity to challenge and change his or her current circumstances;
- promoting continuity of experience by identifying, valuing, linking to, and extending from, prior knowledge and experience;

— taking into account relevance and meaning for the learner;
— identifying and catering for the needs, interests and abilities of individual learners and groups of learners;
— recognising and addressing the expectations and aspirations of the learner;
— recognising the impact of others' expectations on the learner;
— promoting the creative potential of each learner;
— recognising an individual's preferred learning styles, and promoting the development of other learning styles;
— recognising and supporting the holistic development of the learner intellectually, emotionally, socially, physically, ethically and spiritually.

Knowing Oneself as a Learner

Just as there are differences in personality, there are differences in the ways that we learn and use information. Some people are quiet and tend to be reflective in the way they process information. Others are "take charge" kinds of people who need to put information to immediate use and to solve problems. Just as we have different preferences and ways of learning, we also change and adjust our learning strategies based on our own development and on the different learning situations in which we find ourselves. By understanding ourselves and becoming more aware of these differences, we become more capable of adjusting to new situations throughout our lifetime as learners.

Metacognition or "self- knowing" includes the following aspects of understanding our "learning" selves:

— Knowing our learning "style" and how we learn best in different learning situations.
— Our recognition of differences in learning tasks and our ability to match the appropriate learning strategy to the task.

— Our ability to monitor whether we are understanding and learning in a given situation or during the performance or a task.

— When we know that we do not understand, recognizing the problem and identifying a different strategy that will be more appropriate to the learning situation.

— Knowing our learning "style" and how we learn best in different learning situations. By gaining an awareness of your learning style, you can choose the learning strategies that work best for you. For example,

a. If you are a visual/right-brained or holistic learner, you might use mapping, drawings, and color-coding as note-taking strategies to make information visual and to capture the main ideas or "big picture".

b. If you are an auditory learner, you can tape record lectures and ask questions during the lecture to get more information in an auditory format.

c. If you are "left-brained" and a detail/step-by-step learner, you will want to use an outline or Cornell note-taking system that puts the information in a linear format.

You should also consider environmental factors like time of day, temperature, level of sound and size of groupings in which you learn best. Then try to schedule your classes and study sessions around your preferences. Our recognition of differences in learning tasks and our ability to match the appropriate learning strategy to the task. For example, there are different types of reading tasks and different strategies that are appropriate when reading these materials.

When you read literature, you identify the theme and how the author expands on that theme through the use of story, characters, setting, action, etc. When you read a science textbook, you read for important details: critical concepts, definitions of important terms, examples or applications, etc.

When read math word problems, you identify the problem and then determine which processes and calculations will give you the solution to the problem.

When you come to a new kind of task or problem, you go through the following steps:

— Identify what kind of task it is by scanning your memory for a similar task.

— Once you have found a match to the new task or problem, determine the strategies you used to complete the original task.

— Apply the same strategies to the new task.

How we monitor whether we are understanding and learning in a given situation or task. As we apply learning strategies to tasks, we should continuously check the effectiveness of the process by evaluating our progress in completing the task; and the outcome or understanding by asking ourselves the following questions:

— What is this about? (Can I put this information in my own words? Explain it to someone else?)

— Does the answer (or outcome) make sense?

— How am I doing?

— When I am unable to answer the questions above, I might ask:

— What could I do to make this process more effective?

— What other strategies might work more effectively?

To check comprehension and understanding at higher levels of cognition, you might want to refer to the site on cognitive structures. When we know that we do not understand, recognizing the problem and identifying a different strategy that will be more appropriate to the learning situation. If we are unable to explain our new learning, or complete a practice problem applying this learning, we may need to find another strategy that will work more effectively.

UNDERSTANDING ADULTS

The first step to being a successful adult education ESL (English as a Second Language) teacher is to understand your students and their motives for attending your class. Adults are not just large children. Teaching ESL to adults is much different from teaching ESL to first and second grade students. Frequently, teachers trained in elementary education can use many of their ESL skills in teaching adults. However, there are major differences which are outlined below.

— *Life experiences*: Adults bring to the classroom setting a lifetime of experience that should be mutually shared. Sharing experiences makes the content of the class practical and relevant to daily living. This ensures that the content of your instruction includes life-coping skills and it stimulates the motivation of the adult students.

— *Motivation*: Adult students for the most part are highly motivated. They attend class of their own free choice usually at some personal and financial sacrifice. Occasional absences are due more to family obligations rather than a lack of motivation.

— *Immediate goals*: Adult students usually have very specific and immediate goals. They are not looking forward to some long range academic achievement; rather they need English today to get a job tomorrow.

— *Self Concept*: Many adult learners are afraid to return to school for a variety of reasons. They lack the uninhibited enthusiasm of small children. The undereducated adults, in particular, are convinced that they cannot learn or are too old to learn.

Students in Adult ESL Classes

There is no typical adult ESL student. Generally every class will have a wide range of backgrounds, skills and interests. Some of the more important student differences are identified below along with some suggestions as to how these factors may affect how you group your students and teach your classes.

Literacy: One of the most important differences among adult students is whether or not they read in their native language.

FORMAL EDUCATION

Age: Adult education classes generally attract students of widely ranging ages. Often students in their late teens will be taking the classes in order to get into GED or vocational classes.

— Young adults may be taking classes because they need to speak and write English to get a good job.

— Middle aged adults frequently take classes to improve English skills for promotion in their jobs or to change careers.

— Older retired individuals may be taking the classes now that they finally have time.

The wide range of ages suggests that you may need to use a wide variety of activities in the classroom in order to reach all of your students. It also suggests that you can often be most effective by grouping students and doing many activities in the small groups. Age is one natural way to group people.

Motivation: The motivation of your students may fall into a broad spectrum distribution.

— You will have students who are very eager to learn English so they can move on to other classes or so they can advance in their employment

— You may also have students who are required (by their employer, by some social assistance program, etc.) to attend your classes but who do not really care about English at all. Some may be motivated to learn every possible detail about every aspect of English.

— Others may only want as much language as is necessary to do a particular job. As an instructor, you need to explore what your students really want. Regardless of the motivation adult students come with, genuine concern for the student, an enjoyable class and a sense of progress will increase motivation once the students are there.

Native Language Background: Because immigration laws and refugee patterns shift frequently, the native language backgrounds of your students may be as varied as their ages or as homogeneous as a regular English class. The native language backgrounds of the students can affect your teaching about as much as any other single factor. Some languages are more similar to English than others. These similarities can be in vocabulary, grammatical structure, or sound. The languages might also share our alphabet. Teaching people with these language backgrounds is easier than teaching those with language backgrounds less similar to English. Even though it may be more difficult to teach people English when their native language is extremely different form English, it is not impossible. Many of these students become very fluent in English.

Native Culture — One of the most surprising things for many teachers is the influence that the native culture has in the classroom. Students come with their native cultural view of

— what a teacher should say and do

— what should happen in any kind of classroom

— how a language should be taught

For example, in many oriental cultures, the teacher is a highly respected individual and there is a great social difference between pupils and teacher. In other cultures there is less distance between students and teachers, and students expect to have more interpersonal relationships with the teachers. Dealing with culture may mean that you have to modify some of your behavior so as not to offend your students and gain their respect as their teacher. It may also mean that you will have to explain to some of them the differences in cultural expectations and encourage them to move towards the norms of the society in which they are currently living.

Why do people enroll in the ESL classes?

Adult learners attend ESL classes because they choose to, not because they have to. If the class fails to satisfy the need which has motivated them to come, they will simply stop coming. Some of the major motivating forces for the students in your class are the following:

— *Survival*: They realize that learning English is essential to satisfy their most basic physical and social needs. They must speak it in order to get food, clothing, shelter, medical attention, as well as to participate in social and political institutions.

— *Job enhancement*: In many instances they need to be able to speak English in order to get a job. Sometimes they have a job but need better English skills in order to keep the job or to advance in their employment.

— *Education*: Many students attend ESL classes in order to complete their GED or, in some cases, to attend college.

— *Social interaction*: Some students attend ESL classes for social reasons. They enjoy meeting and getting to know new people, and the ESL class is a place where they can fulfill those needs.

One thing in general to remember about adult students is that they are much more likely than younger students to come with specific purposes for their learning. They are more likely to know what they want to learn and why they want to learn it.

How can students be motivated so that they want to keep coming to class? Because students come with specific purposes for learning, one of the best ways to keep them motivated is to help them feel progress towards their goal. In order to do this, you will have to determine somehow what those goals are. One way to proceed is to conduct an informal discussion to determine their goals. This may require the assistance of interpreters because of the variety of the students' native languages. Once the goals have been determined, materials and activities should be selected which will be relevant to the goals.

For example, a student wants to learn English so that he or she can work towards a GED, the materials that are chosen should provide vocabulary and language patterns that are used in basic secondary textbooks.

Students will be further motivated if you remind them how each of the activities that you are doing will help them move towards their goals (e.g., "We're doing this activity so that when you are taking a math class, you will be able to..."). One of the most important factors which motivates students is a sense of progress. There should be clear markers of success so that students can look at what they are doing well. This means that there should be fairly frequent measurements (questioning individual students, short quizzes, corrected homework, etc.). Too often teachers avoid measurements because they are time consuming or because the students have an inordinate fear of examinations. However, a wise teacher will build in easy, convenient ways of showing the students their progress. One simple way of doing this is a simple checklist of tasks which the students would want to be able to accomplish in order to reach their overall goal. As they do the tasks one by one, they sense their progress and feel that the class is worthwhile. This will keep them coming until they reach their major goal.

A second factor which will maintain and increase motivation for your students is enjoyment. Activities should provide opportunities for real social interaction and getting to know other people in a relaxed and, sometimes, even humorous ways. If activities are exciting enough, students will not want to miss class because they know they will be missing the "action." If you help your students develop feelings of respect and friendship for one another, those ties will also draw them back to the class. Relevance is probably the most important motivating factor for adult students. If the students are exposed to and study life-coping skills, e.g. balancing a checkbook, applying for a job, etc., their interest will never waiver.

A second step to being a successful ESL teacher is to become aware of the language and how it is used. Even though you have probably spoken English for years (maybe even all of your life) and have been taught the language formally in school, you may not be aware of many of its aspects which give non-native speakers a hard time. Very often the things which give your students the hardest time are things that come most naturally to a native speaker.

— What is correct English?
— What are some major problems that ESL learners have with vocabulary?
— What are some major problems that ESL learners have with grammar?
— What are some important things to know about pronunciation?
— Some Facts About How Second Languages are Learned
— What is correct English?

Most people believe that there is a very definite set of English rules which, when followed, will produce correct English. In reality, this is not true. A better question to ask is, "What is appropriate English?" The answer to that question depends on many things:

— The relationship of the speakers (e.g., good friends speak to each other different than an employer speaks to employees).
— The situation in which the communication takes place (e.g., people have to provide different kinds of information when talking over the telephone than when talking face-to-face.
— The topic of the communication (e.g., you may speak differently in telling a joke than you would in discussing a math principle), etc.
— You should aim at teaching your students language which will help them achieve their goals appropriately. For example, they may want to be able to request help in a store. You would teach them to do it in such a way that they would get the help and that the people helping them

would not think that they were rude, stupid, nor snobbish. Overall, teachers have a tendency to try to teach styles of English that are too formal for most of the situations their students will encounter. Try to avoid this fault. Contractions (I'm, he's, they'll) are always used except in very formal situations.

The problems that ESL learners have with vocabulary usually depend on the native language backgrounds. Many languages have words which are similar in sound and meaning to English words. These kinds of words are called cognates. They are some of the easiest words to learn, and you can use them initially to help students increase their English vocabulary rapidly.

— To really understand words, students have to know
— What they mean
— What other words they are used with
— Which situations they are used in
— What the social consequences of their use can be (e.g. saying "scram" has different social consequences from saying, "Please leave.").

The best way to make sure that students know these things about vocabulary is to teach the vocabulary through use in realistic situations. If the situation is clear, the meaning and use of the vocabulary item also becomes clear. Teaching vocabulary through lists often results in students knowing how words are pronounced and what one meaning of a word is, but they really do not know how to use the words correctly.

Following are some major problems that ESL learners have with grammar?

Word order: In English, word order is more important than it is in many other languages. Very often ESL students produce sentences which sound strange to the native's ear because the order of the words in the sentences is wrong. The basic pattern for English statements is: *Subject-Verb-Object(S)-Place-Time.* Sentences do not have to have all of these parts, but if all of the parts do occur, they most likely will occur in this order. If a sentence has both a *Place* and a *Time*, one of these is frequently moved to the front of the sentence.

A change in basic sentence order can make an English sentence nonsensical or make it mean something completely different. For example, if part of the verb is moved so it comes before the subject, we have a question. (e.g. "John will be home at eight" becomes "Will John be home at eight?") If you switch the time phrase with the place word you get an understandable sentence that no native speaker would ever say, "John will be at eight home." Word order is also important in English with phrases smaller that a sentence.

Verbs: There are several problems that ESL speakers have with English verbs. Basically, however, the English verb system is fairly simple (more simple than most Western European languages but a little more complicated than most Oriental languages). Here are some of the problems students have:

a. *Present tense*: The present tense in most language refers to actions that are taking place in the present. In English, this is not really true. We use present tense to refer to actions which are habitual, repeated, or always true. (e.g., The sun rises in the East; I get up every day at 6:00 a.m.; We celebrate Thanksgiving in November). English uses present progressive (present continuous) to express actions that are taking place in the present (e.g., I'm reading a teacher training manual; I'm teaching an ESL class; You're preparing to take your GED).

b: *Future tense*: The most common future tense in English does not use *Will* as you may have been taught. The most common future tense is produced with the expression *Going to*(e.g., I'm going to eat...; he's going to show us how...; we're going to study...). You should remember also that in everyday speech this going to expression is pronounced "gonna" and that it is not incorrect to say it that way as long as it is understood.

Two-word verbs: Some actions in English are expressed by phrases which consist of a verb and a preposition or adverb. The action is not expressed by the verb alone. For example, *Get* means 'to obtain, to acquire, to receive, etc.' while *Get Over* means 'to recover from an illness,' and Get up means 'to arise from a reclining position.' There are hundreds of such phrases in English. They are a problem for ESL students because they are often not listed in the dictionary in a separate form and their meaning is hard to find. A good textbook will probably teach many of these two-word verbs, but if yours does not, you should teach them to your students as they arise naturally in the classroom (for example, *Hand in* your papers).

Besides not appearing as separate entries in the dictionary, these two-word verbs present one other problem. Some of them must have their two parts together in a sentence while others may have their parts separated by other things in the sentence.

Examples:

1.The teacher always *calls on* students who are prepared

2.She asked me to *call* her *up* after dinner.

The two-word verbs which can not have their parts separated are called "inseparable" and the others are called "separable." Look at the list below.

Examples:

1.They wanted to *look over* the car.

2.They wanted to *look* the car *over*.

3.They wanted to *look* it *over*.

but NOT: They wanted to *look over* it.

The verb Do:In English, we use the verb *Do*(Do, Does, Done, Did, etc.) in at least four different ways:

1. As a verb like other verbs: Jennifer did the dishes
2. As a sign of emphasis: I *did* comb my hair.

As a verb which can be placed in front of the subject to form a question or to which *Not* can be attached to form a negative statement: Do they want more bread? Mr. Jones doesn't know if the clock is correct. As a substitute to save repetition of another verb or verb phrase: My sister needs a new coat and I do too. They didn't finish their tests, but I did. Your students will probably have difficulty with all of the uses of *Do* except the first example.

Preposition: English prepositions are a problem because different languages use different prepositions to express the same ideas. It will help your students if you do not teach too many prepositions at one time. Also, it will help if you are sure to put the prepositions in context (in a situation where the use is natural).

Noun: In English, as in many other languages, we consider some things countable and some things non-countable. If something is countable, it can have a plural form; If it is non-countable, it can not have a plural form and the singular form is used to refer to any quantity. Some of the things which we consider non-countable in English are: abstractions, ideas, ideals, emotions, gasses, fluids, materials with particles too small to be conveniently counted, and fields of study. Many languages have the same concept of count and non-count but they do not always put items in the same category as we do in English. For example, in English, Homework and Housework are generally noncountable. (We do not say Housework, for example.)

In other languages, these nouns are countable and they do have plural forms. Students have to learn which nouns are which in English because it affects other grammar principles as well (e.g. whether to use *A Little* or *A Few* before the noun). There are other problems with English grammar but most good textbooks can guide you along. The pointers included here are mentioned only to make you aware that there are many aspects of English which are not problems at all for native speakers (even uneducated ones), but which might cause problems for your students.

Importance of Pronunciation

As a teacher, the most important thing for you to know is what factors influence whether the pronunciation is correct or not. You can use your own pronunciation as a model. When you want your students to produce the sounds correctly, sometimes you can give them more help if you are aware of what produces the differences. Here are some of those aspects:

Voicing:One thing which distinguishes one sound from other sounds is voicing. When a sound is voiced, the air used to make the sound causes the vocal cords to vibrate. You can tell if a sound is voiced by placing you hand tightly on your throat and saying the sound in isolation. If the sound is voiced, you will feel vibrations. (Try saying "zzzzz" with your hand tightly on your throat. Now try saying "sssss." You should feel the vibrations with "zzz" but not with "sss.") When a student is saying a sound incorrectly one reason may be that he or she is voicing an unvoiced sound or is not voicing a voiced sound.

Mouth, Tongue, and Lip position: Another thing that makes a difference in sound is the position of the mouth, tongue, lips, etc. (sometimes these are called articulators). For vowels, differences in sounds are produced by how far forward or back the tip of the tongue is in the mouth, by how high or low it is, by how much the jaw is dropped, and by whether the lips are rounded or not. For consonants, differences in sound are produces by where the tongue touches in the mouth, by which part of the tongue touches, and by whether the air is stopped completely or partially and then released. With some consonants the differences are created with articulators besides the tongue (e.g. 'b' is produced by the upper and lower lip) or by the shape of the tongue rather than the position (e.g. 'r' and 'l' are different because the tongue curls up towards the roof of the mouth with 'r'). If your students are producing a sound incorrectly, try to imitate them to feel where your tongue is and how your mouth is shaped; them, move your tongue to the correct position to make the sound. You ought to be able to help your students get their tongues and mouths into the correct position in this way.

Stress and Rhythm: English has a stress and rhythm pattern which is different from most other languages in the world. Most languages give equal amount of time to each syllable. In English, we give an equal amount of time between *stressed* syllables. This means that we say many unstressed syllables very quickly. This difference is one that most ESL speakers will benefit from learning through lots of practice and examples.

Intonation: In English, there are two basic intonation patterns. With one, the speaker raises his or her voice on the last stressed syllable of the sentence and keeps the tone higher to the end of the sentence (called rising intonation). This pattern is used to indicate that what he or she is saying or asking requires a *Yes* or *No* answer. With the other pattern, the speaker raises the tone on the last stressed syllable of the sentence and then drops the tone to a point that is even lower than the tone before the voice was raised (called rising-falling intonation). This pattern is used for regular sentences and for most questions requiring the giving of some information as an answer. There are other patterns, but they are basically variations of the two described. You need to help students be aware of the intonation as often it can completely change the meaning of a sentence (e.g. "You're a high school graduate" can either be a statement or a question depending on whether it is said with rising intonation or rising-falling intonation).

Many textbooks may also give you pointers about English pronunciation. However, if they do not, you can usually figure out what the problems are by looking at the four aspects of sounds which were discussed, namely, voicing, position, stress and rhythm, and intonation.

The third Step to being a successful ESL teacher is to be aware of some common myths about second language learning and teaching that can significantly reduce your effectiveness. They are:

1. *That language can be learned much like other school subjects, i.e. learning facts or rules and applying those facts in a problem solving fashion*: This myth often results in the teacher spending a lot of time talking about the language being learned and not talking in that language. It results in testing the students' knowledge of grammar and not their ability to communicate. Language is not learned primarily by learning the "rules" but rather by first listening to and understanding the spoken language and then practicing speaking. Occasionally, however, learning of rules can help many adults learn and use the language. Just do not make rules the focus of the course.
2. *That language is learned primarily by memorization and repetition of sentence patterns*: While repetition and memorization can play an important role in language learning, they cannot by themselves insure that students will be able to use the language for any real purpose. Repetition and memorization, if used, must be accompanied by other activities requiring the application of the learned patterns in novel situations and with variation in vocabulary and even structure.
3. *That language lessons should be centered around a particular grammatical pattern and that these should be sequenced from simple to complex*: This myth often leads to the teaching of sentences because of their simplicity rather than because of their usefulness to the learner. The first consideration in selecting material for teaching a second language should be to choose vocabulary and sentences that the learner wants and needs to learn. The grammatical simplicity of the sentence should be a secondary consideration.
4. *That language is learned by first gaining mastery over one sentence pattern and then moving on to another*: This myth

often leads to the overuse of mechanical structure drills and causes the teacher to place an inordinate amount of attention on the correction of grammatical errors. Research has shown that grammatical development takes place gradually and that the learner is developing many aspects of the grammar simultaneously. Learner errors are not all bad. They can show the teacher that the learner is progressing normally toward mastery of the whole language system.

The teacher's efforts should be focused on providing the student with lots of opportunities to hear and comprehend communicative language and to interact in as realistic a way as possible.

ESL Placement

The last important step in being a successful adult education ESL teacher is student assessment and placement. It is critical that adult students be properly placed otherwise they will quickly lose interest and drop out. If the material you present in any level ESL class is too easy, students will become bored. If it is too hard, they will not return for the second class. Regardless of the placement technique used for adult students, the first impression is an important one. Many adult students come to the ESL classroom with a lot of fears. In some cases their last experience with school was a negative one (e.g. they may have left school as teenage drop outs). Consequently, it is very important that the teacher establish a friendly, enthusiastic rapport free of any academic pretense. This friendly social approach is especially important for the more undereducated adults. Even though their fear level is very high, it can be broken down by a friendly smile and pleasant small talk.

Adult Student's oral ability

The most common method of assessing adult students' oral proficiency in order to place them in appropriate classes is to engage them in a brief oral interview. For non-literate students this approach is particularly valuable. The following questions are appropriate for this interview:

— What is your name?

— Where do you live?

— Are you married?

— Do you have any children?

— Where were you born?

— What day is it today?

— Where do you work?

— What kind of work do you do?

— How long have you lived in this city?

— What do you need the most help in? Speaking, reading, or writing?

— Why do you want to study English?

— What do you like to do for fun?

-- Tell me something about you family.

At all times be relaxed and friendly with the students. Make them feel comfortable. Reassure them that this is for placement purposes only and it is not an examination. Repeat the question or statement if necessary. You may clarify a response or even prompt the student to help them feel more at ease. If they give a correct and clear answer in English, give them two points for each item. If they give an unclear, inappropriate answer give them one point. For no answer give them a zero. Add up their points for a total score. Students with a total score of about 0-10 should probably be placed in a beginning class. Those with scores of about 10-20 should be in an intermediate class and those who score above 20 should be in an advanced class. These scores are only estimates and the examiner must use his judgment in determining the class which could be appropriate for each individual, especially those whose score fall near the breaking points.

Literary Assessment

In addition to oral assessment and placement, it is very important to assess the literacy skills of your adult students. There are two aspects to this assessment, first determining if the student is literate in his native language and second finding out if the student has some writing skills in English. To assess the literacy skills of the individual you are interviewing, simply ask them to write the answers to the questions that appear on the reverse side of the placement instrument. Encourage the students to write their responses in either English or their native language whichever they find easiest. (You may need interpreters to assess the level of your students' native literacy.) Again, make your students feel comfortable. Repeat the fact that the purpose is only to place the student in an appropriate class. Encourage them to answer as many as possible. The literacy assessment instrument is not to be used as a diagnostic tool; rather its purpose is to distinguish the literate adult student from the totally non-literate student. ESL curricula for these two very distinct groups must be developed to meet their specific needs.

LEARNING/RADICAL BEHAVIORISM

From the 1950s through the 1970s radical behaviorism, as espoused by B. F. Skinner, dominated theories of learning and instruction. Since that time, behaviorism has been replaced almost entirely by cognitive and other approaches. Almost, but not quite entirely. It is still possible to see vestiges of the behaviorist approach to instruction in some forms of computer-based learning and occasionally elsewhere. The greatest stronghold of behaviorism in education is probably in classroom management. Many classroom teachers are familiar with using reward systems, time-out, and other behaviorist approaches to encourage students to pay attention, stay in their seats, and so on.

Although this is a use of behaviorist principles in an educational setting, it is not really the same as using behaviorism as the basis for learning or instructional theory. Although behaviorism should be considered a historical, rather than contemporary, approach to understanding learning, it is still worth knowing about because of its recent, and to some degree continuing, influence.

Important ideas leading up to Skinner

Skinnerian behaviorism had important antecedents, including:

— *Associationism*, and Ebbinghaus's experiments with memorizing lists of nonsense syllables. Why did Ebbinghaus conduct his learning experiments with nonsense syllables? And, in retrospect, why was that perhaps not such a great idea?

— Thorndike's interest in the association between the environment and action (or behavior), rather than just the association between ideas.

— Pavlov's "discovery" of *classical conditioning*, where a previously "neutral" event (e.g., ringing a bell), when paired with a biological stimulus (e.g., food) can come to elicit the same physiological response (e.g., salivation).

Some concepts associated with the classical conditioning paradigm:

— *Higher-order conditioning*: when a conditioned stimulus is paired with another previously neutral stimulus, it too can acquire the ability to elicit a response. So, if Pavlov's dogs were conditioned to salivate when he rang a bell, then he began flashing a bright light at the same time, eventually the light alone might come to elicit the same response.

— *Extinction*: when the conditioned stimulus is presented over a sufficient period of time without the unconditioned stimulus, the conditioned stimulus eventually loses its ability to elicit the response. (I.e., ring that bell enough times without presenting food, and I'll stop salivating.)

— *Counter-conditioning*: Changing the response to a conditioned stimulus by pairing it with a different stimulus.

In the case of Baby Albert, you might pair a pleasant stimulus with the white rat, just in case extinction alone doesn't work. Or, in the case of Pavlov's dogs, you might pair an appetite-suppressing stimulus with the conditioned stimulus (if you could think of something that suppresses a dog's appetite!).

Watson introduced the notion of behaviorism: that psychology should be concerned only with the objective data of behavior, since we can't really know what's going on in the mind. B. F. Skinner followed Watson's lead in emphasizing behavior, rather than thoughts, feelings, attitudes, etc., as the "proper" subject matter of psychology. The interesting difference in Skinner's view is that he was less concerned about the relationship between environmental stimuli and responses; rather, he was mainly interested in behavior (or a response) and its consequences. Attempts by psychologists to link all behaviors to stimuli from the environment had become very cumbersome, and required postulating a lot of intervening mental processes. Just imagine starting only with stimuli that elicit physiological responses (heat, loud noises, hunger, etc.), and trying to account for complex human behavior like building a cathedral or writing a poem!

Skinner said that the environment provides us with "cues" that serve as antecedents for behavior; i.e., they set the conditions for it to occur. Skinner distinguished two classes of behavior: *respondent* and *operant*. Respondent behavior is the kind we perform automatically in the presence of some stimulus from the environment. Operant behavior is "emitted" without necessarily following any particular stimulus. For example, babies grasp at things and babble, just because that's what babies do. To Skinner, it would be the consequences of their grasping or babbling behavior that are important.

According to Skinner, the basic "unit" of behavior analysis is a *discriminative stimulus*, followed by an *operant response*, followed by a *contingent stimulus*. This is commonly diagrammed something like this:

S (discrim) —> R —> S (conting)

Remember that the discriminative stimulus sets the stage for the response, but does not automatically elicit it in the way that an object moving toward your eye can elicit a blink. For example, robins peck for worms when they're on the ground, but not when they're flying. So, the ground is a discriminative stimulus for pecking behavior. The pecking behavior may be followed by getting a worm. If so, the worm is a new stimulus, which is contingent on the pecking behavior, and which may serve to reinforce that behavior.

Humans, too, are very sensitive to discriminative stimuli. We know that very different sets of behaviors are appropriate for different settings. For example, the behaviors that are appropriate at a football game are quite different from those that would be appropriate at an opera. While Skinner had some interest in the role of discriminative stimuli in setting the stage for behavior, he was more interested in the consequences of behavior; that is, in the response-contingent stimulus that follows a response. Skinner noted that the consequences of a response (the contingent stimulus) can be either satisfying or unsatisfying to the person or organism making the response. When the consequence is satisfying, it is said to *reinforce* the behavior; that is, to make it more likely to occur in the future. When the response is not satisfying, or aversive, it is said to *punish* the behavior; that is, to make it less likely to occur in the future.

It's important to remember that we can't always guess what consequence will be satisfying to someone. The final test of whether a consequence is reinforcing to someone is whether or not it increases the behavior of interest. Operant conditioning would be a fairly simple concept if it were concerned only with positive and negative consequences of a behavior or response. But it's a little more complicated than that. Skinner reasoned that we could think not only about situations in which a satisfying or aversive outcome was *presented* following a response, but also about situations in which it was *removed* following the response.

For example, suppose every time a student asks a question in class, the teacher responds in a curt or abrupt way. This may function as a punishing consequence which decreases the question-asking behavior. Then, a new teacher who is more open to questions takes over the class. The punishing or aversive consequence has been removed, so the student may increase the question-asking behavior. In particular, note that both positive reinforcement and negative reinforcement (the upper left and lower right cells in Driscoll's table) serve to *increase* or strengthen behavior.

Positive reinforcement does so by presenting a satisfying outcome after the response; negative reinforcement does so by removing an aversive outcome after the response. Also, both punishment, and response cost, timeout, and extinction (the upper right and lower left cells) serve to *decrease* or weaken behavior. Punishment does so by presenting an aversive consequence following the behavior. The others do so by removing a satisfying consequence following the behavior.

Learning New Behaviors

So far, we've considered only behaviors that the person (or animal or organism) already knew how to perform. The only issue was whether the frequency of the behavior would be increased or decreased. But how does behaviorism account for learning to perform new behaviors? In your text, four processes are suggested:

— Shaping involves the reinforcement of successively closer approximations of some target behavior.

— Chaining teaches complex behavior by reinforcing the performance of simpler behaviors which are then strung together in the proper sequence to make up the more complex behavior.

— Discrimination learning is the process of learning to discriminate between settings in which a particular behavior will or will not be reinforced.

— Fading is the gradual withdrawal of prompts or cues (discriminative stimuli) that guide the performance of a complex behavior.

To this point, behavior is reinforced every time it is performed. However, behaviorists found that this need not be the case. Once a behavior has been established, reinforcement "schedules" other than one reinforcement for every performance turn out to be more effective at maintaining high response rates.

Behaviorism and education

One of the most lasting influences of behaviorism in education is in the use of principles of behavior management. Many teachers have used ideas such as "time out" and token economies to reward on-task classroom behavior and discourage disruptive behaviors. Behaviorism also had a pervasive influence on instruction and instructional design, although that influence has faded considerably over the past two decades. Contemporary computer-assisted instruction is a direct descendant of teaching machines and programmed instruction, both of which were attempts to create a technology of teaching in accordance with behaviorist learning principles. Instruction created according to behaviorist principles (especially programmed instruction, early computer-based instruction, and some contemporary computer-based tutorials and drill-and-practice) typically emphasized these characteristics:

— *Specific, observable learning outcomes*: The target behaviors needed to be specified so that the instructor or designer could provide appropriate reinforcement when they were achieved.

— *Individualized learning*: Each learner worked independently, at his/her own pace. This permitted "reinforcement" to occur at the moment the learner completed a particular objective.

— *Frequent reinforcement*: The material to be learned was broken into very small "chunks", usually somewhere between a paragraph and a page of text. This was so that the learner could be reinforced frequently while working through the material.

— *"Knowledge of correct results" as a reinforcer*: The usual pattern of this kind of instruction was to present a small amount of reading or a problem, then to pose a question. In behaviorist terms, the reading or problem was a discriminative stimulus; when the student answered the question, they were emitting a response; and reinforcement that followed the response was finding out whether they had answered the question properly.

— *Fading of prompts*: In more sophisticated behaviorist instruction, the learner would be provided with less and less guidance or prompting as he/she proceeded through the material.

One of the reasons that this kind of instruction has largely disappeared is that it emphasized lower-order skills such as memorization. It is very difficult to teach higher thinking skills such as synthesis and evaluation in this instructional format.

2

UNDERSTANDING THE LEARNER IN THE LIGHT OF INTEREST

Developing a student profile helps to provide a deeper understanding of an individual's unique interests, styles and abilities. By gathering information from a variety of sources, teachers and school-based teams are in a better position to make educational decisions that will enhance the student's development.

PRINCIPLES OF CREATING STUDENT INTEREST

- — Thinking is interesting.
- — Interest is contagious.
- — Interest is strengthened by a sense of progress.
- — Interest is sustained by a state of suspense.
- — Goals become interest centers.
- — The novel and unexpected are interesting.
- — Humor creates interest.
- — Techniques for Creating and Maintaining Interest
- — Arouse a feeling of need.
- — Use illustrations and personal experiences.
- — Use multiple sensory teaching and learning aids.

— Use a variety of teaching techniques.
— Base teaching on thinking.
— Create doubt and suspense.
— Build genuine interests in your students.
— Create a "felt need" for learning.
— Be enthusiastic.
— Use "real world" examples and situations.
— Expect quality from your students.
— Be professional.

Student Interest Inventories

Having students complete interest inventories gives teachers a greater understanding of student's interests and is a great motivator in the classroom to build on student's interests. Teachers have many ways to find out about student interests. There are some published inventories that can be helpful. One is *My Book of Things and Stuff* written for primary and intermediate students. Another is *The Interest-A-lyzer* appropriate for middle and secondary school students. There are commercially produced interest inventories that can be purchased. For example: Myers-Briggs Type Indicator (MBTI) - This inventory is based on Carl Jung's theory of psychological type. It measures your individual preferences in how you relate to others and the world around you, how you gather information and make decisions, the types of situations in which you feel most comfortable, and the lifestyle you adopt. It has direct applications to your preferred style and interests as a career professional.

Campell Interest and Skill Survey (CISS) -- This inventory is a survey of self- reported interests and skills. It is designed to help you understand how your interests and skills relate to basic job interest orientations and specitic occupations. You will receive a detailed profile based on a computer analysis of the completed inventory. Many curriculum guides contain informal interest inventories or teachers can develop their own. Following are two samples of informal interest inventories,one for Grades 1-6, and one for Grades 7-12. These require less standardized responses and can collect more anecdotal information. You can glean questions from this, however, to add to a more standardized inventory.

Interest Inventory for Grades 1-6

— *Play and Other Activities*

1. What do you like to do in your free time?
2. What do you usually do after school? On weekends?
3. What are your favorite games?
4. Do you like making things? If so, what?
5. What special tools or playthings do you have at home?
6. Is there a tool or plaything you wish you had? If so, what?
7. Do you have pets? If so, what?
8. Do you collect things? If so, what?
9. Do you take private lessons (piano, tennis, etc.)?
10. If you could have 3 wishes, what would they be?
11. Did you ever wish you were someone else? If so, who?
12. Are you afraid of some things? If so, what?
13. About how many hours a day do you watch TV during the week? On weekends?
14. What TV programs do you like?
15. About how many hours a day do you listen to the radio during the week? On weekends?
16. What type of radio programs do you like?

17. How often do you attend movies?
18. What movies have you liked?
19. Do you play with computers? If yes, explain.

— *Reading*

20. Do you like being read to? If so, what?
21. Do you enjoy hearing a story told? If so, by whom?
22. Do you like to read? If so, what kind of reading?
23. Do you like comic books? If so, which ones?
24. Do you like magazines? If so, which ones?
25. Are there books or stories you especially liked? If so, what ones and why?
26. Do you have books of your own? If so, about how many?
27. Do you use the school library? If so, about how often?
28. Do you use the public library? If so, about how often?
29. Which of the following do you enjoy, and are there special preferences?

a. Reading
b. Being read to
c. Attending movies
d. Listening to the radio
e. Watching TV
f. Participating in sports
g. Playing computer games
h. Other (playing piano, sports, dancing, sewing, etc.)

Interest Inventory for Grades 7-12

— *Amusements and Other Activities*

1. What do you like to do in your free time?
2. What do you usually do after school? In the evenings? On weekends or vacations?
3. What are your favorite sports? Do you participate or mainly observe?
4. Do you like to make things? If so, what?
5. What tools do you have at home?
6. Do you have pets? What are they?
7. Do you collect things? If so, what?
8. Do you take private lessons (piano, tennis, etc.)? If so, what?
9. Do you have any hobbies? If so, what?
10. If you could have one wish, what would it be?
11. Are you afraid of some things? If so, what?

— *Television, Radio, Movies, Music, Computers*

12. About how many hours a day do you watch TV during the week? On weekends?
13. What TV programs do you like?
14. About how many hours a day do yo listen to the radio during the week? At other times?
15. How often do you attend movies?
16. What movies have you liked?
17. What singers do you like?
18. What musical groups do you like?
19. Do you enjoy computer games? If so, what kinds?

— *Reading*

20. Do you like to read? What type of books do you like?

21. Are there any books you especially liked? If so, name them:
22. Do you enjoy hearing someone read or tell stories?
23. Do you use the school library? Often, seldom, or never?
24. Do you use the public library? Often, seldom, or never?
25. Do you have a library card?
26. Do you like comic books? If so, which ones?
27. Do you like magazines? If so, which ones?
28. Do you read newspapers? If so, what parts?
29. What kinds of reading do you enjoy (about animals, sports, people, space travel, ow-to books, etc.)?

— *Vocational and Educational Interests*

30. What would you like to do after finishing school?
31. Is there anyone in television or the movies who does the type of work you would like to do? If so, who?
32. Have you done any reading pertaining to this?
33. Do you like school?
34. What subject do you like best?
35. What subject do you like least?
36. In what subject do you get your best marks?
37. In what subject do you get poor marks?
38. Do you plan to go to a post-secondary institution after high school?
39. Has any member of your family been to college? If so, who?
40. Would you like to travel outside Canada? If so, where?

Definition of the Individual Common Essential Learnings

The Common Essential Learnings comprise six categories: Communication, Numeracy, Critical and Creative Thinking, Technological Literacy, Personal and Social Values and Skills, and Independent Learning.

Communication: Communication focuses on improving students' understanding of the language demands in each of the Required Areas of Study, based on a recognition that language is central to learning in all subject areas. Communication does not require that all teachers become language arts teachers, but rather, that teachers understand the role played by language in their subject area(s) and deal systematically and concretely with that role in their instructional methods. The goal is to promote students' learning in all school subjects through improving their language abilities within each subject.

Numeracy: Numeracy is concerned with developing students' knowledge, skills and appreciations of mathematical ideas, techniques and applications. In relation to instruction, Numeracy suggests that a better balance is required between knowing how to compute, measure, estimate and interpret mathematical data, knowing when to apply these same skills and techniques and understanding why these particular processes apply. The goal is to enable students to cope confidently and competently with everyday situations demanding the use of mathematical concepts, as well as developing their ability to learn new concepts when necessary. Further, Numeracy is intended to strengthen students' learning in all school subjects through providing them with grounded understanding of the quantitative aspects of each subject.

Critical and Creative Thinking: Critical and creative thinking is intended to better develop students' abilities to create and to evaluate ideas, processes, experiences and objects. It requires that teachers and students learn to articulate, publicly defend, and change when necessary, their criteria for evaluation. The goal is to develop students who value knowledge, learning and the creative process, who can and will think for themselves, yet recognize the limits of individual reflection and the need to contribute to and build upon mutual understandings of social situations.

Technological Literacy: Technological literacy is concerned with improving students' understanding of how technological systems are integral parts of social systems, and that they cannot be fully separated from the political, cultural and economic frameworks which shape them. The goal is to have students appreciate the value of technology in society within the context of its limitations, and see themselves as having roles and responsibilities in shaping public policy related to technological change.

Personal and Social Values and Skills: Personal and social values and skills examines the personal, moral, social and cultural aspects of each school subject and of the school environment. It reflects a concern with the development of responsible and compassionate individuals and with developing understanding of the rational basis for moral claims. What is desired are students who are capable of self reliance and willing and able to work harmoniously in groups and with other groups. Increased understanding of how culture shapes our thoughts and values is also an important goal of this C.E.L.

Independent Learning focuses on creation of the opportunities and experiences necessary for students to become capable, self-reliant, self motivated and life-long learners. What is desired are students who value learning as an empowering activity of great personal and social worth. All of the other C.E.L.s contribute to the goal of developing independent learners.

Before proceeding with further examination of the Common Essential Learnings, it is important to be clear about how the C.E.L.s will shape curricula and instruction in Saskatchewan. Several understandings are important to note here:

— The Common Essential Learnings are not new school subjects and therefore are not substitutes for content in the Required Areas of Study.

— Students will not be evaluated on their acquisition of the C.E.L.s independently of school subject matter.

— The Common Essential Learnings are not mutually exclusive areas. They overlap and are interrelated in important ways.

Implementation of the C.E.L.s will occur as new curricula are developed and implemented. Because these statements are fundamental to understanding the relationship between the C.E.L.s, the Required Areas of Study, and other school subjects, they require further elaboration.

First, the Common Essential Learnings are perspectives which influence school subject matter and how it is taught, but they are not school subjects themselves. The incorporation of the C.E.L.s into Saskatchewan's core curriculum framework does not mean that teachers will be expected to teach new courses such as critical thinking or independent learning. Rather, the C.E.L.s are to be incorporated into new curricula so that students will be helped in learning how to think critically or acquire some strategies to learn independently within each school subject. The knowledge, skills, processes, attitudes and values contained in the C.E.L.s will be acquired through school subject matter matched with appropriate methods of instruction and a supportive school environment, but not through the direct teaching of any one C.E.L. in isolation from school subjects.

Second, students will not be evaluated on their acquisition of the C.E.L.s independently of school subject matter. The C.E.L.s depend on school subjects for their content, depth and breadth and are shaped in different ways within different subjects. For example, critical thinking in arts education involves different concepts and abilities than critical thinking in mathematics or in social studies. It is necessary, then, that assessment of students acquisition of the knowledge, skills, values or processes associated with the C.E.L.s be achieved largely through assessment within the school subjects. Teacher, peer and self assessments of progress toward achieving the abilities related to Personal and Social Values and Skills, however, will be influenced by subject area learning and by the whole of the school experience.

Third, while the C.E.L.s are discussed as though they were separate and distinct, they contain many of the same values, attitudes, knowledge, skills and processes. Achievement of growth in one of the Common Essential Learnings supports growth in the others and the various C.E.L.s may be developed through similar teaching practices. One lesson can develop abilities and understandings of several of the Common Essential Learnings. Overlap and interrelationships can be expected. The recommendations and understandings of the other C.E.L.s apply equally to Independent Learning.

Fourth, educators will achieve greater understanding of the depth and breadth of each Common Essential Learning as new curricula are developed which incorporate them. Incorporation of the C.E.L.s into teaching practice will be supported through on-going in service developed by Saskatchewan Education in co-operation with key educational organizations and through the on-going development of teaching materials related to the C.E.L.s. Responsibility for implementation of the C.E.L.s will occur as new curricula which integrate them with the Required Areas of Study are developed and implemented.

Foundations for the Common Essential Learnings

The Common Essential Learnings promote active, self-motivated and increasingly independent learners. They are intended to direct content and instruction in ways that will provide students with an integrated and meaningful knowledge base, as well as the understanding and processes necessary to achieve personal autonomy and compassion for others. The C.E.L.s are based upon certain foundational beliefs about the teaching-learning process and the teacher's role, and are developed in part from Saskatchewan's Goals of Education.

Goals of education

The Common Essential Learnings (incorporated into the Required Areas of Study) support the achievement of Saskatchewan's goals for education. Such important goals as "working to create greater social justice" and "participating in the democratic process of governments" are developed through Personal and Social Values and Skills and Critical and Creative Thinking. Lifelong learning goals such as "acting as a self reliant learner, capable of autonomous learning" are developed through such C.E.L.s as Communication, Numeracy and Independent Learning. The promotion of Technological Literacy supports goals such as "making informed consumer decisions" and "respecting and seeking to enhance the environment."

The emphasis provided by the C.E.L.s is one of developing persons committed to both reflection and action, and to participation in the shaping of the future rather than reacting to change. Finally, the C.E.L.s emphasize that one should analyze personal needs in the context of respect for the environment and respect for others.

Teaching-learning process

Foundational beliefs about learning which led to the development of the Common Essential Learnings can be summarized as follows:

— There is more than one type of learning. For example, acquiring information makes different demands upon the learner than acquiring skills, processes, attitudes or values. For this reason, different types of learning may require different methods of instruction.

— Learning is a function of the total environment and is the result of an interactive process, with both students and teachers having an influence on the outcomes of any interaction.

— Important factors which influence learning. include: relevance of the content and methods to the learner's interests, needs and goals; congruence with developmental levels of the learner; and allowances for active participation of the learner.

— The individual C.E.L. perspectives contain - either implicitly or explicitly - an emphasis on learning in order to understand and to apply knowledge in daily life, rather than simply learning by rote. This emphasis requires a compatible vision of the teaching-learning process. The central principles of such a vision can be described in the following manner.

What children learn depends not only on what they are taught but also on how they are taught, their developmental level, and their interests and experiences. In other words, there is not a direct equation between what is taught and what is learned. These beliefs require that much closer attention be paid to the methods chosen for presenting material, as well as the ways in which mediating influences (such as economic circumstances, cultural background, special talents or abilities) affect students' learning. While the goals of the Common Essential Learnings apply to all students, it needs to be recognized that not all students will reach these goals to the same extent or in the same way. For example, expectations for students with special needs are shaped by their particular abilities or disabilities.

Another fundamental of a teaching-learning process shaped by the C.E.L.s is that meaningful learning depends on giving students opportunities to be actively involved in knowledge construction. This does not mean totally embracing a discovery approach to learning, nor does it mean abandoning lecture and drill as methods of teaching. It does mean that new curriculum developments will include analyses of which types of knowledge are best acquired through lectures, memorization or practice, and which are best achieved through teaching methods that lead students to make the important connections themselves.

Teacher's role

"The teacher has to teach both students and subjects, and to do that, he or she must reconcile respect for the child and respect for what is being taught." Teaching is a learned profession, and many of the demands made on teachers relate to their being part of a scholarly community. Teaching requires an understanding of several categories of knowledge, including: content knowledge derived from the various disciplines; general pedagogical knowledge; curriculum knowledge; knowledge of learners and the learning process.

In addition, teachers need to have: knowledge about education as an institution with its own rules and regulations, as well as education's relationship to the larger community and the government; knowledge of educational goals, purposes and values; and understanding of how the body of knowledge in each of these categories is built, codified or changed. While teaching has technical aspects which can be analyzed and prescribed, it is also a dynamic and reflective process.

Changing and improving instruction has implications for teachers' personal values and beliefs and is dependent in part on their unique abilities and experiences. Teachers' understandings of curricula and instruction will grow out of meaningful and concrete learning situations - just as they do for students. Teachers play a critical role in incorporating the Common Essential Learnings into school subjects. The demands of this process are best supported by a belief in the potential of the C.E.L.s to strengthen and enrich students' present learning and future lives.

COMMUNICATION

The goal of incorporating Communication into Saskatchewan's K-12 curricula is to promote students' learning in all school subjects through improving their language abilities within each subject. What is desired are students who can bring order and meaning to facts and experiences and communicate that understanding effectively to others.

Communication as a Common Essential Learning focuses on the language demands of each school subject. The role of the teacher is central to improving students' understandings through the development of communication abilities in all subjects. Thus, Communication is described largely in terms of instructional strategies necessary to help students with this task. It does not require that all teachers become language arts teachers, nor does it replace teachers' responsibilities for teaching the content and processes of other school subjects.

As a C.E.L., Communication recognizes first, that the language requirements of all school subjects must be clarified, and second, that teachers must be supported as they assume responsibility for these requirements. The over-riding purpose of such clarification and support is to assist students in coming to a better understanding of all their school subjects. Communication is based on three important principles which demonstrate the relationship between language, thinking and learning. Learning in all subjects is developed in and through language. Learning and growth in language abilities in the four language modes-listening, speaking, writing and reading are inter-connected and inseparable from learning in each individual field of study. This means that growth in language abilities is necessary for the continuous development of understanding in any school subject.

Growth in language abilities takes place as a result of planned language experiences in all four modes - listening, speaking, reading and writing. One learns to write as one learns to speak as one learns to read and listen. Each ability improves to the extent that all are exercised. Each school subject possesses unique (as well as common) language requirements. For example, while reading a literary passage in order to develop a response to its tone or mood, one needs to have a feel for the overall flow of the passage and suspend word by word analysis. Developing understanding of mathematical problems or algebraic equations, however, requires that one pay attention to each word or individual unit. This suggests that language instruction needs to be incorporated into all courses of study.

Language instruction within school subjects (other than English Language Arts) should focus on the language demands of each subject in terms of teacher talk, textbook language, and the specialized vocabulary and structured forms of expression unique to that subject. The interrelationship between language, thinking and learning is further clarified through an understanding of how students learn. Knowledge exists in the minds of knowers, and students do not develop or acquire knowledge until they can put information into an ordering which has meaning. Language is the means that students generally use to bring order and meaning to facts and experience, either by speaking or writing, or by inner monologue of thought. It is largely by means of language that the school expects learning to take place.

One of the aims of education is to help the student achieve full potential as a language user (including alternative and/or augmentative forms for those students unable to use verbal communication). To support this aim, awareness of the diversity of students' needs is important. When speaking of language, it needs to be remembered that language includes alternative forms of communication such as signing, manual communication systems, electronic communication devices and Braille. These forms are important not only for students with exceptional needs, but also for people with whom these students may wish to communicate. It is recognized that adaptations may be necessary for students with special needs. It is also important to recognize that communication may take different forms in different cultures.

Cultural differences in aspects of communication such as silence, eye contact and ways of expressing emotions need to be respected. When developing Communication, it is critical to be sensitive to cultural norms. Language develops in use, in response to the demands put upon it by learning in different subject areas, as well as students' life experiences. The language that evolves in a particular situation is shaped by a number of factors, including:

— the nature of the speaker or writer and the audience;
— the relationship that exists between the two;
— the purpose in speaking or writing;
— the nature of the subject; and
— the medium being used.

Language development is enhanced by the opportunity to use language in many different situations in order to deal with a wide variety of tasks. Through language, students acquire most of their learning. Methods of inquiry, recording, reporting and theorizing are linguistic processes, sensitive to the context in which they take place. It is in the school's power, as the context in which the learning of the Required Areas of Study takes place, to facilitate these processes. It is through language used for clearly perceived learning purposes that students acquire understanding of what a school education offers. Schools need to become places where understanding of the nature of language as well as general learning can proceed in an integrated manner through reading, writing, speaking, and listening.

The Teacher's Role

Communication as a C.E.L. supports teachers in their efforts "to increase and/or vary the language experiences that help students understand and explore the subject matter and processes of the Required Areas of Study". Students need to become literate in the language of each subject area. Teachers of each subject can help with this achievement by:

— having students participate in directed talk about the subject matter at hand (with the help of a teacher-prepared discussion guide) in pairs, small groups and large groups;

— providing opportunities for practicing the language of each subject area in different modes (listening, speaking, reading and writing) at different levels of complexity and formality related to the concepts of audience and purpose;

— taking students through a section of text, showing them how the subject presents its information and how it links facts or arguments in a particular way, or setting questions that help students identify these techniques for themselves;

— assisting students in the process of organizing information in subject areas (sorting, selecting, summarizing, outlining, taking notes, reviewing, previewing, and reporting on material);

— developing students' study skills through activities such as, analyzing material with students and brainstorming a number of questions or assignments that could be given, or having students compose questions themselves;

— working with the teacher-librarian in the library resource center to show students where subject area resources are located and how to make use of these resources.

Generally, teachers will need to place a great deal more emphasis on expressive language, both oral and written, as students come to terms with learning in the subject areas. Having greater awareness of the contextual nature of language and learning suggests that teachers should use a variety of instructional contexts - including individual, small group, whole class, pairs, and even across-age groupings - to take advantage of different language and learning possibilities.

Teachers should be aware of the different capabilities of students at different ages, as they deal with language in the various modes-listening, speaking, reading and writing. Students' development in language, thinking and learning is enhanced when teachers:

— provide students with examples of language - how it looks, works and is used (e.g. labels for classroom objects, charts on classroom walls, books displayed on shelves or ledges);

— value their students' existing language competencies and plan learning experiences that build on these;

— provide opportunities for second-language students to draw upon their first-language skills in order to allow students to engage in higher order thought processes such as generalizing, hypothesizing, persuading, arguing and reporting;

— provide extended wait time to allow for students' reflection and solicit responses in such a way that each student has an equal opportunity to respond;

— follow student responses with requests for clarification, elaboration, extension and evidence;

— provide opportunities for tentative, exploratory and inexplicit discussion in small groups;

— set some pre-listening, pre-speaking, pre-reading and pre-writing activities such as brainstorming, prior questions or personal reflective writing;

— provide assignments which incorporate process writing and meaningful classroom talk and listening such as: student journals and logs, small-group projects, student-teacher dialogues, role playing and educational drama;

— further develop thinking (both the level and type of thought) through the language which teachers use themselves and require of students, including analysis, reasoning, formulating, synthesis and decision making;

Teachers' roles in fostering Communication abilities often overlap and reinforce their roles in fostering other C.E.L.s - such as Critical and Creative Thinking and Independent Learning.

Students' language needs

Studies of the problems which teachers most frequently

encounter in students' writing and reading abilities in the content areas typically include the following situations and difficulties:

— Students often copy sections of text, rather than attempting to translate the text or reference book into their own words.

— Many students can recognize and pronounce the words but do not understand what they read.

— Often students cannot write clearly and logically about what they have read.

— Students frequently cannot apply what they have learned from a text or lecture to a new situation or context.

— Many students have limited vocabularies which restrict their reading and writing potential.

— Many available textbooks are too difficult for students, and teachers have to translate them for students.

Working from concerns such as these, strategies have been developed which assist students in understanding and applying subject matter from the content areas. The activities which appear to be most useful are those which focus on having students think through and actively construct the meaning of texts, lectures or films for themselves, and which require students to translate this knowledge into another form (such as concept mapping and diagramming). Retention rates from such activities are longer and material is more likely to be related to previous knowledge, past experience and/or other areas of study.

Activities which incorporate listening and speaking in pairs, small or large groups with reading and writing activities promote the most growth. Such activities can be categorized to reflect students' needs in the content areas (cited previously as frequently encountered problems). These categories include: preparation for reading, listening or viewing; reflection on text read; extraction and organization of text; and translation and sharing of new learning. While two of these categories will be discussed briefly, the list of practical resources related to Communication provide support in all of these areas.

Whenever we learn something, we make connections or forge links between what we already know and what we are learning. At the same time, learning something new involves putting aside content judged to be irrelevant. This dual process involves thinking that is not simply receptive (where students passively take something in), but rather thinking that is active and constructive. To engage students in this type of thinking-learning activity is one of the surest ways to promote genuine understanding of content.

Understanding can be fostered through preparatory activities, such as questioning of various types, discussion, analysis and categorization tasks, and process writing. Whether students are in kindergarten or in grade twelve, exploration of a topic within one of the content areas proceeds best when linked to an activity which focuses students' thoughts on the underlying meaning of the topic. Meanings can be personal, reflecting students' own experience related to the topic, or meanings can be more formal, exploring for example, the relationship between the new topic and knowledge of other school subjects.

The strategy of having students establish prior questions is valuable at any age. Teacher questioning and discussion in an introductory or preparatory lesson should be designed to elicit responses from students about what they already know on the topic. The second step in such a, process would require students to reflect on what they don't know and what they would like to know about this same topic. Such exploration can be achieved through a variety of formats.

Some appropriate methods, beginning with students in kindergarten, are class brainstorming and preparation of the group's set of questions (recorded on an experience chart). Teachers of older students may ask their classes to reflect on the topic, and then to write individual sets of questions. In all grades, such an initial activity should be followed by an activity at the end of the unit which leads students back to their original questions, in order to see if they have been answered. A somewhat more formal technique used to prepare students for new learning is that of the structured overview or concept map. Teachers print these concepts on sheets, which are cut into cards by students. Students are instructed to read the words or phrases on the cards, then to sort them into two piles of concepts - first, ones they are familiar with or have a basic understanding of, and second, ones they don't understand.

Recording and working specifically with the collection of concepts that students do not know is a useful offshoot of this activity. Students could also be expected to work further with the concepts they do know, arranging them on their desks to reflect their present understanding. They could move cards closer together to demonstrate which concepts belong in the same category, or alternatively, order them from the most general or inclusive concepts (top of their desk), to the sub-topics (middle), to specific examples of sub-topics (bottom).

Much new information that is presented to students comes in the form of material which they are required to read. Strategies for helping students make sense of what they read in the content areas include those which focus attention on the underlying structure or framework of how the text or section of text is organized. All print materials in schools do not follow an ideal and consistent structure. This lack of consistency makes extracting and organizing material a difficult task for most students. Beginning in the middle years, teachers should assist students in developing some common structures for reading factual material. Students should become familiar with and recognize a number of the most common structures, including:

— ideas, people, situations or settings are compared or contrasted one with another;
— main ideas are broken into sub topics;
— sub topics are supported by examples;
— solutions are suggested to problems;

— items in a category are listed; such items may be described in word, sentence or paragraph units (that is, lists are not always lists of words);

— causes are explained in terms of their effects.

Just as young students come to recognize predictable story patterns, older students should come to recognize organizational structures. Reading the table of contents in a variety of textbooks as the basis for discussion of some common organizational schemes, would be a useful preliminary activity in any of the content areas. Having pupils draw diagrams which summarize a text, chapter or passage is also helpful. Teachers might present several types of diagrams as models, such as graphs or flow charts, but students should be encouraged to develop their own diagrams whenever possible.

Organizing print material into a visual display is a valuable small group activity which stimulates understanding, because it requires so much re-reading and checking of facts. At the same time, it gives teachers an effective way of assessing students' levels of understanding. Many activities promote meaningful learning in the content areas. One final activity discussed here is that of note-making. The making of notes is an intrinsic part of learning, which can help students better organize and understand information from text, talk or film. It is an activity which is useful for research and essay writing, as well as for studying.

Teachers have a role to play in helping students develop the ability to make notes. In the early years, children need to be encouraged to put ideas and information into their own words. Asking students to share with their classmates a sentence about the report they have just heard or the program they have recently watched, can lead to thinking about the main idea of the presentation. After students' initial offerings are given, teachers can focus discussion further with comments and questions such as: "We have heard a lot of things that people remember about the book I just read. What do you think is the most important part of the book?"

By the time students have some rudimentary abilities in reading and writing, they should be encouraged to summarize new information by writing one or two sentences which describe what they have learned from an activity, book or film. Young students should also be given tasks such as writing down one word which best tells what a book, recording, or film was about. In the middle years, note-making should be preceded by having students set prior questions (as individuals or in groups) which will guide them in looking for specific information. Two activities which are useful for middle-years' students include:

— having pupils make a set of notes on a short selection (2 - 3 pages) which they have read;

— having students make notes on a short passage which a teacher has read to them.

In both instances, students profit most from the sharing and group discussion which follow such an activity. During discussion, teachers will need to find ways to have students reflect on some of the following observations:

— It is advantageous to wait until you have read or heard the entire selection before beginning to make notes (providing the selection is relatively short).

— In note-making, students must pay attention to economy (keeping the notes brief), precision (making the point clearly and accurately), and creativity (finding ways to organize notes that work best for them and best express their own thoughts and understanding).

— Note-making activities should be accompanied, at least part of the time, by an activity where the notes are used or applied - such as using the notes to give a talk to the class, or as the basis for writing a short research summary or report. Continuing into the secondary school years, students need opportunities to use note-making as a thinking activity - one which links their reading, viewing and talking with their writing.

Some general guidelines for developing students' abilities with regard to note-making and report writing include:

— setting up purposeful note-making tasks based on the content being taught;

— involving students in discussing ideas and thereby checking on their understanding of what they have read (or viewed or heard) before they begin note-making; insisting that students write projects and assignments in their own words;

— providing students with time in class to talk about and develop their own notes and reports;

— providing students with clear guidelines on content, presentation, approximate length and assessment criteria for reports;

— beginning a lesson with sustained writing about the previous day's work, starting with key words, extending into sentences and linking sentences into paragraphs.

Finally, it should be noted that the preceding discussion of note-making and other strategies for organizing information are consistent with the role of the teacher-librarian in a resource-based learning approach. Co-operation between teacher and teacher-librarian in incorporating Communication strategies into library research projects is important.

NUMERACY

The goal of incorporating Numeracy into Saskatchewan's K-12 curricula is to develop individuals who can cope confidently and competently with everyday situations demanding the use of mathematical concepts, as well as developing their ability to learn new concepts when necessary. What is desired are students who know how to compute, measure, estimate and interpret mathematical data, know when to apply these same skills and techniques, and understand why these particular processes apply. Further, Numeracy is intended to strengthen students' learning in all school subjects through providing them with grounded understanding of the quantitative aspects of each subject. Numeracy can be described as the knowledge, skills and appreciations needed for students to understand and utilize mathematical ideas, techniques and applications.

Numerate people demonstrate an "at-homeness" with numbers and are able to understand information that is presented quantitatively: in graphs, charts and tables; through reference to percentage increase or decrease; and in timelines. Numeracy involves students in integrating such skills as interpreting quantitative information, performing straightforward calculations mentally, estimating values that are known and unknown, and developing an intuitive knowledge of measurement units. Alternative processes and basic skills are needed for students with severe disabilities, as some students may not proceed beyond simple ordering, one-to-one correspondence or an elementary knowledge of numbers.

A focus upon Numeracy in Saskatchewan's core curricula is justified by the demands of modern life - both within and outside the workplace. It is also justified by the demands of acquiring an education. Numeracy can be considered as a way of knowing - one which helps students better understand all of their school subjects. Strengthening students' mathematical abilities by exercising them in other subject areas may offer students another means of comprehending these subjects. Increasing students' opportunities to apply their numeracy skills should result in more students integrating them into their everyday understandings.

An examination of the demands of modern life reveals that numeracy skills are drawn upon daily. Numeracy demands encompass a number of routine tasks such as counting objects, reading clocks, counting money and finding the page location of a book. Non-routine tasks such as completing an annual tax return or estimating the amount and cost of new carpeting are often accomplished with outside help. Adults do, however, exhibit flexibility of thinking while performing everyday tasks and tend to select techniques according to a number of criteria, including: the purpose of calculation, the degree of precision and accuracy needed, the size and types of numbers, and (most importantly) helpful contextual cues in the environment.

For example, shoppers use a variety of ways to compare prices and take into account contextual cues when they compare the prices of two products of equal size or quantity. A great variety of mathematical demands are placed on people in contemporary Canadian society (both inside and outside educational institutions); a review of these demands illustrates the general types of abilities and competencies required. These can be discussed under the general headings of: data analysis and interpretation, calculation, and measurement.

Computers are forcing more and more members of society to become familiar with numbers and statistics, and in particular the interpretation of quantitatively expressed information. Most government agencies and business groups produce statistics. Business managers, administrators, public servants and consumers need to be sufficiently numerate to interpret the data that are now routinely used for decision making. Consumer reports, cost of living indexes and surveys are examples of data-oriented messages that people receive and need to process. Adults see graphs, tables, charts, scales and dials almost every day and are expected to synthesize information from them. In order to function in an information society, it is essential for students to learn how to read and interpret quantitative information which may be presented in tables of figures or visually displayed in graphs.

One of the most common mathematical tasks carried out by adults is that of calculation, using pencil and paper methods, calculators, mental calculations and estimations. Adding, subtracting, multiplying and dividing with whole numbers are done frequently, but rarely with large numbers. Multiplying and dividing usually involve only one-digit factors and divisors. Adults use a wide variety of methods for such tasks; these methods are usually either self-invented or taught by other adults. Calculations involving decimal fractions to two places are common in relation to money - especially addition and subtraction. The use of percentages is widespread in laboratories and offices; again, most uses involve money. Since the changeover to metric few common fractions are seen, but recognizing fractional parts such as halves and quarters is needed by most people. Common fractions almost always have denominators that are powers of 2, such as 2, 4, 8 and 16. The ability to calculate with whole numbers and fractions increases students' understanding in subject areas such as social studies (e.g. calculating the population density or GNP of a country).

In order to increase speed and accuracy, and ultimately productivity, most employers encourage the use of calculators for the tasks described above. Calculators are faster, and in many instances, more accessible than computing with pencil and paper. Opposition to the use of calculators in classrooms or workplaces may be based on the fear that students will not gain knowledge of basic calculation skills or that workers will fail to notice errors produced by the inappropriate use of calculators. These difficulties can be largely overcome by instruction in the optimal use of calculators, supported by instruction in estimating approximate answers in order to check the accuracy of calculations.

In a large number of situations, there is no choice but to estimate because exact values are not obtainable. Predictions about the future, guesses about the past, and estimates of military strength would fall into this category. Sometimes estimates are easier to use and are clearer than the more precise actual figures. For example, a newspaper headline may state that the population of a city is 30 000 people, instead of using the actual figure of 29 876. Further, the use of estimates usually gives consistency. Government reports on the percentage of people unemployed give that percent to the nearest tenth and sports columns customarily round off a winning "percentage" to the nearest thousandth.

The ability to estimate is a highly valued work skill and can take several forms. Numerical estimation is used to detect calculation errors produced by calculators or pencil-and-paper methods. Another form of estimation involves measurement, as some decisions often have to be made based on visual inspection. Although skills of measurement estimation develop further on the job, it is essential that workers demonstrate an intuitive knowledge of or "feel" for measurement units. Students' understanding in the Required Areas of Study and other subjects is increased when they are able to estimate the accuracy of calculations or the length of time a particular assignment, such as an essay, will require.

A knowledge of measurement is vital. Even adults who do not take an active part in the measurement process need to be aware of the meaning of measurement, as they are likely to be consumers of measurement information - ordering supplies, calculating profit margins, or evaluating the success of a program. Understanding in school subjects such as science also require that students have a feel for measurement, understand the options presented by specific measurement situations and take into account their margin of error.

The Teacher's Role

Mathematics teachers will continue to be primarily responsible for developing an understanding of mathematical concepts, rules, principles, relationships and procedures, but Numeracy must also be supported in other subject areas. Almost all subjects can include some meaningful opportunities for students to apply mathematical knowledge. Most students in the elementary and middle grades learn best if they are involved in meaningful activities that require the use of manipulative materials. Secondary students also benefit from hands-on experiences with instruments and tools. A great deal of discussion and work with concrete materials should precede any introduction of symbolic abstractions. Opportunities to support the achievement of Numeracy can be discussed under the general headings of: problem solving, calculation, measurement, space and shape, and data analysis and interpretation.

Problem solving

If students encounter only the simplest of problems, or use formal procedures they don't. understand when solving problems, their approach to problem solving can become mechanical. When students are given problems to solve, instruction should focus on the understanding of the problem statement, the analytic tools or general problem-solving strategies that might be profitably used, and the assessment of the reasonableness of a solution. Even after a solution has been determined and discussed, analysis of the problem should continue. Students could discuss other methods of solution, make any generalizations, and show how other problems could be created by changing some of the features of the original problem. A few problems studied intensively contribute far more to developing the ability to solve problems than many problems treated superficially.

It is important to include examples of real-life problem solving in all school subjects, especially those problems that require continual reformulation, involve the collecting of information, and allow students to try a number of methods of solution - including ones that may not appear to be mathematically elegant. To discuss and solve real-life experiences, a teacher of second-language and other special needs students must be well aware of the level of language competency of students and then direct discussion through appropriate questioning in order to make use of what students know. By participating in practical activities, students develop their abilities to carry out routine tasks and approach non-routine problems with some confidence that solutions can be found. Older students can estimate the amount of food or money needed for a 3-day class trip. A school subject such as social studies can provide students with the opportunity to participate in examining solutions to real-life problems, such as inner-city poverty or where to locate a community recreation center.

Opportunities for students to practice and apply calculation skills can be found in all school subjects. In the Required Areas of Study, students can be encouraged to select the most appropriate means of performing any necessary calculations from pencil-and-paper methods, calculators, mental calculations, and estimations. Although not a replacement for thinking and reasoning, the hand-held calculator can provide teachers with additional time to help students become numerate. It is critical, as well, that students learn to distinguish between appropriate and inappropriate uses of calculators. "Just as literate people do not rely entirely on a dictionary to carry out their daily communication tasks, numerate people do not rely entirely on a calculator to carry out their computational tasks".

Despite the obvious advantages of using calculators, the ability to calculate mentally and to provide quick estimates of the accuracy of a calculation, whether produced electronically or manually, continues to be extremely useful. Since the great majority of everyday problems are solved mentally, it is important that students are taught a variety of ways to calculate in their heads. Once the students understand how and when to apply a mental calculation technique, practice is needed to increase speed and accuracy. Students also require considerable help and practice if they are to learn to distinguish between situations calling for rough estimates or exact answers. Teachers can develop students' intuitive notions of mathematical concepts through practical activities with varied materials.

Students can perceive the attributes of mass (weight) by comparing the differing weights of objects balanced in their hands. By pouring liquids from one container into another. students can observe the properties of volume. Direct experiences related to measurement ideas can lead students to realize that area requires a "covering" of surfaces and perimeter forms a "boundary" around those surfaces. If students have an intuitive notion about what they are measuring, they will be able to distinguish between—and be less likely to confuse - measurement processes which appear to be similar.

Unconventional instruments and non-standard measurement units, such as feet or hands, can be used initially to help students develop an understanding of the measurement process.

Students of all ages benefit from experiences in carrying out measurements using a variety of conventional measurement tools. Providing students with extensive practical work ensures that they will have less difficulty in learning to use and select tools and instruments encountered outside of school. Whenever measuring takes place in any subject area, it should be done primarily for the purpose of gathering data needed for the solution of a problem, with some discussion about precision and error and their effects on computation. Perhaps the most significant contribution schools can make to a student's understanding about the nature of measurement is the establishment of a wide variety of everyday equivalencies that can be used whenever measurement units are being considered. For example, if students know that doorways are usually 2 m high, then students can be asked to compare the length or height of people or objects in relation to the standard height of a doorway.

Most subject areas can contribute significantly to the development of a measurement sense. Whenever a country is being studied in social studies, its size can be compared with the size of other geographical areas familiar to the students. For example, a chart portraying a map of Saskatchewan can be overlaid with an outline of the country of France to demonstrate comparative size. In the physical sciences, where measurement is commonplace but the units are not, teachers can facilitate students' understanding of units such as light years, pascals, joules, newtons, milliamperes and nanometres by providing them with a concrete reference. For example, a dollar bill lying flat on a table exerts a pressure of about 1 Pa. It is the responsibility of all subject areas to help students to think and estimate with metric units.

All measurements and measuring tools seen in school should continue to involve metric units, especially in the elementary and middle grades. As students need considerable practice in converting from one metric measurement unit to another, teachers can provide opportunities for students to convert from cm to mm, and back again. Although it is important for students to learn the terminology used to describe geometric shapes (i.e. diagonal, perimeter, square and radius), the focus of instruction should be on the properties of plane and solid objects and how such knowledge can be applied to real-world situations. Spatial concepts are developed best through kinesthetic experiences.

Plane and solid shapes should be available for pupils to handle, measure, and use in building. Students can learn a variety of ways that plane and solid objects can be constructed from simple materials or drawn with conventional instruments. All students can learn to use such drawing instruments as a ruler or compass. Students can also learn how to read a variety of scale drawings and plans, make reasonably accurate sketches of simple or complex structures, and occasionally construct a full or scale model using a plan or drawing. Such activities can help students learn spatial concepts and relationships, use appropriate terminology, and improve their ability to visualize. Knowing how to read and interpret quantitative information presented in any number of forms is essential for functioning in an information society.

At a minimum, students need a facility with the base ten number system and an understanding of how symbols can be used to represent quantities. Emphasis in all subject areas should be on the practical handling of numbers, such as interpreting graphs, using an instructional manual or reading prices. Structured concrete materials - such as base 10 arithmetic blocks, bundling sticks, place value charts and containers, abacuses, money and metric measuring instruments - should be used to develop an understanding of decimal place value relationships. An important aspect of data analysis is the reading and interpretation of information organized in tables and charts or displayed as graphs.

To develop a facility with reading these types of data presentations, it is important that almost all school subjects contain some instruction on reading and using tables, charts and graphs commonly seen in a particular area of study. One of the most important areas of Numeracy utilized in our technological society is statistics. Statistics refers broadly to the collection, analysis and interpretation of numerical data. Because of its importance, students should become familiar with rudimentary statistical notions; in all school subjects students should be encouraged to critically examine any statistics cited as evidence for an argument or used to express a point of view. It is important that students learn to withhold judgments about any argument based on statistical information until they find out how this information was obtained.

The study of elementary probability should emphasize its use in estimating risks, chances, odds and proportions. Students should see how probability is used, as in forecasting weather conditions, in estimating risks to the environment from chemical pollutants, or in determining the chances of winning a lottery. In all subject areas an attempt should be made to help students understand common expressions and uses of probability.

CRITICAL AND CREATIVE THINKING

The goal of incorporating critical and creative thinking processes into Saskatchewan's K-12 curricula is to develop individuals who value knowledge, learning and the creative process, who can and will think for themselves, yet recognize the limits of individual reflection and the need to contribute to and build upon mutual understandings of social situations. What is desired are students who have purposes for learning, know how and when to question, who recognize when more information is needed and the type of knowledge which is required, know how to find and organize information, and who can generate and evaluate a number of alternatives to human problems.

Critical and Creative Thinking can be described as qualities of good thinking processes and as types of thinking. Creative thinking is generally considered to be involved with the creation or generation of ideas, processes, experiences or objects; critical thinking is concerned with their evaluation. Critical and creative thinking are interrelated and complementary aspects of thinking. Almost all of the thinking which we undertake contains some critical and some creative aspects. For example, when we try to solve real life problems we move back and forth several times between creative and critical reflection as we develop solutions or weigh the consequences of any one solution. It is important, therefore, that any attempts to improve thinking abilities pay attention to both critical and creative aspects of thinking.

Critical and creative thinking processes are combinations of abilities, knowledge, values, attitudes, skills and processes. While the knowledge base required for critical and creative reflection varies from subject to subject, the underlying values and attitudes remain constant across school subjects. Although skills and processes are somewhat dependent upon specific subject matter for their form, these same values and attitudes are required in all subjects for their execution. It is also important to note that the content of each category is descriptive of the area but not a final or all inclusive list. Educators are encouraged to evaluate these lists and to generate others as they become more familiar with incorporating critical and creative thinking into their teaching.

Critical and creative thinking contribute to achieving such crucial goals for education in Saskatchewan as developing students who work towards the creation of greater social justice, exercise the right to dissent responsibly, and act in accordance with an ethical framework which reflects qualities such as honesty, integrity and compassion. A final aspect of how Critical and Creative Thinking is defined by Saskatchewan Education is related to these goals and can be stated as the intention to develop "strong sense" critical and creative thinkers.

Paul distinguishes between "weak sense" and "strong sense" critical thinking in the following way. People who have the abilities necessary for undertaking quality critical and creative thought but use them only to their own advantage are critical and creative thinkers in the weak sense. Strong sense critical and creative thinkers, however, are committed to using their abilities to seek out the most accurate and fair positions regardless of or in spite of their own particular interests or desires. Such thinking takes into account the needs, viewpoints and arguments of others and is built upon analysis of one's own motives.

The importance of having students develop good critical and creative thinking abilities has to do with the foundations needed for a democracy and with the tools needed for independent and life-long learning. A democracy is only as strong as its citizens are informed, capable of, and willing to engage in critical and creative reflection. Critical thought is necessary for analyzing arguments and for rational decision making, while creative thinking is necessary in order to develop alternatives to ways of life not considered upon reflection to be desirable. Students also need to develop these thinking abilities in order to move their learning beyond memorization or passive acceptance, to understanding and the commitment to persevere until clarity and insight are achieved. Without a commitment to critical and creative thinking the values of rationality, truth and justice achieve little substance in the classroom.

Given the above purposes for developing students' critical and creative thinking abilities, it is important to examine teaching methods or means of instruction in terms of their consistency with these purposes. While the last decade saw the development of many commercial thinking programs designed to teach thinking as generic skills which could be developed in isolation from school subjects and from analyses of underlying values and beliefs, most researchers today argue that critical and creative thinking processes are more than simply technical skills. A technical skill is one which can be taught in the same way across a number of contexts without involving an individual's basic feelings, beliefs or motives in any significant way.

A technical skill, then, can be learned in the same manner regardless of whether one is a fair-minded or compassionate individual or whether one has foundational knowledge in any particular school subject. Critical and creative thinking are not these types of skills. Rather, developing these thinking abilities involves will or desire on the part of the thinker to go beyond what is given and to make an attempt to understand the self and question the motives of others. Such thinking is highly dependent upon human purpose. Treating critical and creative reflection solely as technical skills is not consistent with the purposes for which they are being developed in Saskatchewan schools.

In addition, it is important to recognize that critical and creative thinking takes different forms in different disciplines or arts and that critical and creative reflection do not develop in a vacuum. Every occasion of thought requires some content to reflect upon. Thought is shaped by content - by the facts, concepts, principles and theories of various disciplines or fields and by one's experiences and observations. While critical and creative thinking may contain some common elements, they also take unique forms in unique areas of study. For example, critical thinking in mathematics does not necessarily involve the same mixture of knowledge, skills and processes as critical thinking in social studies or the arts.

The criteria for good critical or creative thought in an area of knowledge depends upon the methods developed in that area for establishing the truth of its claims. This implies, then, that being able to think critically about literature is no guarantee that one will also be capable of critical and creative reflection using the concepts and principles of algebra as subject matter. While the values which move people to attempt such reflection remain constant, the knowledge base required does not. Part of the teacher's role in fostering critical and creative thinking abilities is that of building students' understanding of the concepts, skills and processes of the various disciplines and fields and of their methods for constructing and evaluating knowledge.

Teachers need curricula and instructional methods which support inquiry into methods for knowledge construction, such as how scientists "do" science or how historians establish historical facts. In summarizing the purposes and definition of critical and creative reflection, it is important to understand the relationship between why one would undertake such reflection and how one would best go about it. Methods follow from purpose. This understanding may be developed further through an analysis of the teacher's role in assisting students to become critical and creative thinkers.

The Teacher's Role

The role of the teacher in helping to improve students' critical and creative thinking abilities includes examining the personal qualities required of teachers by such a goal and the classroom climate and teaching practices which best support it.

Discussion of the teacher's role in fostering critical and creative thinking must begin from a recognition of the teacher as a person whose unique character, interests and desires can not be separated out from the idea of the teacher's role. Good teachers are doing more when they teach than acting according to prescribed roles. Their desire to nurture a love for learning, to help students recognize and act upon their capabilities, and to establish a classroom climate which is based upon mutual regard and respect gives their teaching purpose and meaning beyond any technical description of the teacher's role. What is required is that teachers be authentic individuals who are striving to improve their practice through the use of critical and creative thought. Acting upon their belief in the importance of critical and creative reflection, teachers would attempt to:

— analyze their own thinking processes and classroom practices and provide reasons for what they do;
— be open-minded, encouraging students to follow their own thinking and not simply repeat what the teacher has said;

— change their own positions when the evidence warrants, being willing to admit a mistake;

— consistently provide opportunities for students to select activities and assignments from a range of appropriate choices;

— exhibit genuine interest, curiosity and commitment to learning;

— undertake the organization and preparation required to achieve learning goals;

— seek imaginative, appropriate and ethical solutions to problems;

— be sensitive to others' feelings, level of knowledge and degree of sophistication;

— show sensitivity to the physical elements which contribute to a stimulating learning environment through the physical arrangements and displays they provide or facilitate;

— allow for student participation in rule setting and decision making related to all aspects of learning, including assessment and evaluation.

An integral part of teaching methodologies designed to foster critical and creative reflection is the type of classroom environment which the teacher helps to create. The type of climate which appears to be most desirable is one which fosters psychological safety and intellectual freedom within a structure where individuals respect one another as persons of unconditional worth. Teachers can move towards making their classrooms more thoughtful places by making judgments and decisions from a base of empathy and understanding, by valuing originality and authenticity, and by using differences of opinion as teaching situations which invite thoughtful analyses.

More specific activities and strategies for the improvement of thinking abilities will also be proposed, with the qualification that the best ways to foster critical and creative thinking will continue to be developed by reflective practitioners as they come to know their students. What is needed are teachers who engage their students in meaningful activities - ones which incorporate students' unique interests, abilities, backgrounds and community needs. The ideas presented here are only intended as starting points for further reflection, and like all good ideas will be improved by critically appraising their application to individual situations.

Teachers can foster critical and creative thinking within the various school subjects by

— Using the vocabulary of critical thinking themselves. For example, asking questions such as: "What can you infer about the effects of this action from the statements given? What can you conclude about the person who took this picture from the evidence contained in the picture? Is honesty a necessary condition of friendship?"

— Involving students in role plays or simulations of historical events where people held conflicting views. For example, the constitutional debate between the federal government, the governments of the provinces, and the leaders of The First Nations, the Metis and non-status Indians.

— Organizing for "structured controversy." That is, involving students in discussions and debates which tackle more than one side of an issue and require students to back arguments with evidence and reference to consequences.

— Being alert for and encouraging students to notice where material presented in texts, films and other communications over-simplify or distort reality as students understand it.

— Encouraging students to use qualifiers and recognize contradictions.

— Supplementing regular textbooks with additional curriculum materials (including nonprint forms) which could provide local, regional or provincial applications, appeal to more than one of the senses, offer alternative ways of knowing, and/or provide a wider variety of perspectives on the subject matter.

Having students attend community meetings, watch television programs or read newspaper articles which express different viewpoints. Following this by an analysis of the relative strengths and weaknesses of the arguments, including analysis of the possible motives or human purposes underlying the viewpoints.

— Having students attempt to solve real life problems where there is the possibility of more than one adequate solution and where several different types of information are required.

— Exploring with students the methods used to develop knowledge in a particular discipline or field.

— Asking students questions with multiple answers or several equally correct answers.

— Requiring students to defend their assertions with reasons. For example, when students answer a question the teacher would follow the students' answers, whenever appropriate, with a further question which asks the students why they believe this version or think their answers are reasonable, plausible or accurate.

— Having students analyze the content of popular media - music, movies or TV - for the accuracy and completeness of its portrayals and the consistency of the reality presented with life as they know it. For example, exploring the contradictions between the existence of poverty and commercials which portray the acquisition of material possessions as being largely a matter of choice between competing brands rather than requiring that one have the money to afford them.

— Having students analyze the content of popular media using standards which compare the media's portrayal of human behavior with ideals, such as treating people with respect and tolerance and refraining from stereotypical, sexist or racist views. Inquiring into media's portrayal of the consequences of human actions.

— Requiring students to analyze objects and artifacts, either man-made or in the natural environment, from a design perspective which examines their purpose, structure, model cases and the criteria for their evaluation.

— Using, and encouraging students to use, analogies and metaphors in descriptions, comparisons and attempts to understand new concepts, ideas, principles or theories.

Practices such as these do not need to be restricted to middle years or secondary students. Critical and creative reflection can be improved beginning in the early grades when teachers understand these thinking processes themselves. Before students can analyze arguments, tease out the assumptions contained in them, or recognize possible motives which shape people's views or restrict their objectivity, they must have a sense of themselves and of others as persons of worth. This sense is built from an understanding of human feelings and of how individuals' behavior affects the persons around them. Kindergarten teachers begin to develop such understandings from the first day of school, through activities which engage students' emotions while helping them acquire a language to express these emotions. It is also important for teachers of young children to offer support to students in solving their own social problems and conflicts, but not to impose solutions upon them.

Critical and creative thinking begins when a child is expected to confront in their own thinking, the reasons for treating other people with respect and the ways in which one can do so. Quality of thought also improves through direct encounter with reality - with the concrete and with the natural materials which can be provided in an expanded school environment. An important aspect of the teacher's role in providing students with concrete materials and real life experiences is to ask critical questions which foster student reflection about these materials and experiences. Some general guidelines for teachers, which apply to developing critical and creative capacities in students of all ages, would be to:

— choose real objects and experiences over workbooks and textbooks in developing understanding whenever possible. For example, when studying ponds and pond life, a trip to the pond is important and more appropriate than the use of books or films alone.

— consistently allow for students' input into establishing the criteria for the evaluation of classroom activities, assignments and behaviors.

— choose to display students' work over commercially prepared displays. For example, while commercial alphabet displays are readily available, only students can create an alphabet which will be personally meaningful to them and contain their own experiences and categories.

— consistently offer and encourage students to seek alternative ways of responding to structured art activities, fulfilling learning requirements, or completing a craft, project or assignment. While 2 + 2 should always equal 4, there are at least 100 ways to make a paper mouse.

Perhaps the most important aspect in developing a climate conducive to critical and creative thinking is to increase students' will or motivation to behave reflectively. While there are many ways to learn and to know, the knowledge retained by students is that knowledge which they find relevant to their daily lives or which can be integrated into larger systems of knowledge. This does not mean that learning should always be easy or that all knowledge should have immediate relevance. It also is not intended to imply that memorization and drill are necessarily inappropriate or meaningless activities. Rather, the suggestion is that students will voluntarily exercise their own willpower and persevere at difficult learning tasks (including memorization when necessary), if they see the learning task as personally meaningful.

For educators, this means portraying knowledge as valuable in itself and as a means to important human ends. Thus, the knowledge which students encounter in schools must not be presented solely as isolated or discrete elements, but rather should be explored as parts of meaningful wholes. Knowledge must be examined in terms of its relationship to other knowledge and to students' experiences and understandings. Teaching which encourages students to reflect upon and build these relationships supports critical and creative thinking. Finally, because teacher-questioning is such an important aspect in the development of critical and creative thinking processes, a brief overview of types of critical questions would be useful. The following types of questions can be used to stimulate individual reflection, process writing, and small or large group discussion in a subject area.

TECHNOLOGICAL LITERACY

The goal of incorporating Technological Literacy into Saskatchewan's K-12 curricula is to develop individuals who understand how technology and society influence one another and who are able to use this knowledge in their every day decision making. What is desired are students who are able to analyze the technological influences on their lives and see themselves as having roles and responsibilities in shaping public policy related to technological change.

Technological Literacy can be described as the intellectual processes, abilities and dispositions needed for students to understand the link between technology, themselves and society in general. Technological Literacy is concerned with developing students' awareness of how technology is related to the broader social system, and how technological systems cannot be fully separated from the political, cultural and economic frameworks which shape them. In order to achieve an informed, balanced and comprehensive analysis of the technological influences on their lives and then be able to act on the basis of their analysis, students require certain levels of knowledge, skills and abilities. These include:

— understanding that technology includes hardware, know-how, cultural needs and desires, and economic and political decision making;

— understanding how technology shapes and is shaped by society;

— understanding that technological issues involve conflicting assumptions, interpretations and options;

— having the necessary data collection and decision making skills to make intelligent choices;

— having the ability and desire to take responsible action on social issues.

A Technologically literate person is someone who critically examines and questions technological progress and innovation. To be critical about technology means to have "the intellectual skills to analyze the pros and cons of any technological development, to examine its potential benefits, its potential costs, and to perceive the underlying political and social forces driving the development". Decisions about the creation and use of new technology involve human, social and environmental issues which place constraints and limits on the solutions. Values also influence intellectual processes, since anything that involves choice also involves consideration of whose values are shaping a particular technological development. The capacity to make critical judgments involving technology increases the ability of students (as citizens) to use such knowledge to shape and influence their environment.

Many changes have occurred in society as a result of advances in science and technology. Some of the changes have been good; other changes have entailed risks that were either not known or only dimly perceived. Science and technology touch the lives of all people in basic ways every day, affecting the manner in which they obtain food, transportation, clothing and housing. As science and technology play increasingly vital roles in peoples' lives, it is important to develop a basic understanding of both forces in this technologically-rich society.

Science is a process of discovery. It is a set of ongoing procedures including hypothesis testing, observing and synthesizing information, in order to better understand the world. Scientific knowledge is the result of humans reaching a consensus about some aspect of the physical world. That is, the acceptance of data depends upon psychological and social factors, such as the beliefs, and values of the scientist and of the society, as well as agreements related to methods for acquiring scientific knowledge. This reflects the nature of both scientific data (which tend to be theory-laden) and science as a human activity (with its personal and social aspects). The findings of scientific experiments result from the interaction of scientists, scientific knowledge and the community.

What distinguishes science from technology is that its role is to extend and modify knowledge - to change knowledge rather than to preserve it. This role arises from an interest in acquiring knowledge for its own worth and not as a means to other ends. It is critical that students appreciate the need for scientific knowledge above and beyond technical applications. In order to assess the value of fundamental research (as opposed to applied research) it is necessary to have an understanding of how scientists proceed with their work.

Technology

— Technology can be defined through the following understandings:

— Technology is more than the "hardware" or the non-natural objects manufactured by humans.

— Technology includes "know-how", i.e., having the information, skills and procedures necessary to design, produce or use technology. Such "know-how" is not sufficient in itself.

— Technology is the process of manufacturing the hardware, which includes the economic, social and political environments that make this manufacture possible. (For example, an important part of understanding a technological development is understanding how and, as a consequence, why it is funded.)

— Technology is the use of hardware and people in order to extend human capabilities. (For example, the use of automobiles leads to a system of roads, gas stations and driving laws. It is this combined system that extends the human capability of moving about.)

— Technology is an ordered, rational effort to solve definable problems.

— Technology enriches and eases daily life, but can carry with it unanticipated side effects. It is important to consider the benefits compared with the costs - in terms of resources, value and money—before and during the development of a technology. There is always a degree of risk involved, because of the difficulty in predicting all the effects of a particular technological development.

As technology is at the heart of many of the critical issues facing today's society, students need to develop an understanding of both the benefits and the risks inherent in any given technological innovation. In order to make intelligent decisions on technological issues, it is important for students to understand how technology and society influence each other and then be able to use this knowledge to shape public policy in a democracy.

An understanding of how technology shapes and is shaped by society is based on two principles. First, technology is an agent of social change. Technological systems have produced great increases in the speed of communication, made mass production possible, and reduced physical labor for human beings. Technology has also provided an abundance of products and services; this requires individuals to make wise consumer decisions. Second, societies influence the course of technological development.

Social, historical and cultural factors determine if, and how, a technology is used. More than ever before, students are immersed in an environment shaped by human technology. Citizens' responsibilities in a technological age are defined as the exercising of democratic rights on issues that affect the direction to be taken by society and its technological developments. Becoming technologically literate means coming to grips with the problems of living in, and exerting influence upon, the constructed world.

In a democracy, it is believed that people of differing abilities and roles can communicate to create answers to problems of living; it is also felt that citizens can have some influence upon which technologies are advanced or restrained and how this process occurs. As citizens become better informed, they can begin to exert some measure of control over technological change. Public policy agendas at the national and provincial levels include issues and problems that require a level of technological literacy. For example, people might need to assess how a technological development would affect their personal health.,

The active, informed and effective participation of citizens in the governing process requires information about matters and issues, understanding of the workings of political systems and of the processes of participation, rational decisions about those matters and issues, and finally, action based on those decisions. Further, it is critical to understand who makes decisions about particular technological innovations and from what bias these decisions are made. Value claims are implicit in any positions regarding technological innovation and development. Therefore, critical analysis of these positions - including an examination of both the underlying values and the factual information provided by experts - is necessary in order to create citizens who are informed decision makers.

In order for students to live effectively in a technologically-sophisticated society, they need critical understandings which include:

— understanding of science as a process of discovery and consensus-making;

— understanding of technology with its inherent risks and benefits;

— understanding of how technology shapes and is shaped by society;

- understanding of the relationship between technological decisions and human values;
- understanding of the roles and responsibilities in shaping public policy related to technological change.

It should be noted that not all students may be able to integrate these critical understandings to the same degree. Some students with special needs may not be capable of reaching a level where they can analyze issues. These students may be more involved with the "know-how" aspect of technology, and may need to be assisted in the development of abilities to use technology in order to enhance the quality of their lives.

The role of the teacher in developing technologically literate students includes:

- building increased awareness, knowledge and understanding about technological developments of interest to students and to society as a whole through a contemporary view of technology;
- fostering critical thinking and decision making, based on evidence and on moral principles such as respect for persons or respect for the environment;
- providing opportunities for students' active involvement in local, regional and national issues.

A Contemporary view of technology includes both the more explicit concepts (contained by the solid lines in the lower portion of the inverted triangle) and the more implicit concepts (outlined with dotted lines in the expanded upper portion of this triangle). The intellectual processes, such as debating or problem solving, can be used to develop Technological Literacy. Some of the technological issues and areas that can be explored with this development are also illustrated.

A contemporary view of technology

This perspective requires that technological developments be related to students' lives and to the society in which they live.

For certain disabled students, technology can be the key to greater independence. For example, a personal computer with voice output can be used by students unable to speak or by blind students as a notetaking device and word processor. The use of adaptive devices by students with challenging needs can unlock the doors to communication, to participation in activities, to independence and to learning. Through the use of appropriate strategies, materials and experiences students with special needs can be assisted in using technology to enhance their daily living, safety and health, leisure and recreation, and decision making. Such abilities will enable these students to function as full members of society. One area in which students can examine the impact of technology on their lives, is the development of computer technology.

Computers are becoming more familiar in the school system at all levels. Computer literacy - as one aspect of technological literacy - requires more than programming skills. A curriculum for computer literacy should reflect a blend of the technical, cultural and organizational aspects of computer technology; it should also familiarize students with the public policy issues posed by information technologies. With access to vast amounts of information through databases, students need to understand the importance of distinguishing between what information is available and the purposes for which that information can be used. In order to deepen students' understandings about the effects of technological developments on their lives, it is important to relate these developments to issues and interests that are real to students.

By linking subject matter with everyday life and developments in society, students become involved in authentic and understandable experiences related to technology. In the earlier grades, technology can be looked at in terms of smaller and more local issues. For example, a unit on magnets could provide students with the opportunity to brainstorm about how their day would change if there were no magnets (for example, fridge doors wouldn't close). A subsequent discussion of what life would be like without magnets would help students consider the impact of this technological development on society as a whole (for example, the absence of large industrial magnets would create more jobs for people). It is important to have students draw relationships in their studies to larger world issues and to discuss both the positive and negative aspects of technology. This provides an accurate view of the role that technology plays in both meeting human needs and creating human problems.

Anderson has developed a guide for analyzing technological innovations that helps students understand the interrelationships between technology and social change, as well as the trade-offs and unexpected side effects that result from technology. Just as technological developments change societies, teachers can help students understand that societies also influence the course of technological developments. Understanding technology requires a consideration of the social forces brought to bear on those who make decisions about a technological innovation. The direction of technological development is often guided by the needs of managers, who may not be trained in the technical aspects of technology. Statements presented by developers, in support of their position for a particular technological innovation, require critical examination. The values that underlie such statements also need to be considered. Students who are acquainted with the values that underlie technological decisions are better able to participate in the shaping of public policy.

The interactions between technology and society sometimes lead to issues that can only be resolved by examining all sides of the question, as well as the beliefs, values and alternate solutions associated with each side. It is critical, then, to develop issue investigation and action strategies which students can apply to the issues they will face as citizens. Teachers can develop the necessary knowledge and skills within the Required Areas of Study through:

— involving students in locating information both from print and non-print sources, structuring relevant information and critically comparing information from different sources;

— modelling and encouraging the critical evaluation of data/ information;

— providing class time for student debate and analysis;

— giving students time to reflect verbally and in writing;

— structuring questioning and discussion (related to technological developments) so that implicit judgments based on assumptions and values become explicit;

— having students make comparisons of differing views by charting the differences and similarities, and then drawing conclusions;

— having students list the advantages and disadvantages of each side of a technological issue;

— helping students develop a broad perspective on the role that technology has played in the evolution of civilizations (both past and present);

— developing in students good habits of inquiry such as respect for evidence, care in drawing conclusions, curiosity and a healthy skepticism;

— encouraging student inquiry with an emphasis on how the student reached his or her solutions;

— exploring other cultures to understand the diversity of ways in which humans relate to their environment and to technology;

— modelling and encouraging the use of problem solving and decision making strategies.

An example of the last point is Patrick and Remy's "decision tree". This strategy can be a useful aid in developing alternatives and reaching a rational decision. The 4 basic elements are:

— discover the need for a decision;

— explore the values and goals relevant to the decision opportunity;

— develop alternative courses of action;

— predict likely consequences (positive and negative) of alternative courses of action.

Most skills are learned very gradually. For instance, "critically comparing information from different sources" cannot be learned quickly. It is important to widen students' concept of learning so that they recognize gradual learning as real learning. Assessment techniques should include an evaluation of this gradual learning process.

Responsible action related to decision making can be encouraged by:

— introducing decision making strategies and providing opportunities for students to use the strategies in reaching decisions related to technological issues;

— providing students with practice in exercising "control" over situations involving technology at different levels - personal, local, then regional;

— developing students' abilities to take persuasive consumer, legal or political actions in the resolution of issues (e.g. writing letters to newspapers or speaking at public meetings).

To summarize the theory and practice of promoting Technological Literacy:

— learning in the content areas should provide a contemporary view of technology related to students' interests so that students have an understanding of the social, economic and political forces which affect technological developments;

— it is critical for students to realize that technology both shapes and is shaped by society, and that as citizens, they can be a powerful influence in shaping the course of technological innovations;

— it is important that teachers promote the development of critical thinking and decision making and encourage students to act on the basis of their decisions.

PERSONAL AND SOCIAL VALUES AND SKILLS

The goal of this Common Essential Learning is to assist in the development of compassionate and fair-minded persons who can make positive contributions to society as individuals and as members of groups. What is desired are individuals whose actions reflect an educated, rational and empathetic sense of social responsibility. In the classroom, this Common Essential Learning has two related aims: to support students in treating other persons with respect; and, to support students in coming to a better understanding of the personal, moral, social and cultural aspects of school learning.

Personal and Social Values and Skills is that complex of knowledge, values, attitudes and abilities which contribute to the development of a sound moral character, a sense of community, and competence in responding to the personal, social and cultural aspects of life. This C.E.L. is intended to contribute to an understanding of the rational basis for examining moral questions and the resolution of conflicts between individuals' needs and desires on the one hand, and their responsibilities to others and to the environment on the other. It involves the development of self knowledge and understanding of the feelings, experiences, needs, purposes and rights of oneself and others. Other Common Essential Learning's contribute to the achievement of this one, particularly Critical and Creative Thinking and Communication. While not all of our students will have the same mental or physical capabilities to reflect upon and communicate their understandings in this area, all students will benefit from a caring environment wherein teachers model respect for all persons.

A basic understanding in this area involves distinguishing between different types of values. For example, one can make a distinction between fundamental moral values and aesthetic, economic or other kinds of relative values. Values within these categories can be held either by individuals or by cultural, social or political groups. Although a democratic society does not establish absolute standards for aesthetic, economic or recreational values, certain fundamental moral values are considered necessary for all citizens to hold. Further, while many personal values might be relative to the needs and interests of the person, fundamental moral values such as truth, rationality and justice are not.

The most basic moral value underlying development of this Common Essential Learning is that of respect for persons. By making a claim for fundamental moral values stemming from a respect for persons, a foundation is established which can be used to develop rational arguments about actions or issues of concern. Moral values, which form one reference point for such reasoning, include values such as: truthfulness, compassion, fair-mindedness, justice, respect for the environment, respect for the rights and property of others, and respect for democratic processes (the rights of majorities and minorities).

A focus upon Personal and Social Values and Skills is justified through: its contributions to a just society; the preservation and growth of cooperation and harmony within and between social and cultural groups; self knowledge; and a fuller understanding of the personal and social aspects of school knowledge. Development of the understandings and abilities of this C.E.L. are further justified through the support which they provide to learning situations. While personal and social values and skills are developed from a rational base, it is important to acknowledge both the affective and cognitive dimensions of human rationality. All learning in schools is acquired in social contexts where, for example, the behavior of an individual can affect the quality of the learning experiences of others.

The abilities and understandings promoted in this Common Essential Learning contribute to the establishment of an open and caring environment and thus support students' learning and their desire to learn. Schools are not value-neutral environments: "In transmitting knowledge to children and young people and developing their understanding of the world the school of necessity has to be committed to the value and the ideals of truth". Schools within a democratic society must also maintain a commitment to such foundations of a democracy as freedom of speech, equality and fairness in the treatment of persons. While families and communities will continue to take responsibility for the maintenance of certain societal and cultural values including moral values, this does not exempt schools from their responsibilities in this area.

The emphasis desired by Saskatchewan Education is to help students acquire fundamental moral values stemming from respect for persons through rational and humane processes. Thus, the concept of moral relativism (a belief that when dealing with moral issues any decision is as good as any other) is not sanctioned. While we are not repeating our descriptions of the teacher's role in fostering the abilities contained in the other C.E.L.s, it is important to remember that they apply equally here. This is particularly true of the role for the teacher developed in Critical and Creative Thinking and Independent Learning.

Within what is perhaps the most demanding, challenging and comprehensive of all the responsibilities which educators share, several interrelated areas need to be examined. These areas include: the models of moral reasoning and moral behavior which teachers display in their actions and the classroom structures which they establish; the overall climate of the school; institutional supports for Personal and Social Values and Skills; and the opportunities provided within the Required Areas of Study for developing moral reasoning and promoting self, interpersonal, and cross-cultural understandings.

While the abilities and understandings of this C.E.L. develop gradually and are shaped both by negative and by positive experiences with others, a single compassionate and fair-minded teacher has a powerful and long-lasting positive affect. A good starting point for understanding this potential is to look at teacher behavior that is consistent with respecting persons. Within the larger aim of coming to understand and ground one's behavior in a basic respect for persons, several crucial themes will be explored. These include examining the role of contradiction, consistency, and balance in developing personal and social values and skills. When we respect other people we acknowledge their language, their history and their culture as important aspects of their personal identity.

While respect implies causing no harm and supporting the rights of individuals and groups to make decisions about what is in their best interest, it also involves active attempts to do well by others. By conferring the status of persons onto others we oblige them to adopt these same responsibilities. That is, respect must be reciprocal. In the classroom, teachers model respect for persons in two important and related ways:

— by treating students, colleagues and parents with respect (showing genuine interest and regard and abstaining from ridicule or abuse);

— by not accepting a lack of respect from others.

As most classroom teachers can acknowledge, the difficult part of this modelling comes in understanding how to translate these general guidelines into the specific practices demanded by unique classroom situations. The concepts of contradiction, consistency and balance are useful here.

Consistency

Consistency within a respect for persons involves teaching practices like the following:

— Establishing classroom rules and norms for behavior with students through open discussion supported by questions such as: "Is this a good rule for all of us to live by?" (The consistency here is one of trusting, that is, respecting students' instincts and desires towards fairness.)

— Being clear about when and in what way students (or one's self) are not acting respectfully towards others, and expecting the behavior to cease. (The consistency here is between having a rule and applying it in the same manner with all people including one's self.)

— Establishing consequences for disrespectful behavior which do not violate the basic rule of acting with respect for persons. (The consistency here is in treating offenders with respect while demanding improvement. For example, it is inconsistent to shout at students when admonishing them for arguing loudly with each other, or to resort to ridicule and derogatory personal remarks when reprimanding a student for their disrespectful treatment of others.)

— Maintaining expectations that respect for persons is a value shared by all and being worked on by all, through responding to offenses with opening remarks such as: "It is not like you to..."; or "I realize you did not want things to happen in this way..."; rather than, "I knew you couldn't be expected to..."

— Acting on a belief that all persons are capable of growth and improvement in their treatment of others. (The consistency here is one of starting each student's day with a clean slate and not allowing ourselves to become cynical about the intentions or the potential of our students to respond to fair treatment.)

— Having the same expectations for and offering the same support to both sexes. Avoiding sexual stereotyping through language or action and being sensitive to sexual bias in the materials selected for classroom use. Encouraging greater understanding and friendship through grouping practices, seating arrangements, and other practices which do not unnecessarily segregate the sexes.

— Being clear that sexism, racism, and all forms of bias or discrimination are acts which violate respect for persons.

— Fostering an understanding that respect for the religious, spiritual or cultural values and beliefs of others is a necessary condition of respect for persons—one which supports the achievement of self esteem and self respect for all. (To be consistent, one would qualify this by saying this applies so long as those religious or cultural beliefs do not violate the more fundamental moral value of respect for persons or a commitment to truth.)

Acting in accordance with respect for persons also involves knowing when to treat people differently in order to achieve this goal. Respecting students' differing cultural backgrounds requires that teachers become knowledgeable about the behavioral norms of cultures other than their own. (For example, eye contact is not respectful in some cultures.) Ways to behave consistently and respectfully towards students with special needs should also be examined. In some cases it will not be appropriate to expect the same level of understanding and action from all students, but it is important to give all students as much responsibility for their personal, social and moral behavior as their physical and mental capabilities will allow.

When attempting to act in a manner consistent with valuing and respecting persons, contradictions begin to surface which must be dealt with. Schools are social institutions containing people, and people do not always act in accordance with their own moral values and beliefs. While persons in authority are expected to be good role models in this area, at times they are not. This needs to be acknowledged with students in a manner that does not undermine the legitimate authority of teachers, administrators or parents. If disrespectful behavior is glossed over when it belongs to adults but acknowledged when it belongs to students, students may become confused about or mistrustful of the genuineness of our belief in respect for persons and of our commitment to it. They may also doubt our commitment to truth.

We need to develop an understanding of the importance of truth and respect for persons, alongside an understanding of the need for some forms of legitimate authority in social institutions and families. This will enable students to choose to behave well, even in those difficult situations where others do not. The choice would be made from a commitment to the moral values first, and a belief in the communication process second. Where contradictions arise between what people say and how they act, our students need to feel that they can discuss the contradictions, present their viewpoints about injustices or misunderstandings in a respectful manner, and be heard. For adults and students in schools, the important goal here is that of continuously reflecting upon one's own behavior using the standards of truth and respect for persons, and attempting to act in accordance with them. A belief in the capability and the desire of all persons to improve in their treatment of others is a necessary condition of acting on a respect for persons.

Nowhere does the need for constant reflection and the subtlety, the complexity, the artfulness of teaching become more evident than in establishing and maintaining the kind of role model we want to be and the kind of classroom environment we want to achieve. No simple formulas will suffice. The idea of balance is a useful device for weighing the alternatives in individual situations. As educators we need to be sensitive to and constantly adjust the balance between:

— the rights of the individual and the rights of the group. (While we need to develop some general rules and procedures for the whole class to follow, on occasion, for good reasons, we need to allow a student to be exempted from rule or established procedure.)

— freedom and responsibility; variety/choice and ritual/routine. (Students need to experience both the freedom to experiment and to change their mind and the demands of seeing a difficult task through to completion.)

— teacher as facilitator with teacher as final authority.

Teachers need support from other members of the educational system if they are to fulfill the demands of this role to the extent that they desire. Any examination of teachers' roles is incomplete if it does not acknowledge the reciprocal relationships between teachers' rights and responsibilities and those of administrators, trustees, parents, students and fellow teachers. Thus, the consistencies and balances demanded by the teacher's role and the contradictions which need to be examined should also apply to the school, the school system, and the provincial institutions of education.

The more authority over decisions affecting the rights and choices of others that persons have, the more responsibility they have for acting in accordance with a commitment to truth and respect for persons. With power comes the obligation to exercise it wisely, thoughtfully and fairly. Thus, habits of personal reflection upon the rights and needs of others must be part of the daily life of all members of an educational system. Before one makes a decision or takes action, one should feel confident that all perspectives have been examined, that the history of the situation is understood, and that the intended goals of the action are sound and potentially worthwhile for all students. Self reflection must be supported by knowledge of the situations and lives of those affected by the decision.

The best assurance for educational administrators that the decisions they make will support growth in personal and social values and skills is based on:

— knowledge of self;
— commitment to truth and a basic respect for persons; and,
— a commitment to the processes of co-operation and open communication. Dialogue is as important a tool for moral reasoning outside the classroom as it is within it.

Supporting Personal and Social Values and Skills Across the Curriculum

In developing Personal and Social Values and Skills in all school subjects, three areas require particular examination. These areas are: developing understanding of and experience with moral reasoning; examining the content of curriculum materials in relation to this C.E.L.; and, examining social issues in the classroom.

Moral reasoning

Moral reasoning is concerned with thinking as it relates to the treatment of persons (in the context of their environment) through the use of moral principles derived from the most fundamental principle of respect for persons. Since it is possible to consider these moral principles and their application objectively, it is also possible to be rational in our treatment of moral issues and dilemmas. Although the principle of respect for persons should be the foundation for one's general treatment of oneself and others, the very general nature of this principle makes it a difficult one to apply in concrete situations. Therefore, mediating principles are needed. These mediating principles are logical extensions of the most fundamental moral principle of respect for persons.

Examples of such mediating principles would be the commitment to: transmit and promote that which is true; treat all persons equally unless there are relevant differences; maximize anther's freedom; and, consider the rights and needs of persons. These principles can be further translated into substantive values which provide rules of conduct. For example, one can derive rules regarding discrimination according to sex or race from the principle of equality. Similarly, since respect for persons is developed within the human context and humans depend upon their physical environment for survival, respect for the environment can also be considered a mediating principle. The process of moral reasoning involves critical reflection upon how to translate the fundamental moral obligation of respect for persons in specific situations. This requires that teachers, together with their students, use mediating principles, moral rules and moral values to arrive at moral arguments. This process involves substantive knowledge, fact-finding and open dialogue. Such dialogue should be developed by persons committed to the employment of strong sense critical thinking.

Examining Curriculum Content

Curriculum development in all subject areas needs to be concerned that the material presented to students is non-sexist and non-racist. As all materials presented for study will not be totally free of bias, teachers should help students examine materials for the biases that they may contain and the possible effects such biases produce. In studies of individuals in science, the arts, social studies, health or literature, students should be exposed to a balance of males and females from differing cultural backgrounds, in both historical and contem1porary settings. "Students should come to see that greatness and goodness have found, and can find expression among men and women in different cultures and races". The study of literature and the media can contribute to a heightened awareness of stereotypes, an analysis of why they are used and a better understanding of the ways in which biased presentations affect minority groups.

In social studies, developing understanding of the relationships between history, climate, resources and cultural patterns can lead to a better understanding of persons from different cultural backgrounds and religious groups. The use of quality children's literature in language arts and drama can provide elementary students with opportunities to learn about human feelings and about other cultures. Middle years' students can begin to explore how values influence behavior through the narratives of, for example, Louis Riel or Mother Theresa.

Secondary students can move from these particular illustrations to discuss understandings such as: whether a character in history, drama or a novel acted in a morally correct way; whether an individual challenged the prevailing moral codes, and why; or whether there were conflicting moral values in the situation being studied. Throughout their school years and in all their school subjects, material about people should become an important source for thinking about human needs and human rights and how these can be reflected through acting upon a respect for persons.

Examining Social Issues in the Classroom

The demand that school curricula be relevant and applicable to the challenges of modern life involves educators face to face with the social issues of their time and place. Social issues surface through the content of school curricula in the Required Areas of Study and through the content of students' daily lives - their own real experiences and their exposure to the media. When such important social issues as racial prejudice or poverty are explored through the themes and concepts of units in social studies, history or health education curricula, they are clearly part of a teacher's responsibilities. The nature of that responsibility is not always clear, however, - particularly when instruction shifts from the prescribed textbook or film to classroom discussion.

When a social issue is the focus of study, teachers need to consider how to ensure that treatment of the issue is comprehensive and fair, and also how to avoid moral relativism without stifling student reflection upon perspectives which violate fundamental moral values. Curriculum decision making related to the treatment of social issues in the classroom can be strengthened by reflecting upon the following guidelines:

— study of social issues should be incorporated into existing curricula and studied as a means of integrating important knowledge, values and abilities rather than in isolation from the content of school subjects.

— study of social issues should strengthen students' understanding of the need for a sound knowledge base in the disciplines or fields related to the issue. Students should develop a greater respect for factual knowledge - its uses and limitations.

— study of social issues should strengthen students' abilities to understand the rights, feelings and viewpoints of others and strengthen their knowledge of themselves. Through collaboration, co-operative research and problem solving, and engagement in meaningful dialogue, respect for others is fostered.

— study of social issues should strengthen students' reasoning abilities. Students should be involved in the examination of value positions implicit in the issue and the construction of logical arguments built upon moral principles. Students should develop their critical and creative thinking abilities through such processes as basing arguments upon fundamental human rights and creating ethical alternatives to practices they consider to be unfair or unsound.

— study of social issues should strengthen students' knowledge of and commitment to fundamental moral principles stemming from a respect for persons. The Canadian Charter of Rights and the United Nations Charter of Rights and Freedoms can be used as sources for establishing these principles.

Four key factors in the examination of social issues:

— commitment to achieving a perspective on the issue which is factually and ethically grounded.

— stating the value positions involved in the issues.

— establishing arguments based upon human rights, human needs or needs of the environment.

— fact-finding to back arguments.

One other element of social issues research not treated explicitly in this model should also be considered. That is:

— generation of alternative solutions based on human rights, human needs or environmental needs.

INDEPENDENT LEARNING

Independent learning focuses on creation of the opportunities and experiences necessary for students to become capable, self-reliant, self-motivated and life-long learners. What is desired are students who value learning as an empowering activity of great personal and social worth. All of the other C.E.L.s contribute to the goal of developing independent learners.

"Independent Learning is that learning in which the learner, in conjunction with relevant others, can make the decisions necessary to meet the learner's own learning needs." In this process, independent learners develop the values, attitudes, knowledge and skills needed to make responsible decisions and take actions dealing with their own learning. Independent learning is fostered by creating the opportunities and experiences which encourage student motivation, curiosity, self-confidence, self-reliance and positive self-concept; it is based on student understanding of their own interests and a valuing of learning for its own sake.

Independent learning is part of an ongoing, lifelong process of education that stimulates greater thoughtfulness and reflection and promotes the continuing growth of students' capabilities and powers. More than the rote learning of facts and skills, this approach to learning encourages students to make meaning for themselves, based on their understanding of why and how new knowledge is related to their own experiences, interests and needs. Independent learning is a direction for the process of education, not an absolute standard; this process takes different forms for different students and it varies according to subject matter and students' interests and abilities in the subjects. Independent learning involves the teacher and learner in an interactive process that encourages students' intellectual development and their capacity for independent and reflective judgment.

Independent learning is fostered by a school environment which is sensitive, flexible, democratic and responsive to the needs of students. This encourages a strong sense of purpose and motivation on the part of students. Independent learning makes full use of the resources of the school and the community and fosters the development of independent learners in every grade and in every subject. Independent learning addresses the needs of individual learners for independence and active participation in their own learning, both in school and in the larger society. This approach to learning is an important part of core curriculum: "It is essential for schools to reduce students' dependence on schools and teachers for their learning and increase students' capability to set and meet their own learning goals."

Since learning extends beyond the school context, learners require independence as a life skill, to assist them in preparing for new situations and experiences. Independent Learning can assist students in acquiring the knowledge, abilities, skills, values and motivation that enable them to analyze learning situations and develop appropriate strategies for action. Independent learning requires that people take responsibility for their own learning. Individual responsibility stems from the belief that learning can be affected by effort, and this belief is the critical factor which leads to individuals' perseverance in the face of obstacles. Teachers can help students take responsibility for their learning by providing opportunities and strategies for learning independently and by encouraging them to initiate and actively participate in their own learning. Students need to explore issues that have meaning and relevance for them.

Individual students bring different perspectives and experiences to learning situations, and in the final analysis, it is the learner who achieves learning and creates meaning from any new material or experience. A sense of social responsibility will be fostered by teaching which supports the examination of new knowledge in terms of its relevance and meaning for students in particular and human purposes in general. An important motivating factor in independent learning is the encouragement of students' own interests and their desire to learn. Students will be motivated to learn if the learning activity is meaningful, and if the knowledge is useful and provides a means of achieving a desired goal. Such learning activities provide a stimulus to reflective inquiry and continuing intellectual development.

In contrast, learning activities in which the student has no interest lead to increasing dependence on external motivation and extrinsic rewards. This approach to teaching has the effect of diminishing student initiative, rather than encouraging student participation in learning for its own sake. Students will move towards independence in varying degrees, depending on factors such as age, skill level and ability in a particular subject. It is important to establish the conditions for enlarging student learning in all its variety, thereby encouraging the growth and development of all students towards greater responsibility for their own learning. Independent learning cannot be achieved in isolation. Learning is an interactive process among students and between teacher and students. Students engage in learning activities as individuals who are interdependent with other individuals in the classroom and in the wider society.

Independent learning has implications for responsible decision making, as individuals are expected to analyze problems, reflect, make decisions and take purposeful actions. To take responsibility for their lives in times of rapid social change, students need to learn on a life-long basis. As most aspects of our daily lives are likely to undergo profound changes, independent learning will enable individuals to respond to the changing demands of work, family and society. For example, changes in work life will require retraining, job change and life-long learning, and technological change will demand the values, attitudes and skills associated with independent learning. As in the case with Critical and Creative Thinking, Independent Learning is an important foundation for maintaining democracy and promoting social justice.

Citizens are called upon to independently assess problems, make rational decisions and take actions - not based on what others decide is best for them, but based on an assessment of their own interests and the interests of others in Society. As guardians of the future, today's youth require the independent learning abilities that will empower them to act in accordance with the principle of social justice and for the survival of our planet. Finally, it is through Independent Learning that all the other Common Essential Learnings become an integrated whole. Independent Learning is a vehicle for consolidating the understandings developed through all of the Common Essential Learnings.

The Teacher's Role

Three aspects of the teacher's role in fostering Independent Learning are: the learning environment created by the teacher; the relationship established between teacher and learner; and the teaching and modelling of skills needed for independent learning. Children enter the formal education process as intuitive independent learners. It is important to create a learning environment which furthers this process of independence, and enables students to consciously accept responsibility for and make decisions about their own learning. The teacher plays an important role in providing a supportive environment that encourages students' motivation, self-confidence, curiosity and desire to learn. Independent learning will be fostered by a climate that is sensitive, flexible and responsive to the learners' needs.

The atmosphere, environment and structure of the school itself must support independent learning, with teachers, principals and others in the school modelling independent learning behaviors. The process of education creates the context within which students can progress towards greater responsibility for their own learning. Working with teacher-librarians in the library resource center program will also further encourage student inquiry. Resource-based learning will enable students to access resources, and will involve them in a process of active learning in the school and community. Strong library programs can offer students guidance, support and freedom as they increasingly take responsibility for their own learning.

In a school system based to a great extent upon competition and grades, it is particularly important to encourage students' intrinsic interest in learning - learning for its own sake, not as a means to an end. Independent learning strategies that address the interests and concerns of students, make the curriculum content relevant to students' needs and demonstrate the purpose of learning will contribute to the development of autonomous learners.

Relationship between teacher and student

The relationship between teacher and learner should foster increasing learner responsibility. As students grow in maturity and understanding, they are able to take on greater responsibility for their own learning. As this happens, teachers need to relinquish control of decision making. This transfer of control is best supported by a school environment that is "organized to encourage and support a continued, increasingly mature and comprehensive acceptance of responsibilities for one's own learning".

Teachers assist students in mastering the decision making processes as instructors, guides and facilitators. In this role, teachers not only enable students to acquire a solid base of knowledge and experience, but they also help students to discover the personal meaning of this knowledge and experience in terms of their own needs. This process leads to a more meaningful learning experience for students; they are motivated to take greater control over their learning because it is relevant to their needs, both as individuals and as members of society. As teachers encourage students to take greater responsibility for decision making, they must also judge students' readiness for such responsibility.

Such judgments are based on the learner's age, maturity, ability and knowledge, and can only be made by teachers who know their students well. As in all Common Essential Learnings, teachers' instructional techniques will be an important basis for implementation of Independent Learning. The attitudes, skills and knowledge of independent learning will be fostered in students, in large part, through the ways in which teachers organize their classrooms and instruct their students. It is important that teachers utilize instructional techniques, strategies and approaches based on collaboration between learner and teacher. This will encourage student participation, both in determining goals and in monitoring the learning process. Also desirable are teaching approaches that foster student self-confidence and empower students to take responsibility for their own learning.

An important aspect of the teacher's role is the teaching and modelling of skills needed for independent learning. Consistent with the discussion of the other C.E.L.s, it is important to note that such skills should not be taught in isolation, but rather developed through school subject matter. Five principles, adapted from Herber and Herber, provide an outline of how teachers can incorporate skill teaching and create a learning environment which frees their students to become independent life-long learners.

Modelling and practicing learning skills: Independence in the performance of a task is the logical extension of having learned and practiced a task. Students are taught activities which facilitate the transition to independence through modelling, demonstration and direct instruction of learning skills. These are followed by practice opportunities provided by the teacher, who monitors students' progress towards their goals of independent decision making. As part of this process, it is important to share with students what is being done and why an activity is useful. The goal is that learners will eventually make their own decisions, connect what they already know with what they are learning, make judgments and inferences, apply new ideas and derive pleasure from learning.

The following example outlines this learning process: Students might undertake a class project on time management in conjunction with doing an assignment. The teacher and students would do the assignment together. As the teacher models the actions involved in time management through thinking aloud, the students are learning ways to manage time during this assignment as well as why this is important. The teacher then models and prompts student action in doing another assignment and attending to the time management needed. This modelling is repeated until the student can do the activity without cues from the teacher, and gradually takes over the actions. As an important part of this process, students are reminded often that there are other solutions to a problem such as time management; they are encouraged to seek the solutions that work best for them. Discussion of students' personal adaptations should follow completion of the assignments. The teacher-librarian·has an important role to play in developing independent learning skills, such as narrowing a topic or identifying sources.

Transfer of responsibility from teacher to learner: Independence is developed by design, not chance. Four steps involved in the skill aspect of independent learning are: show students how: provide practice; have students structure activities: finally, have them use the activities independently. The pace of this sequence is dependent upon the age and background of the student, the level of the task to be done and the attitudes of both teacher and student. The transfer of decision making responsibility from teacher to student is a key part of the teacher's role in fostering independent learning; the transfer needs to be accomplished without either over- or under-controlling the process. This shift is enhanced by a teachers' positive attitude to independent learning, as well as a good knowledge of the needs, interests and abilities of individual students. This transfer of control is crucial; it leads to students discovering how their efforts can affect their learning. Students then experience control of the learning task, and from this control they acquire motivation to continue learning.

Knowledge and understanding of students: Independence is a relative state. Independent learning is a cyclical process, whereby students learn a skill at one level, then use the skill to learn other skills or content, repeating the cycle many times over. This process is related to the developmental level of the student, the requirements of the material and the effective transition from learning a skill to using the skill to learn.

As part of this independent learning process, it is important that teachers know their students well. Teachers need to observe and reflect upon students' learning processes. This role is a proactive one, since in order to help the students succeed as independent learners, the teacher needs to anticipate difficulties and offer support at crucial intervals. Teachers need to develop a good understanding of their students' strengths and weaknesses - socially, emotionally, intellectually and physically - their exceptionalities, their health, their cultural backgrounds. Students become motivated when they believe that they have the ability to control their own learning. This motivation is enhanced by learning which builds on students' own interests; basing learning experiences on students' needs and interests helps develop enthusiastic learners. For independent learning to proceed, student choice must become a regular part of the classroom environment, including the structuring of assignments, topics, group processes and timelines.

Collaborative instructional techniques: Independent learning is not carried out in isolation; it includes co-operative, small group and whole class learning. Independent learners select from a variety of settings, resources and styles that meet their needs and interests. The teacher's role is to facilitate learning in a variety of ways which are age appropriate, subject appropriate, related to available resources and related to students' needs for a balance between structured experience and independence. Instructional approaches which facilitate independent learning include the following:

— divergent thinking

— concept mapping

— journal writing

— learning centers

— inquiry process

— independent research

— student-teacher conferences

Teachers can also vary the setting, topic, assignment, time, depth and group processes. All variety and choices should include provisions for learning study skills, as well as student input into evaluation.

Support and encouragement to students: Becoming independent is an ongoing process which takes time, patience and support. To be lifelong learners, students are ever in the process of becoming independent. It is the responsibility of the educator to foster this developmental process of learning. The teacher's role is to be a patient facilitator, showing students how to learn independently, encouraging them, providing feedback and supporting their efforts. These are all crucial factors in providing a learning environment which fosters independent learning and which motivates students to pursue independent learning skills.

3

UNDER STANDING THE LEARNER IN THE LIGHT OF NEEDS

LEARNING STYLES

"Learning style" refers to the way you perceive, organize, process, and understand information. For example, do you prefer to use a tape recorder during lectures or take notes and rely on instructor handouts? Do you prefer to work alone or in a group? Do you prefer to read a software technical manual or explore the software via the interface? Do you prefer to listen to an explanation of a process or look at a graphic depiction? Do you prefer to be given all of the project criteria or negotiate aspects?

Bridging Differences

In 1987, Arthur W. Chickering and Zelda Gamson published the "Seven Principles for Good Practice in Undergraduate Education" with support from the American Association of Higher Education (AAHE), the Association of American Colleges (ACE), and the Johnson and Lilly Foundations. The seventh principle states: *Good practice respects diverse talents and ways of learning*. "There are many roads to learning. People bring different talents and styles of learning to college. Brilliant students in the seminar room may be all thumbs in the lab or art studio.

Students rich in hands-on experience may not do so well in theory. Students need opportunity to show their talents and learn in ways that work for them. Then they can be pushed to learn in new ways that do not come so easily." (Chickering & Gamson).

Some questions to ask yourself:

— Do you encourage students to speak up when they do not understand?

— Do you select readings and design activities related to the background of your students?

— Do you provide extra material or activities for students who lack essential background knowledge or skills?

— Do you find out about your students' learning styles, interests, or backgrounds at the beginning of each course?

— Are your course materials accessible – face-to-face and online?

— Do you use different assessment methods – written, oral, projects, etc.?

The most effective teaching strategy is variability. Understanding how different learning styles affect approaches to learning can assist teachers in developing strategies that best serve individual differences. Some approaches to consider:

— Use different activities in class – videos, discussion, lecture, groups, pairs etc.

— Use mind mapping for visual presentations.

— Engage in full-group discussion following small-group discussion.

— Encourage the use of email or bulletin boards.

— Value every answer and find some relevance to encourage participation.

— Offer contract learning to help students define their own objectives, determine the learning activities, and define the criteria and methods of evaluation.

— Utilize multimedia presentations.
— Consider field trips – physical and virtual.
— Diversify delivery methods.
— Give students a problem to solve that has multiple solutions.

DIFFERENTIATED CLASSROOM

A different way to learn is what the kids are calling for.... All of them are talking about how the one-size-fits-all delivery system—which mandates that everyone learn the same thing at the same time, no matter what their individual needs—has failed them.

In the United States more than a century ago, the teacher in a one-room prairie schoolhouse faced a challenging task. She had to divide her time and energy between teaching young children who had never held a book and could not read or write and teaching older, more advanced students with little interest in what the young ones were doing. Today's teachers still contend with the essential challenge of the one-room schoolhouse: how to reach out effectively to students who span the spectrum of learning readiness, personal interests, culturally shaped ways of seeing and speaking of the world, and experiences in that world. Though today's teachers generally work with single classes with students of nearly the same age, these children have an array of needs as great as those among the children of the one-room school.

Hallmarks of Differentiated Classrooms

In differentiated classrooms, teachers begin where students are, not the front of a curriculum guide. They accept and build upon the premise that learners differ in important ways. Thus, they also accept and act on the premise that teachers must be ready to engage students in instruction through different learning modalities, by appealing to differing interests, and by using varied rates of instruction along with varied degrees of complexity. In differentiated classrooms, teachers ensure that a student competes against himself as he grows and develops more than he competes against other students.

In differentiated classrooms, teachers provide specific ways for each individual to learn as deeply as possible and as quickly as possible, without assuming one student's road map for learning is identical to anyone else's. These teachers believe that students should be held to high standards. They work diligently to ensure that struggling, advanced, and in-between students think and work harder than they meant to; achieve more than they thought they could; and come to believe that learning involves effort, risk, and personal triumph. These teachers also work to ensure that each student consistently experiences the reality that success is likely to follow hard work.

Teachers in differentiated classes use time flexibly, call upon a range of instructional strategies, and become partners with their students to see that both what is learned and the learning environment are shaped to the learner. They do not force-fit learners into a standard mold. You might say these teachers are students of their students. They are diagnosticians, prescribing the best possible instruction for their students. These teachers also are artists who use the tools of their craft to address student's needs. They do not reach for standardized, mass-produced instruction assumed to be a good fit for all students because they recognize that students are individuals.

Teachers in differentiated classrooms begin with a clear and solid sense of what constitutes powerful curriculum and engaging instruction. Then they ask what it will take to modify that instruction so that each learner comes away with understandings and skills that offer guidance to the next phase of learning. Essentially, teachers in differentiated classrooms accept, embrace, and plan for the fact that learners bring many commonalities to school, but that learners also bring the essential differences that make them individuals. Teachers can allow for this reality in many ways to make classrooms a good fit for each individual. Although differentiated classrooms embody common sense, they still can be difficult to achieve. In part, it is difficult to achieve a differentiated classroom because we see few examples of them. The examples that are out there, however, offer a productive way to start exploring differentiated instruction.

Teachers work daily to find ways to reach out to individual learners at their varied points of readiness, interest, and learning preference. There is no one "right way" to create an effectively differentiated classroom; teachers craft responsive learning places in ways that are a good match for their teaching styles. as well as for learners' needs. Following are samples from classrooms in which teachers differentiate instruction. Some are lifted directly from an observation in a classroom. Some are composites of several classrooms, or extensions of conversations with teachers. All are intended to help in forming images of what it looks like and feels like in a differentiated classroom.

Snapshots from Two Primary Classrooms

For a part of each day in Mrs. Jasper's 1st grade class, students rotate among learning centers. Mrs.Jasper has worked hard for several years to provide a variety of learning centers related to several subject areas. All students go to all learning centers because Mrs. Jasper says they feel it's unfair if they don't all do the same thing. Students enjoy the movement and the independence the learning centers provide. Many times, Isabel breezes through the center work. Just as frequently, Jamie is confused about how to do the work. Mrs. Jasper tries to help Jamie as often as she can, but she doesn't worry so much about Isabel because her skills are well beyond those expected of a 1st grader.

Today, all students in Mrs. Jasper's class will work in a learning center on compound words. From a list of 10 compound words, they will select and illustrate 5. Later, Mrs. Jasper will ask for volunteers to show their illustrations. She will do this until the students share illustrations for all 10 words. Down the hall, Ms. Cunningham also uses learning centers in her 1st grade classroom. She, too, has invested considerable time in developing interesting centers on a variety of subjects. Ms. Cunningham's centers, however, draw upon some of the principles of differentiated classrooms. Sometimes all students work in a particular learning center if it introduces an idea or skill new to everyone.

More often, Ms. Cunningham assigns students to a specific learning center, or to a particular task at a certain learning center, based on her continually developing sense of their individual readiness. Today, her students also will work at a learning center on compound words. Students' names are listed at the center; one of four colors is beside each name. Each student works with the folder that matches the color beside his or her name. For example, Sam has the color red next to his name. Using the materials in the red folder, Sam must decide the correct order of pairs of words to make familiar compound words. He also will make a poster that illustrates each simple word and the new compound word they form.

Using materials in the blue folder, Jenna will look around the classroom and in books to find examples of compound words. She will write them out and illustrate them in a booklet. Using materials in the purple folder, Tjuana will write a poem or a story that uses compound words she generates and that make the story or poem interesting. She then can illustrate the compound words to make the story or poem interesting to look at as well as to read. In the green folder, Dillon will find a story the teacher has written. It contains correct and incorrect compound words.

Dillon will be a word detective, looking for "villains" and "good guys" among the compound words. He will create a chart to list the good guys (correct compound words) and the villains (incorrect compound words) in the story. He will illustrate the good guys and list the villains as they are in the story, and then write them correctly. Tomorrow during circle time, all students may share what they did with their compound words. As students listen, they are encouraged to say the thing they like best about each presenter's work. Ms. Cunningham also will call on a few students who may be reticent to volunteer, asking them if they'd be willing to share what they did at the center.

Two Elementary Classrooms

In 5th grade, students at Sullins Elementary work with the concept of "famous people" to make connections between social studies and language arts. All students are expected to hone and apply research skills, to write effectively, and to share with an audience what they have learned as a result of the unit. Mr. Elliott asks all his students to select and read a biography of a famous person from the literature or history they have studied. Students then use encyclopedias and the Internet to find out more about the person they have chosen. Each student writes a report about a famous person, describing the person's culture, childhood, education, challenges, and contributions to the world. Students are encouraged to use both original and "found" illustrations in their reports.

Mr. Elliott gives a rubric to the whole class to coach students in areas such as use of research resources, organization, and quality of language. In her 5th grade class, Mrs. May gives her students interest inventories to help them find areas where they may have a special talent or fascination, such as sports, art, medicine, the outdoors, writing, or helping others. Ultimately, each student selects an area of special interest or curiosity. The students and teacher talk about the fact that in all areas of human endeavor, famous people have shaped our understanding and practice of the field. She reads them a biographical sketch of a statesman, a musician, and an astronaut. Together, students and teacher describe principles about these famous people.

For example, famous people often are creative, they take risks to make advances in their fields, they frequently are rejected before they are admired, they sometimes fail, they sometimes succeed, and they are persistent. Students test the principles as they discuss historic figures, authors, and people in the news today. In the end, students conclude that people can be famous "for the right reasons" or "for the wrong reasons." They decide to research people who become famous by having a positive impact on the world. The school media specialist helps each student to generate lists of "positive" famous people in that student's particular categories of interest. She also helps them learn how to locate a variety of resources that can help them research famous individuals.

This includes brainstorming possible interview sources. She talks with them about the importance of selecting research materials they can read and understand clearly. She also offers to help them look for alternatives if they find materials that seem too easy or too hard for them. Mrs. May and her students talk about how to take notes and try various ways to take notes during their research. They also consider different methods of organizing their information, such as webs, outlines, story boards, and matrices. They talk about all the ways they can express their understandings: through essays, historical fiction, monologues, poems, caricatures, or character sketches.

Mrs. May provides students with a rubric that guides them on the content, research, planning, and outcome of their work. Students also work with Mrs. May individually to set their own goals for understandings, working processes, and final products. As the assignment continues, Mrs. May works with individuals and small groups to assess their understanding and progress and to coach them for quality. Students also assess each other's work according to the rubrics and individual goals. They ensure that each report shows someone who has made a "positive" contribution to the world. In the end, the whole class completes a mural in the cafeteria that lists the principles of fame in the shape of puzzle pieces. On each puzzle piece, students write or illustrate examples of the principle from their famous person's life. They then add ways in which they believe the principles are or will be important in their own lives. Students also share their final products with an adult who knows something about, or is interested in learning about, the person they researched.

Comparisons from the Middle Grades

In Mr. Cornell's science class, students work in a specific cycle: read the text chapter, answer questions at the end of the chapter, discuss what they have read, complete a lab. and take a quiz. Students do the labs and complete their reports in groups of four. Sometimes Mr. Cornell assigns students to a lab group as a way of managing behavior problems. Often, students select their own lab groups. They read the text and answer the questions individually. Mr. Cornell typically conducts two or three whole-class discussions during a chapter. All students enter the science fair in the spring, with a project based on a topic studied in the fall or winter. Mrs. Santos often assigns students in her science class to reading squads when they work with text materials.

At this stage, group assignments usually are made so students of similar reading levels work together. She varies graphic organizers and learning log prompts according to the amount of structure and concreteness the various groups need to grasp essential understandings from the chapter. She also makes it possible for students to read aloud in their groups or to read silently. Then they complete organizers and prompts together. As students read. Mrs. Santos moves among groups. Sometimes she reads key passages to them, sometimes she asks them to read to her, but she always probes for deeper understanding and helps to clarify their thinking. Sometimes Mrs. Santos asks students to complete labs, watch videos, or work with supplementary materials before they read the chapter so they have a clear sense of guiding principles before they work with the text.

Sometimes they read the text for awhile, do a lab, and go back to the text. Sometimes labs and supplementary materials follow text exploration. Frequently, she will have two versions of a lab going simultaneously: one for students who need concrete experiences to understand essential principles and one for students who already grasp the important principles and can deal with them in complex and uncertain contexts. Mrs. Santos gives quizzes and diagnostic learning log entries several times in the course of a unit. Thus, she is aware of which students need additional instruction with key understandings and skills and which students need more advanced applications early in the unit. Students have several choices for a major science project:

— Work alone or with peers to investigate and address a problem in the community that relates to the science they are studying.

— Work in a mentorship role with a person or group in the community using science to address a local problem.

— Study scientists past and present who have positively influenced the practice of science in an area they have studied.

— Write a science fiction story based on the science they have studied with the goal of submitting the story to the school's literary arts anthology.

— Use classroom cameras to create a narrated photo essay that would help a younger student understand how some facet of the science they have studied works in the world.

— Propose another option to the teacher and work with her to shape a project that demonstrates understanding and skill in science.

In Mr. O'Reillys 8th grade English class, students read the same novels and have whole-class discussions on them. Students complete journal entries on their readings. In Mrs. Wilkerson's 8th grade English class, students often read novels around a common theme, such as courage or conflict resolution. Students select from a group of four or five novels on the same concept, and Mrs. Wilkerson provides classroom sets of the books. Mrs.

Wilkerson also makes sure the novels span a considerable reading range and tap into several interests.

Mrs. Wilkerson's 8th graders meet frequently in literature circles with students reading the same novel. There they discuss what they are reading. Although the various literature circles reflect different degrees of reading proficiency, students in each group take turns serving in one of five leadership roles: discussion director, graphic illustrator, historical investigator, literary luminary, and vocabulary enricher. There are printed guides for each role to help students fulfill them well. Mrs. Wilkerson also varies journal prompts, sometimes assigning different prompts to different students. Often, she encourages students to select a prompt that interests them. There also are many opportunities for whole-class discussion on the theme that all the novels share, allowing all students to contribute to an understanding of how the theme "plays out" in the book they are reading and in life.

Samples from High School

In Spanish I, Mrs. Horton's students complete the same language pattern drills, work on the same oral exercises, read the same passages, and take the same quizzes.

In French I, Mr. Adams's students often work with written drills at differing levels of complexity and with different amounts of teacher support. Their oral exercises focus on the same basic structures, but completion requires different levels of sophistication with the language. Sometimes students can "opt out" of review sessions to create their own French dialogue or to read a French language magazine. Students often work in teacher-assigned, mixed-readiness pairs to prepare for what the teacher calls "fundamentals quizzes." Students who wish to do so can, from time to time, select a partner to prepare for a "challenge quiz."

Success on a challenge quiz nets students "homework passes" they can use to be excused from homework assignments when their work on the quiz indicates they have mastered the homework material.

In Mr. Matheson's Algebra II class, students typically complete the same homework, work independently on in-class drills, and take the same tests. In her Algebra II class, Mrs. Wang helps students identify key concepts and skills in a given chapter. After various chapter assessments, students are encouraged to look at their own assessment results and select homework assignments and in-class miniworkshops that will help them clarify areas of confusion. She encourages students to decide whether they work most effectively alone or with a partner and to make that choice when there are opportunities to do so.

Toward the end of a chapter, Mrs. Wang also gives students individual "challenge problems," which they can tackle alone or with a classmate. She designs the problems to be a mental reach. On end-of-chapter tests, students find challenge problems similar but not identical to the ones Mrs. Wang gave them earlier. There may be five or six different challenge problems distributed among the tests of 30 students. In physical education, Mrs. Bowen's students usually all work with the same exercises and basketball drills. Mr. Wharton helps his students diagnose their starting points with various exercises and basketball skills, set challenging goals for personal improvement, and chart their personal progress. He particularly stresses growth in two areas: a student's best and weakest area.

In U.S. History, Miss Roberson and her students cover the information in the text sequentially. She lectures to supplement information in the text. Miss Roberson includes a special emphasis on women's history and African American history during the months designated by the school for those emphases. Mrs. Washington's U.S. History students look for key concepts and generalizations that recur in each period of history they study. They also look for concepts and generalizations unique to each period. They study various points of view and the experiences shared by various cultural, economic, and gender groups. They use a variety of text, video, and taped materials of varying degrees of difficulty.

Mrs. Washington sometimes lectures, but she always uses overhead transparencies that provide key points of her lecture to help visual learners. She also stops throughout the lecture to encourage students to talk about key ideas in the lecture and to ensure their grasp of those ideas. Essays and projects often ask students to take their understanding of a period in U.S. history and contrast it with what was going on in another culture and in another geographical area during the same period. Project assignments always offer several options for how a student can express his or her understanding. At the end of each quarter, students have the option of taking their whole grade from an exam, or they can take half of it from an alternative assessment proposed by the teacher and modified by the student with teacher guidance and approval.

Differentiated classrooms feel right to students who learn in different ways and at different rates and who bring to school different talents and interests. More significantly, such classrooms work better for a full range of students than do one-size-fits-all settings. Teachers in differentiated classrooms are more in touch with their students and approach teaching more as an art than as a mechanical exercise. Developing classrooms that actively attend to both student similarities and student differences is anything but simple. The chapters that follow describe classrooms with differentiated, or responsive, instruction, and they offer guidance on how you can, over time, make such classrooms a reality for your class or school.

RETHINKING HOW WE DO SCHOOL—AND FOR WHOM

Think back 75 or 100 years ago. Now, fast-forward to today. In many ways, those years reflect more change for humans than all the years before in recorded history. Think about farming 100 years ago—and today. Think about the practice of medicine 100 years ago—and today. Imagine transportation 100 years ago—and today. Consider the 20th century's changes in engineering, clothing, and communication. The transformation is dizzying! While most of us succumb to occasional nostalgia for "the good old days," few of us would opt for yesterday's physicians, communication systems, or fashion. Although we think of school as a static enterprise, the field of education has grown and changed, too.

Today we understand many things about teaching and learning that we had no way of knowing a century, or even a few decades, ago. Some of these insights stem from psychology and the science of the brain. Others come from continuing observation in classrooms. Whatever their genesis, these educational changes are every bit as revolutionary as moving from the pencil to the typewriter to the personal computer.

New Ways of Thinking

We could fill volumes with the expanding understandings of how children learn. We could fill other volumes with the implications of this knowledge for teachers. Differentiated instruction is first and foremost good instruction. Many current understandings about learning provide strong support for classrooms that recognize, honor, and cultivate individuality. Following are three principles of effective teaching and learning that educators have not always known or clearly supported.

We can draw at least three important conclusions from the study of intelligence over the past half century. First, intelligence is multifaceted, not a single thing. Howard Gardner suggests that humans have eight intelligences: verbal-linguistic, logical-mathematical, visual-spatial, bodily-kinesthetic, musical-rhythmic, interpersonal, intrapersonal, and naturalistic. Robert Sternberg suggests three kinds of intelligences: analytical, practical, and creative. Before them, other researchers, such as Thorndike, Thurstone, and Guilford, identified varied types of intelligence. While the names of intelligences vary, educators, psychologists. and researchers have drawn two significant. consistent conclusions:

— We think. learn, and create in different ways.

— Development of our potential is affected by the match between what we learn and how we learn with our particular intelligences.

A second important conclusion about intelligence is that it is fluid, not fixed. In other words, providing children with rich learning experiences can amplify their intelligence, and denying them such richness of experience can diminish their intelligence. A third understanding stems from the burgeoning field of brain research. Neurons grow and develop when they are used actively; they atrophy when they are not used. Vigorous learning changes the physiology of the brain. These theories suggest several clear implications for educators. For exampie. teachers must be effective in developing many types of intelligence. not just one. Also, students who come to school lacking rich learning experiences can make up lost ground if they find rich experiences in their classrooms. All students must continue vigorous, new learning. or they risk losing brain power.

The Brain Hungers for Meaning

Thanks to progress with imaging technology in the field of medicine, we can now look inside the human brain and see how it functions. Such observations have rapidly expanded the understanding of teaching and learning. We now know important details about what works best for the brain in learning. The brain seeks meaningful patterns and resists meaninglessness. Though the brain retains isolated or disparate bits of information, it is much more efficient at retaining information that is "chunked." Chunked information is organized around categories and ideas that increase the information's meaningfulness. The brain constantly seeks to connect parts to wholes, and individuals learn by connecting something new to something they already understand.

The brain learns best when it can come to understand by making its own sense out of information rather than when information is imposed on it. The brain doesn't respond much to things that carry only a surface meaning. It responds far more effectively and efficiently to something that carries deep and personal meaning, something that is life shaping, relevant, important, or taps into emotions. These and many other understandings tell us much about the individuality of learners and about the nature of effective curriculum and instruction. Brain research tells us that each learner's brain is unique, and educators must provide many opportunities for varied learners to make sense of ideas and information.

The research tells us that when we set out to have students connect the novel to the familiar, what is novel to one child already may be familiar to another and vice versa. Brain research tells us that curriculum must cultivate meaning making. It should be organized around categories, concepts, and governing principles. A meaningful curriculum is characterized by high interest and high relevance, and it taps into learners' feelings and experiences. If we want students to retain, understand, and use ideas, information, and skills, we must give them ample opportunity to make sense of, or "own," them through involvement in complex learning situations.

Brain research also makes clear that if learning is a process of connecting the unfamiliar to the familiar, teachers must create abundant opportunities for students to link the new with the old. This is a three-part task. First, teachers must identify the essential concepts, principles, and skills of their subjects. Then they must become experts about their students' learning needs. Then they must use this information about learning needs to provide differentiated opportunities for students to construct understanding by connecting what they know with the essentials they are trying to learn.

Humans Learn Best with Moderate Challenge

Through increased understanding of both psychology and the

brain, we now know that individuals learn best when they are in a context that provides a moderate challenge. That is, when a task is far too difficult for a learner, the learner feels threatened and "downshifts" into a self-protection mode. A threatened learner will not persist with thinking or problem solving. On the other hand, a simple task also suppresses a learner's thinking and problem solving. He or she coasts into a relaxation mode. A task is appropriately challenging when it asks learners to risk a leap into the unknown, but they know enough to get started and have additional support for reaching a new level of understanding.

Put another way, students who consistently fail lose their motivation to learn. Students who succeed too easily also lose their motivation to learn. For learning to continue, students must believe that hard work is required, but the hard work often pays off with success. Teachers also must remember that what is moderately challenging today won't offer the same challenge tomorrow. Challenges must grow as students grow in their learning. Again, this new knowledge offers important guidance for educators. What is moderately challenging and motivating for one learner may offer far too little challenge (and therefore little motivation) for a classmate. The same task just may be too stressful for yet another classmate. Learning tasks must be adjusted to each student's appropriate learning zone. Further, tasks must escalate in complexity and challenge for students to learn continually.

Over the past half century or more, the student population has changed dramatically. Today, all children are expected to come to school, whatever their gender, socioeconomic status, or physical or mental challenge. Yet at one time, not all children came to public school. Children with physical disabilities and severe learning problems stayed home. Children from poor homes, including new immigrants, worked in factories or at other jobs to help support the family. Farm children worked the fields and didn't come to school, except in seasons when crops didn't require planting or harvesting. Girls were often excluded from advanced education because of the perception that they would marry, raise children, and run a household, roles not believed to require much education.

Children of the very rich often had tutors or went to exclusive boarding schools. Not too long ago, most children who came to school had two parents in the home. At least one of those parents usually was at home when the child left for school and when the child returned. We now teach many children whose homes have only one parent. Most children no longer have a parent at home at both ends of the school day. While that fact alone is not necessarily negative, it complicates children's lives. Sometimes children are frightened by this isolation. Many lack a steady hand to monitor school progress or homework—or even to listen to the events of a school day. We teach children who, for better or worse (and probably both), are offspring of the electronic era.

Their world is both larger and smaller. They know more things, but they understand less of what they know. They are accustomed to quick and ready entertainment, and yet their imaginations are less active. They have to cope with realities and problems that once would have been unknown to children, and yet many have markedly smaller support systems for wisely navigating these problems. They are aware of all sorts of positive possibilities in the adult world, but they have little sense of how to build bridges to reach them. These young people are at ease with and itchy to use technologies that frighten many of the adults "in charge" of their worlds.

Today, more kinds of children come to school and stay in school, bringing with them a greater range of backgrounds and needs. Many of these children lack the "givens" of early life that a teacher once took for granted. They are at once enriched and impoverished by their environments. Further, there is a chasm between children who have benefited from rich childhood experiences and those who haven't had the same opportunities.

Many of today's students come from homes where support and encouragement are in short supply. These children have immense learning potential, but they arrive at school with that potential weighted down by a lack of experience, support, models, and plans that, if present,, would make education a fundamental expectation of life. On the other hand, many other learners come to school with skills and knowledge months or years ahead of where their learning is "expected" to be according to the standard curriculum.

Schools must belong to all of these children. Educators often speak of equity as an issue with children of the former group and excellence as an issue for the latter. In truth, equity and excellence must be at the top of the agenda for all children. We cannot achieve equity for children who come to school at risk of falling behind in learning unless we ensure that these learners enter classrooms where teachers are ready to help build the sorts of experiences and expectations that the world outside the classroom may have been unable to build for the child. We cannot achieve excellence for children at risk of school failure without emphatically, systematically, vigorously, and effectively seeing to the development of their full potential. We must dream big dreams with them and be persistent partners in helping them soar toward those dreams.

Both equity and excellence must be a part of road map for these students. Similarly, children who come to school advanced beyond grade expectations in one or more areas also require equity of opportunity to grow from their points of entry, with teachers doggedly determined to ensure that their potential does not languish. These children, too, need teachers who commend, and command, excellence—teachers who help them dream big, who cause them to experience, accept, and embrace personal challenge. Every child is entitled to the promise of a teacher's enthusiasm, time, and energy. All children are entitled to teachers who will do everything in their power to help them realize their potential every day. It is unacceptable for any teacher to respond to any group of children (or any individual child) as though the children were inappropriate, inconvenient, beyond hope, or not in need of focused attention.

Grouping and the Quest for Equity and Excellence

Schools have tried to meet the needs of struggling and advanced learners by pulling them from regular classrooms for part or all of the school day. They were assigned to special classrooms with similar students and teachers who have the knowledge and skill to meet their unique needs. In full accord with common sense and classroom experience, much of the best research suggests that for struggling learners, such homogeneous learning experiences go awry. Too often in these settings, teachers' expectations for the struggling learners decline, materials are simplified, the level of discourse is less than sterling, and the pace slackens. Too few students escape these arrangements to join more "typical," or advanced, classes. In other words, remedial classes keep remedial learners remedial.

Also in full accord with common sense and classroom experience, much of the best research suggests that when we place advanced learners in accelerated, homogeneous classes, they benefit from a brisk pace, stimulating discourse, raised teacher expectations, and enriched materials. In other words, they continue to advance. In theory, creating heterogeneous classes should address equity and excellence for all learners. There are three major flaws in that assumption, at least as schools have practiced it to this point. First, struggling learners will not experience more long-term success by being placed in heterogeneous classes unless we are ready and able to meet them at their points of readiness and systematically escalate their learning until they are able to function as competently and confidently as other learners.

We have often claimed that such heterogeneous classes represent high expectations for struggling learners, but we then leave them to their own devices to figure out how to "catch up" with the expectations. Such an approach does not result in genuine growth for struggling learners. Advanced learners highlight a second, similar, problem. Once in a heterogeneous classroom, advanced students often are asked to do a greater volume of work that they already know how to do, to ensure the success of other students through much of the school day by serving as peer coaches, or to wait (patiently, of course) while students with less advanced skills continue to work for mastery of skills already mastered by the advanced learner.

Implicitly, and sometimes even explicitly, the advanced learners are fine without special provisions because they are "up to standards" already. Again, this approach won't achieve genuine growth for advanced learners. A third problem with heterogeneity, as it is typically practiced, is the assumption that what happens in heterogeneous classrooms for "typical learners" is what it needs to be. When we create effective communities of learning in which the needs of all learners are specifically and systematically addressed, we will go a long way toward addressing both equity and excellence in schools.

However, heterogeneity usually is a one-size-fits-all endeavor where the learning plan swallows some learners and pinches others. Such classes provide for neither equity nor excellence. Despite compelling new educational knowledge, classrooms have changed little over the last 100 years. We still assume that a child of a given age is enough like all other children of the same age that he or she should traverse the same curriculum in the same fashion with all other students of that age. Further, schools act as though all children should finish classroom tasks as near to the same moment as possible.

A school year should be the same length for all learners. To this end, schools generally adopt a single textbook, give students a single test at the end of the chapter, and another test at the end of designated marking periods. Teachers use the same grading system for all children of a given age and grade, whatever their starting point at the beginning of the year. The curriculum typically is based on goals that involve having students accumulate and retain a variety of facts and skills that are far removed from any meaningful context.

Drill-and-practice worksheets are the chief educational technology, and teachers tell students things they must then tell back. a legacy of behaviorism rooted firmly in the 1930s. Teachers still largely "run" classes, and they are likely to work harder and more actively than students much of the time. To the degree that we focus on developing intelligence in schools, educators seem convinced that only narrow, analytical slices of verbal and computational intelligence are important. This is almost the same as nearly a century ago when the public believed that a bit of reading, writing, and computation would serve learners well in an adulthood dominated by assembly line and agrarian jobs. Schools still prepare children for tests more than for life.

Many observers have written wisely and well about why schools seem so resistant to change. The point here is that while the rest of the world seized upon progress over the last century, the *practice* of education remained static. To overcome this, we need to begin our investigation of how to differentiate instruction for a diverse student population with some important assumptions.

— Students differ in experience, readiness, interest, intelligences, language, culture, gender, and mode of learning. As one elementary teacher noted, "Children already come to us differentiated. It just makes sense that we would differentiate our instruction in response to them."

— To maximize the potential in each learner, educators need to meet each child at his or her starting point and ensure substantial growth during each school term.

— Classrooms that ignore student differences are unlikely to maximize potential in any student who differs significantly from the "norm." This is an issue even in "homogeneous" classrooms where student variance is inevitably great.

— To ensure maximum student growth, teachers need to make modifications for students rather than assume students must modify themselves to fit the curriculum. In fact, children do not know how to differentiate their own curriculum successfully.

— Best-practice education should be the starting point for differentiation. It makes little sense to modify practices that defy the best understanding of teaching and learning. As noted educator Seymour Sarason reminds us, any classroom efforts that aren't powered by an understanding of what keeps children eagerly pursuing knowledge are doomed to fail.

— Classrooms grounded in best-practice education, and modified to be responsive to student differences, benefit virtually all students. Differentiation addresses the needs of struggling and advanced learners. It addresses the needs of students for whom English is a second language and students who have strong learning style preferences. It addresses gender differences and cultural differences. It pays homage to the truth that we are not born to become replicas of one another.

As Howard Gardner suggests, even if we could figure out how to make everyone a brilliant violinist, an orchestra also needs top-quality musicians who play woodwinds, brass, percussion, and strings. Differentiation is about high-quality performance for all individuals and giving students the opportunity to develop their particular strengths.

HOW DO TEACHERS MAKE IT ALL WORK?

We all have our own images of "how to do school." Parents base their images on the 13 or more years they spent in school. As teachers, we create different images of school: from our own early schooling through professional training to our first years teaching in the classroom. Students create their images of school day after day in their pilgrimages to become "educated." Images of school also are fueled by cartoons, movies, television, and books. As a rule, these images are dominated by rows of desks and a teacher working in front of the group.

Students wait passively—slouched or wiggling—for the teacher to do whatever she had in mind for the day. Few of these images prepare us even to envision, let alone craft, classrooms that are differentiated in response to the array of children's learning needs. Alas, there is no fail-safe way to master the alternate approaches to teaching and learning that common sense (and tomes of research) tells us would be more effective. If the notion of a student-centered, differentiated classroom is new to you, here are a few suggestions to help you steer your thinking and planning in that direction.

Examine Your Philosophy About Individual Needs

A young teacher working hard to implement a differentiated classroom recently reflected, "Differentiated instruction isn't a strategy. It's a way of thinking about all you do when you teach and all that the kids do when they learn." Not only is she correct, but her insight offers important guidance. Instead of first focusing on what to do in the classroom, it's wisest to focus on how to think about teaching and learning.

— Which makes better sense to you: that you do most of the work in the classroom, or that students are the primary workers and thinkers? Why?

— Does it seem more likely to you that everyone should always need the same book, math problem, or art lesson? Or are students likely to show up at different points of readiness for reading and math and drawing? Why?

— Do students all seem to learn in the same way or at the same pace? Or do some process information differently and at a different pace than others? How do you know?

— Do you learn more about students by talking *to* them or talking *with* them? Why?

— Do students become independent learners in classrooms where they are always told what to do? Or do they become independent when teachers systematically give them more responsibility for learning and teach them how to use the independence wisely? Why?

— Do learners care if they have choices about what and how to learn? Do they care a lot or a little? Why?

— Are we most motivated to grow when we try to reach our own ceilings or when the ceilings are someone else's? Why do you say so?

— In general, are you more effective and efficient at teaching with small groups of students and individuals, or are you more effective with the whole class? Why do you say so?

— Is learning richer and more permanent when it's rote or meaning based? How do you know?

Like students, teachers are ready for differing degrees of challenge. Many teachers successfully start differentiating instruction with small, well-organized changes. Here are some suggestions. Use the ones that make sense for your starting point.

— Begin the process of differentiation by teaching all of your students to do an "anchor activity," which is meaningful work done individually and silently. This could be journal writing, free reading, foreign language pattern drills, seatwork in math, or sketchbook assignments. It's something useful and important for students to do on a relatively regular basis throughout at least a portion of the year. It may seem a bit of a paradox to begin differentiation by *not* differentiating. But when you ask all students to learn to work absolutely quietly on one (or more) anchor activities, you pave the way for breaking off individuals or small groups to do other tasks while the remaining students continue with the comfortable, predictable anchor activity.

— Early on, you may want to ask some students to work with an anchor activity and others to work on a different task, which also requires no conversation or collaboration. This introduces the idea that students won't always do the same work. You create an atmosphere that's conducive to individual focus, and you emphasize attending to one's own work rather than focusing on what someone else does.

— Try a differentiated task for only a small block of time. In a primary classroom, for example, begin a language arts period with all students doing paired reading from the same "reading boxes." After 10 minutes of paired reading, differentiated by reading readiness, call all students to the reading corner to listen to a story together. Now discuss it as a whole class. Or, in a middle school history class, begin with a whole-class discussion and common use of a graphic organizer to compare two time periods. For the last 10 minutes of class, ask students to do one of two journal entries in their learning logs. The entries can be at different levels of complexity or based on two different interest areas. Starting small like this is the "think-versus-sink" approach. You think your way to success without sinking beneath too many changes. You also teach your students to succeed in an independent, learner-centered class. You don't ask them to manage too many routines and processes for which they are unprepared.

Envision How an Activity Will Look

Olympic athletes often pause before an event, close their eyes, and see themselves completing the competition. They envision clearing the vault, making the ski jump, or completing the dive. This is a good idea for a teacher in a differentiated classroom, too. Take time before the day begins to ask yourself how you want a differentiated activity to begin, what you want it to look like as it progresses, and how it should end. Think about what could go wrong along the way. Then plan to keep those things from happening. Write out procedures for yourself and directions you'll give students. Of course you can't envision every possible snafu, but you get better and better at second-guessing and at making plans and giving successful directions. Especially in the early stages, improvisational differentiation is less likely to succeed than choreographed differentiation.

As you work your way into a differentiated classroom, be sure you think your way into it as well. When you try something new, take time to reflect before you take the next step. You could ask yourself many questions. Here are a few.

— Which students seemed to be engaged in learning? Which were not? Do you know why in either case?

— What evidence do you have that each student understood or "owned" what you hoped would come from the lesson? Do you need to get more evidence to answer this question?

— How did you feel about the introduction you gave to the activity or lesson?

— In what ways did the activity or lesson begin as you wished? Did it get off track? How? What worked and what didn't as students began to work? Were your directions clear? Were materials easily accessible? Did you specify the time for moving (to stations, centers, or small groups, for example)? Did you specify and reinforce the time allotted to settle down?

— As the activity or lesson progressed, how well did students remain focused? If there was point where focus was ragged, can you figure out why? If focus was maintained throughout, why did things work so well? How did group size work? Do any students need to sit in a different place in the room? Did you see any pairings or groups that were unproductive? Were there any students who do not work well in groups, or do not work well alone? Did students know how to monitor the quality of their work? Did they know how to get help?

— How was the conclusion to the activity or lesson? Was there enough warning for students to stop their work in an organized way? Did they know where to put materials and supplies? Were a few students specified to put away materials, move furniture, or handle other clean-up tasks? Were things well organized for the next class or the next day? Did students make the transition to the next class or next activity in a self-controlled way?

— Did you have a sense of who was learning what as the lesson progressed? How did you interact with individuals and groups as they worked? What useful information did you gather as you moved among groups? What effective coaching were you able to do? How might you improve your data gathering and coaching?

Make notes of things you want to retain the next time you try a differentiated activity. Also note things you want to improve. Make specific plans to use the insights you gain from your reflection.

If your teaching philosophy embraces attention to individual students, and if you develop routines and procedures for a differentiated classroom in a systematic and reflective way, differentiation gradually will become a way of life. It won't be something you do every once in a great while. At that point, you need to incorporate at least three things in your routines. As you develop a clear philosophy about what it means to do differentiated instruction, share your thinking with your students. Be a metacognitive teacher; that is, unpack your thinking in conversations with students. Compared to the images many students have about school, you're changing the "rules." Let them know why and how. Here are some ideas that may help you involve your students in creating a responsive classroom.

— Use an activity that helps students reflect on the fact that they differ from one another in how they learn and what they like to learn about. (They already know this fact quite clearly, by the way.) Depending on the students' ages, the activity will vary. Some teachers ask their students to graph their strengths and weaknesses on a range of skills related and unrelated to the class in question. Some teachers have their students write autobiographies about themselves as learners. They reflect on questions about positive and negative school experiences, best and worst subjects, and effective and ineffective ways of learning. A teacher of young children sent home a survey asking parents to provide ages at which their children sat up, walked, ran, talked, got their first tooth, lost their first tooth, and rode a bike. She helped students create bar graphs that clearly showed how children do things on different timetables. They concluded it wasn't nearly so important when someone learned to talk as it was that they learned. Throughout the year, she brought students back to the graphs to remind them it was fine if some students learned a skill before or after others. In the end, what mattered was learning the skill and using it well.

— When you complete the above activity, let students know that their differing strengths, needs, and learning preferences present an interesting problem to you as a teacher. Ask them if they believe you should pay attention to developing their individual strengths and helping them improve in difficult areas by focusing on the ways that work best for them individually. Or do they believe you will do a better job of teaching by ignoring those things? Chances are, they won't choose the "forget-who-we-are" approach.

— Now you can begin an ongoing discussion of how a differentiated classroom looks and operates. Talk about how your role will differ. For example, you'll work with small groups and individuals rather than only the whole class. Students' roles will differ, too. They'll help and support one another's learning in different ways, making it possible for you to work with individuals and small groups. Students will take more responsibility for class operation, using time wisely so everyone can learn. Their assignments will differ. Not everyone will always have the same assignment in class or for homework. The classroom will look different, with small groups or individuals working on various tasks. Students will see more movement, and they'll use a wider range of materials.

— From this point, you are ready to ask students to help you establish guidelines and procedures to make the classroom work. Let them help you decide how to begin class, how to give directions when multiple things are about to begin at once, how they should get help when you are busy, what they must do when they finish an assignment, how to keep the class focused as activities progress, and how to conclude an activity smoothly. These conversations can occur as the need for each procedure emerges, but they are pivotal in establishing and maintaining a successful learning environment.

Continue to Empower Students

There will always be classroom roles only the teacher can fulfill. However, many teachers have found it easier to do things for students rather than teach them to do those things for themselves. Look for things you don't have to do, and gradually prepare your students to do them effectively. For example, can students learn to move furniture efficiently and quietly when the room needs to be rearranged? Can students hand out or collect work folders or other materials? Can students check one another's work in a responsible way at any point? Can students learn to straighten up the room?

Can they learn to file their own work in designated places rather than bring it to you? Can they learn to keep accurate records of what they complete and when? Can they keep records of their grades to gauge how their performance is progressing? Can they learn to set personal learning goals and to assess their progress according to those goals? The answer to all those questions, and many more like them, is yes—as long as you teach them how! Helping students master these things not only develops more independent and thoughtful learners, but it creates a classroom that belongs to kids as much as to adults. It's also a classroom where the teacher is not frazzled from trying to do everything for everyone!

Classrooms are busy places. We often get caught in the undertow of "doing," and we fail to take time for reflecting. Learning to facilitate a differentiated classroom is like learning to conduct a large orchestra. It calls for many players, many parts, many instruments, and many skills. A skilled conductor hears and sees many things at once, but she also takes time away from the podium to reflect on things like the intent of the composer and balance among the sections. She listens to recordings of rehearsals and compares those to performance goals. She identifies a need for additional attention to particular passages and a need for sectional rehearsals.

As your differentiated classroom evolves, cultivate your analytical skills. Some days, just look at how students get into and out of groups, or look only at students who are currently advanced in the subject. Take notes on who elects to work with visual materials and who gravitates to kinesthetic opportunities. Videotape the class every once in a while, or ask a colleague to be a second pair of eyes in your classroom. In either case, you'll identify things that are going well that you'd have missed otherwise, and you'll discover areas that need additional work. Be analytical with your students, too. Ask them to recall the guidelines you established together for working effectively in a group.

Have them analyze with you those procedures that are working well for them and those that are not. Let them make suggestions for how to get even better at working together (or beginning class or moving around the room). Express your pleasure to them when you see them growing in responsibility and independence. Let them tell you when they feel proud. And work together when there is dissonance, too, not to eliminate the passage from the piece, but to attend to it as a whole or in "sectional rehearsals."

When you give directions for multiple tasks simultaneously, don't give everyone directions for all the tasks. It wastes time, it's confusing, and it calls too much attention to task variance. The trick, then, is how to let everyone know what to do without giving whole-group directions. Here are some hints and possibilities:

— Start the class with a familiar task. Once students settle in, meet with one small group at a time to give directions for differentiated tasks.

— Give directions today for tomorrow. That is, today, give directions to a careful listener and a careful follower in each group. They can give directions to their group when the task begins tomorrow.

— Use task cards. Students can go to assigned (or selected) spots in the room and find out what to do by reading a carefully written task card. With younger students, assign more fluent readers to read task cards to the group at the start of the activity.

— Use tape-recorded directions. Tape-recorded directions work wonderfully for students who have difficulty with print, when you don't have time to write a task card, or when directions are complex enough you'd like to explain them a couple of ways.

— Put directions on an overhead or a flip chart for some activities.

— Be sure you think twice about introducing a completely new format in a small-group task. For example, it makes better sense to use graphic organizers several times with the whole class before you ask a small group to use them. It is better to have all students work at the same learning center until they understand how to work there; then, differentiate work at the center.

— Make yourself "off limits" at strategic times in the instructional sequence. You may want to make it "standard procedure" that no one can ask you questions during the first five minutes of any activity. That way, you can walk among students, making sure they settle down and have their materials. You won't be cornered by one student, giving others the opportunity to remain off task. You also need uninterrupted time for meeting with small groups and individuals. With older students, you just might announce those times. With younger ones, you could indicate you're off limits by wearing a ribbon around your neck or a baseball cap. In either case, make certain students understand why they cannot come to you at those times.

Establish Routines for Getting Help

For a variety of reasons, students in a multitask classroom must learn to get help from someone other than you much of the time. Teach them how to do that, and make provisions for help from other sources.

— Work with students on being good listeners. Kids often learn sloppy listening habits because they know someone will reexplain what they miss. Help them learn to focus on you when you talk, ask them to "replay" what you said in their heads, and ask someone to summarize aloud essential directions. They'll learn to need less help if they listen to you well in the first place. That takes time on their part and perseverance on yours.

— Ask students to go through a four-step RICE process if they are stuck about what to do next. They first should try hard to Recall what you said. If that doesn't work, they should close their eyes, see you talking, use good practical intelligence, and Imagine logically what the directions would have been for the task. If that doesn't help, they can Check with a classmate (someone at their table or nearby doing the same task). This should be done in a whisper. If there's still no sense of direction, designate one or more "Experts of the day" who have the independence or skills necessary to provide guidance. The "expert" should continue with his work, stopping only long enough to help someone who is genuinely stuck. (Over time, most students can serve as an expert of the day for one or more tasks.)

— Make sure students understand that in the rare instances where even the RICE procedure fails, they must then move to a preapproved anchor activity. Let them know it's acceptable to tell you how they tried the RICE procedure, came up empty, and began working with the preapproved alternative until they could get your help. It is not acceptable to sit and wait, or to hinder others. Always be sure students know how much you value time. Help them understand that there are many important things to accomplish and little time for doing them. Wise use of time should be a classroom ethic.

Many teachers fear a sense that they will not know what's going on when students work with a variety of tasks in a differentiated classroom. Plus, an effective teacher can't afford to be "out of the loop." In a differentiated classroom, the teacher should have more awareness of what and how students are doing, not less. Teachers must look at the issue of staying "on top of" student progress in a different way. Here are some helpful ideas for accomplishing a new way of staying organized and aware for your classroom.

— Use student work folders. These always stay in the classroom and contain all work in progress (including partially completed tasks, independent study work, and anchor options). The folders also should contain a record-keeping sheet. Here, students document work they have completed and date of completion. Students also should note individual conferences they've had with you, reflecting your conversations about progress and goals. Older students can keep running records of grades on the inside cover of their folders. Such folders provide you a ready way to review student progress and also can be useful for parent-teacher conferences and conferences among parents, teachers, and students.

— Make a list of all skills and competencies you want your students to master in each facet of your subject (for example, in writing, spelling, reading, and grammar). Then extend the list to skills more basic than the ones you're working toward and skills more advanced than the targeted ones. Then turn the skills into a checklist. Sequentially arrange the competencies on the left, and put spaces for several dates and comments across the rest of the page beside each competency. Make one checklist for each student, and keep the lists alphabetically in a notebook. Periodically spot-check students' work using the checklist, or do a formal written or oral assessment with individuals or the group from time to time. As you record observations over time, you should see a clear pattern of individual growth. Not only will that help you monitor student progress, it also should be a great help in developing differentiated assignments targeted to student need. These observations aid in student-teacher planning conferences, too.

— Establish carefully organized and coded places where students should place completed assignments (for example, stack trays, boxes, or folders). This is much more effective than having assignments brought to you, and it is more effective than having a variety of assignments all piled together.

— Carry a clipboard around the class with you much of the time. Make brief notes about nifty things you see students do, "Aha's!", points of confusion, or working conditions that need to be tightened. Use the notes for reflection, planning, and individual and classroom conversations.

— Don't feel compelled to grade everything. (You'd never think of grading a piano student's every practice session!) There's a time for students to figure things out, and a time for seeing if they did, but the two shouldn't always be the same. Help your students see how important it is to complete activities so they become more and more skilled and insightful. Use peer checkers or "experts of the day" when an accuracy check is necessary. When it's time for formal assessment, help students see the link between good practice and success.

— When students are working with sense-making activities and you feel a need to "grade," choose things like whether the student stayed on task, worked hard, got help appropriately, or moved to anchor activities when work was completed. On your clipboard, you might keep a class list with spaces for a daily assessment of these sorts of things. If you see a student have a breakthrough or make a real leap of progress, put a plus in today's space. If a student has real difficulty staying on task despite reminders, put a minus in today's space. Later, put checks in the other spaces. Look for patterns over time, and work with what they tell you. Though you can convert the pattern into a single daily work grade if necessary, there are plenty of other opportunities for formal grading. Remember that grading means more to students if it's infrequent. Continual grading of everything impairs students' willingness to learn from mistakes, makes them teacher dependent, and teaches them to learn for grades, not for its own value. All this grading also makes you crazy and robs you of important thinking and planning time.

Consider "Home Base" Seats

In a differentiated class, it's often helpful to have students assigned to "home base" seats where they begin and end class every day. Students always begin the class in those seats. Some days they will remain in them. If differentiated activities lead them to other parts of the room, they will return to their "home base" seats when the class ends. "Home base" seats help you check attendance quickly. They make it simple for students to distribute work folders for you. "Home base" seats also make it easier to ensure that the room is straight at the end of an activity, and they provides an orderly format for dismissal or transition. Assigned seats also let you develop positive peer groupings for those times when students work at "home base."

Before students begin to move to various work areas, let them know how quickly they should be in their new places and working. You should make the time realistic, but you also should be a bit on the stingy side. After students move through the room, let them know how they did. Work with them so they get used to settling in efficiently. During the activity, keep your eye on the clock. Give students about a two-minute signal that their work time is about to end (flash the lights or just walk to each table and tell them). Follow that with another signal to return to "home base" seating. Students should know that you expect them to return to those seats within 30 seconds.

Teach Students to Work for Quality

A few students in every class seem inclined to measure their success by how quickly they complete their work rather than by how thoughtful they were in doing it. Be clear with your students that craftsmanship and a sense of pride in work are what matter. Help them know why. Let students analyze the differences in work that is hastily finished versus work that shows persistence, revision, and creativity. Sometimes, students finish work quickly because it's too easy for them or the directions don't clearly state standards of excellence. When those are not problems, patiently and persistently insist that only quality work is acceptable.

One teacher called it "working for a Bingo." She taught her students to resist the urge to turn in work until they had done absolutely everything they could think of to improve it. Then they could say, "Bingo! That's it! That's my very best." At least four groups can help you on your path to a differentiated classroom. Colleagues, administrators, parents, and community members all can aid you and your students. With all four groups, you'll probably have to take the initiative to enlist their help. Here are some thoughts about seeking their goodwill and active support.

The unhappy truth in many schools is that some of your colleagues will be resentful if you do something innovative or expend more energy than the norm in your work. A happier truth is that in these same places, there are always a few soulmates who are energized by their work, catalyzed by someone else's ideas, and ready to take the risk of growth. Find one or two people from the latter group and work together. In many schools, an art teacher, a special educator, a teacher of the gifted, and a few classroom teachers already differentiate instruction. They may not feel like experts, but neither do you. They have great ideas and routines already in place. You have ideas and questions to enrich them. At the very least, they'll feel enriched by the compliment you pay them in wanting to learn from and with them. Meet with them regularly, ask for time to spend in one another's classrooms, plan together, troubleshoot as a team, share lessons and materials, and take turns teaching and watching as peer coaches. The synergy from such collegial partnerships can be one of the most amazing benefits of a job that all too often is isolating.

Bringing Parents Aboard

Most parents want appropriate things for their children in school. They want them to grow, to maximize their strengths and minimize their weaknesses, to find the classroom exciting, and to wake up eager to go to school the next morning. Yet as surely as a differentiated classroom must confront children's images of how we do school, it also must deal with parents' stereotypical images of school. Ask parents to write out for you, or tell you, their wishes for their child's year in school. Really listen and learn. Then systematically show parents how a differentiated classroom acknowledges and builds on their child's strengths, provides opportunities to bolster weaker areas, keeps track of individual growth, and promotes engagement and excitement.

Use a variety of ways to help parents understand that you are building a curriculum and way of instruction that includes the same goals they desire for their youngsters. For example, periodic class letters, weekly or monthly newsletters, parent conferences with work folders or portfolios, and student evaluations help achieve this goal. You might want to invite parents to take an active role in the class. Parent volunteers can review math concepts with struggling learners, read with advanced readers who want adult conversation about their advanced books, or work on a project with any student who enjoys the pride of knowing an adult finds him worthy of time and attention. Parents also can be a treasure trove of novels, computer expertise, maps, or hands-on learning materials—all things that expand the learning options for their own and others' children.

Parent-teacher partnerships are important to differentiated classrooms. A parent always knows a child more deeply than a teacher possibly can. There's much for the teacher to learn from that depth of knowledge. On the other hand, a teacher knows a child in ways that a parent cannot. There's much for a parent to gain from that breadth of knowledge. Looking at a child from both parent and teacher viewpoints increases the chances of helping that child realize her full potential. The wisest teachers teach parents as well as children. They eagerly seek opportunities to learn from parents as well.

The world outside the classroom offers more opportunities than even the most magical classroom. It makes sense to open up a differentiated classroom to that larger world. Frederick learns best when he builds models of things. Phan needs someone to toss around ideas in his native language before he writes in English. Saranne is more advanced in computers than anyone in her building, and 4th grade Charlie has pretty well finished 6th grade math. Francie desperately wants to know how to dance, Philip is itchy to learn about archeology, and Genice wants to use a 35 mm. camera to take pictures for her history project. The teacher who can facilitate all those things is rare, indeed.

However, a service club can volunteer regularly to make audiotapes for struggling readers and students with learning disabilities. Mentors can help students discover a world of possibilities with photography, baseball statistics, or jazz. A church can provide volunteers for students trying to communicate in two languages. A company can provide old carpet to cover a reading corner in the classroom. Museums and galleries can provide ideas, materials, or guidance on independent projects. A senior citizens center can provide guidance for a wide range of orbital investigations. The world is a classroom replete with resources and mentors. A generous teacher links learners with those wide options. As mentioned before, don't try to do everything at once. Each year, devise one new way to link up with a colleague, gain insight and support from an administrator, learn from and teach parents, or invite a bit of the world into your classroom. Remember that becoming an expert at differentiation is a career-long goal. One step at a time, you can get there.

AGE-RELATED CHANGES: INSTRUCTIONAL IMPLICATIONS

Learners' Needs and Experiences

- Learning activities and instructional approaches should be based on learners' needs and interests
- Differing needs, interests, and abilities will exist and change over time among older learners so instructors must be flexible
- Life stages and life changes will impact on learning needs
- Social interactions among learners may have value as a learning motivator
- Small group discussion can be used for analyzing individual and group needs
- Learners should be helped to relate new knowledge to past experiences
- Learners should be helped to understand the advantages and disadvantages of being an older person in terms of educational needs
- Help learners tie any necessary text material to their own current knowledge base
- Instructional approaches for should be tailored for different cognitive styles

Involving Learners in Instruction

- Learners should become active in all aspects of efforts to individualize the instructional process

- Learners should be encouraged to be self-directed in determining personal goals, learning approaches, and learning resource needs
- The development of confidence and a positive self-concept can be enhanced when learners engage in completing learning contracts
- Increasing opportunities for personal responsibility reduces learner dependency on the instructor
- Learners should be encouraged to become more efficient and self-motivated in the educational planning efforts
- Discovery teaching techniques can be used to involve and motivate learners
- Use a process orientation to increase perceptions of control and lead to improved self-confidence

Personalizing the Instructor's Approach

- Be helpful, positive, and supportive
- Assist older learners to compensate for intellectual or non-cognitive changes
- Promote learning confidence, self-discipline, and self-respect
- Provide a learning environment of informality and levity
- Help learners feel welcome in any new learning setting
- Help learners feel at ease

The Learning Pace

- Provide long periods of time between stimuli for discussion or answering questions
- Provide adequate time for all aspects of the learning experience
- Eliminate sudden surprises or changes
- Be aware of learner perceptions about life satisfaction and locus of control

— Provide information in short sessions (50-60 minutes)
— Minimize time pressures
— Provide for self-pacing by learners
— Move from easy to difficult material to promote success

Assessment and Evaluation

— Use outside validators if they are the most knowledgeable
— Reduce any chances for failure or making errors
— Utilize peer review or feedback, positive feedback on progress, and various review strategies
— Reduce or eliminate homework and testing procedures
— Help learners talk about their learning, problems, and aspirations
— When testing is required use multiple-choice questions
— Utilize recognition techniques rather than more traditional recall methods

Learning Activity Organization and Meaningfulness

— Become highly organized as an instructor
— Provide instructional goal suggestions and help learners develop personal objectives
— Provide outlines, study guides, and various advanced organizing techniques
— Encourage a belief in personal learning ability
— Assist learners in processing received information
— Facilitate and increase learners' ability and self-perception in terms of reading proficiency
— Assist learners in organizing planned learning activities
— Encourage learners to use learning contracts
— Facilitate practicing techniques

— Show learners how to take notes and make outlines
— Have organizing material be part of the learning process
— Encourage the learner to connect concepts or information with a personal experience base
— Use materials with real meaning to learners
— Appeal to several senses
— Have concrete examples that tie to a learner's past experiences
— Be aware of differences in cognitive or learning styles
— Use various cueing devices
— Urge learners to use mnemonic devices
— Tie new learning to past knowledge
— Utilize headings, summaries, and review aids
— Facilitate a recognition of personal meaning
— Provide clear instructions in an attention-getting manner

Recognize Barriers, Obstacles, and Physiological Needs

— Be sensitive to diminishing hearing and associated problems for some older adults
— Assist learners to move closer to sound sources if needed
— Utilize voice and media amplification whenever appropriate
— Be sensitive to diminishing vision and associated problems for some older learners
— Provide time for adjustments when an older learner moves from light to dark areas
— Provide adequate light for classroom and visual aids
— Insure that glare or direct sunlight is not a problem
— Utilize adequate contrast on visuals and reading material
— Emphasize visual as well as interactive approaches
— Be sensitive to short-term memory problems

— Read material aloud when feasible
— Utilize both auditory and visual presentation modes
— Diagnose learners' needs, abilities, and limitations
— Minimize any learning distractions
— Be sensitive to various obstacles that can interfere with learning
— Be sensitive to physical environment problems
— Check for comfortable heating and proper ventilation
— Have periodic bathroom or refreshment breaks
— Help any learners with limited mobility or declining energy
— Reduce the use of color coding as a category discriminator
— Accommodate those learners who need or desire to sit near the front
— Determine if all learners can focus on and see all visual aids
— Be alert to differences in ways of learning by gender categories
— Help responsible administrators become aware of troublesome barriers

POLICIES FOR OLDER WOMEN

— *Older women should be acknowledged as having unlimited learning potential and given respect as self-directed learners.*

Implementation Strategies

1. Use small group discussion or create learning networks, including electronic networks, for assisting older women to discover personal talents.

2. Provide opportunities for older women to discover their own individual strengths.

3. Make educational resources broadly available that teach about personal potential, learning skills, and using learning materials.
4. Assist teachers and trainers to understand their role in promoting individualized, self-directed learning.

— *Older women should be encouraged to examine personal strengths and weaknesses.*

Implementation Strategies

1. Assist older women to complete self inventories or self-concept measures.
2. Ensure that teachers and counselors have skill in discussing self inventory information with older women.

— *Older women should be helped to develop or strengthen internal reinforcement mechanisms.*

Implementation Strategies

1. Promote skill in using various reinforcement resources (meditation techniques, diary writing processes, and critical thinking techniques).
2. Train teachers to assist older women in strengthening personal growth skills.
3. Secure learning resources that assist older women with internal reinforcement.

— *Older women should be helped to understand personal learning or cognitive style and use such information in their educational efforts.*

Implementation Strategies

1. Assist older women in completing learning and cognitive style measures.

2. Train teachers and counselors to interpret and use learning style information in helping older women with their planning.

— *Older women should be encouraged to form autonomous learning and support groups.*

Implementation Strategies

1. Create learner information sources in libraries, universities, and senior centers.
2. Develop learning exchange or support networks in various settings.
3. Develop peer support groups related to various content areas.

— *Older women should be provided with opportunities for taking individual responsibility for their own learning.*

Implementation Strategies

1. Create necessary administrative support to facilitate individual adult initiative (convenient scheduling, adequate resources, transportation support, adult counseling, etc.).
2. Facilitate workshops or learning materials to develop learning skills in time management and planning.

— *Older women should be provided with opportunities to assume leadership roles in educational organizations.*

Implementation Strategies

1. Establish necessary administrative support to enable and support older women as they develop their leadership skills and become more empowered.
2. Develop mechanisms for more social interaction and networking among older women in leadership roles.

3. Create advisory council of older women who can support organizations and providers in their efforts to meet older women's learning needs.

4. Provide opportunities for older minority women to assume leadership roles.

— *Continue the research necessary to understand various aspects of individualized, self-directed learning.*

Implementation Strategies

1. Determine learning techniques and skills necessary for learners and teachers.

2. Determine means for enhancing learners' problem-solving skills.

3. Study reasons why some older women are reluctant to utilize self-directed approaches.

4. Examine the relationship between life stages and individualized, self-direction learning approaches.

— *Educators and providers should be helped to become aware that older women possess unique strengths, skills, and experiences that have relevance for educational programs and instructional approaches.*

Implementation Strategies

1. Provide opportunities for older women to identify their strengths, skills, and experiences.

2. Facilitate older women to share their self-knowledge about strengths, skills and experiences with other older women.

3. Utilize the inherent nurturing characteristics of older women to facilitate positive lifelong learning experiences.

— *Educators of adults should be provided with training in utilizing theories and practices related to adult learning.*

Implementation Strategies

1. Students in formal adult education or educational gerontology training programs need an understanding of adult learning concepts and approaches, including aspects related specifically to older women.
2. Develop in-service training programs on older adult women as learners for the many educators of adults who have not received any related formal training.

— *Organizations serving older adults should be helped to incorporate concepts of individualized, self-directed learning into normal operating procedures.*

Implementation Strategies

1. Develop individualized resources, create self-study materials, and establish appropriate learning settings.
2. Carry out learner needs assessments to determine possibilities for individualized, self-directed learning and provide the information to administrators.
3. Help organizations coordinate the delivery of necessary resources and services related to individualized, self-directed learning.

— *Organizations or providers working with older women as learners need to provide opportunities for administrators, faculty, and staff to become knowledgeable about older adult learning.*

Implementation Strategies

1. Promote an awareness of research and literature pertaining to older adult learning.

2. Provide workshops, in-service training, and resource material related to older adult learning to employees.
3. Support additional university credit courses for employees so they can study adult learning knowledge in a more formal manner.

— *Organizations or providers working with older women as learners should develop and maintain various measures or criteria for accountability and evaluation.*

Implementation Strategies

1. Create reporting systems that accommodate non-traditional data collection and reporting mechanisms (learning contracts, internship reports, credit for work experiences, etc.).
2. Try innovative evaluation methods (interviewing, networking assessments, validation via outside experts, etc.).

— *Organizations or providers working with older women as learners should seek national legislation and funding to promote and facilitate adult learning at all levels.*

Implementation Strategies

1. Provide learning resources and study opportunity information to a multitude of community agencies.
2. Influence legislation through professional associations.

— *Organizations or providers working with older women as learners should be helped to provide support services that facilitate those desiring to be more self-directed in their learning efforts.*

Implementation Strategies

1. Create centers or special locations within agency

settings where older women as learners can gather, obtain learning resources, and support each other.

2. Ensure that personnel have the expertise to counsel with and help older women make effective use of self-directed learning skills.

— *Organizations or providers working with older women as learners should be helped to provide learning environments that accommodate learning.*

Implementation Strategies

1. Examine the learning environment in terms of physical, emotional, and social issues and make any necessary changes.
2. Maintain on-site specialists on learning environments who can work with educators and learners to design appropriate learning conditions.

4

Understanding the Learner in the light of Individual

Daily observations and experiences as well as recent scholarly traditions suggest that some learning takes place beyond the confines of the individual mind. Learning appears to have social aspects to it. Are there any theoretical and empirical grounds to justify social learning as a distinctive phenomenon? Is there anything qualitatively different in this kind of learning to distinguish it from the familiar solo learning? Can one make the case that social learning is more than an epiphenomenon or solo learning multiplied, that the social aspects of learning are anything more than the kind of secondary help a learner might get from audiovisual displays, bookmarks, and road signs?

If we can raise the question of whether social learning is a valid and viable phenomenon, the opposite question might equally well be raised: Is it not possible that solo learning is just a figment of the traditional laboratory-based psychology on the one hand, and of a socially shared respect for the individual qua individual, on the other? The idea of social learning is not really new, having been an important part of early developments of the science of psychology—"folkspsychology" as formulated, for example, by Munsterberg. This branch of psychology fell into neglect because of its Gestalt-like nature and thus its alleged lack of rigor, its central phenomena left to anthropology and sociology to handle. It was distinguished from the more rigorous laboratory-based, experimentally oriented and far more prestigious psychology of Ebbinghouse.

Social learning has thus continued to be largely ignored by psychologists over the years, relegated at best to the study of background context, not really on a par with the learning of the individual. This relative neglect now appears to have been corrected. With the growing interest in Vygotsky's theory, retrospective examinations of the role of social interactions in Piaget's works, Bandura's reformulation of the individual in reciprocal relations with the social environment, the conception of learning as a constructive, hence socially and culturally situated process, and newly designed empirical work, the study of individuals' learning has come to be embedded in social and cultural contexts and interactions.

A focus on the individual learning in social and cultural solitude is increasingly seen as conceptually unsatisfying and ecologically deficient. As Bronfenbrenner has pointed out, "in ecological research, the principal main effects are likely to be interactions", and these interactions are, to a large extent, between an individual, his or her social surrounds, and the artifacts culture provides. Two conceptions of learning seem to be involved here, each with its own metaphor. On the one hand we have the conception of the individual learner, emphasizing the acquisition of knowledge and cognitive skill as transferable commodities. On the other we have the socio-cultural conception of learning as a collective, participatory process of active knowledge construction, emphasizing context, interaction, and situatedness.

Teasing the varied meanings of social learning apart and illuminating their nature is a daunting endeavor. To make the mission easier, some researchers adopt a loose but unifying information processing perspective on learning, within which different views of learning can be described, compared, and contrasted. As used here, the idea of information processing includes no biasing presumptions about where those processes lie or what entity they serve. The information processes in question might occur within the mind of an individual or within complex webs of social interaction. The entity learning might be an individual or a social entity such as a team or corporation.

From the standpoint of information processing, learning for individual humans, teams, or organizations is a considerable challenge. The learning agent in question, solo or collective, must be able to construct new representations or behaviors based on prior experience. It must have the opportunity to test and select among alternative representations or behaviors, or refine one or combine them. It will need feedback of some sort about how well an alternative fairs. It can benefit greatly from information sources—anything from a text to the incidental or deliberate modeling provided by another wiser agent performing the activity in question, as well some guidance, through self-regulation or provided by others. To learn, it will need to face an approachable but manageable level of challenge, not too hard to cope with but not so easy as to yield completely to the existing repertoire.

The system will also need conditions that sustain motivation and energy. And so on. In other words, learning by any system in any setting has what might be called *critical conditions.* Such conditions figure not only in the logical story of how learning can come about but in the practical story of ensuring that it does come about. Often learning fails not for subtle reasons such as the learner missing the point but for gross reasons such as the lack of a source to provide an important point, not for subtle reasons such as misinterpreting feedback but for gross reasons such as not having informative feedback, only the teacher's "okay" or "X" that tells little about what went right or wrong or where.

With such general challenges in mind, it is useful to speak of a *learning system*—in the individual or group, animal or human or even a computer—as an information processing system aimed at facilitating these critical conditions of learning. Thus, simple trial-and-error learning through reinforcement of an individual organism embodies one kind of learning system, with certain ways of dealing with the critical conditions of generating alternatives (accidentally varying behaviors) and selecting alternatives (through reinforcement). Learning that involves deeper understanding aided by peers in a collaborative setting embodies yet another kind of learning system in which alternatives are provided by different team members, and the selection of the best one is a matter of detailed deliberations and agreements. Learning as in the first example might be called "low road learning" to signify its relatively mindless automatic character.

However, asH the second example suggests, not all learning is low road. Human learners, as well as some computer systems, learn by the low road but often display "high road learning" as well, entailing mindful management of the learning process that deals with the same conditions in far more sophisticated ways, for example by generating alternative hypotheses, testing them, and selecting among them or modifying them based on feedback from the testing. The ideas of critical conditions for learning on the one hand and learning systems designed to facilitate those conditions on the other provide a backdrop for addressing the first question posed earlier: What are the distinctive meanings of social learning as contrasted with solo learning and with one another? They distinguish six meanings for the sake of conceptual clarity.

1. *Active social mediation of individual learning*: In human society, one of the most fundamentally social forms of learning occurs when a person or a team helps an individual to learn. A teacher teaches reading, writing, and arithmetic; parents correct a child's ungrammatical utterances or misuse of words on the fly; a master takes on apprentices and guides their development; children work together to master mixture problems in algebra, each learning from the other. In such cases the facilitating agent and the primary learner form a joint learning

system, the facilitating agent helping the learner to achieve critical conditions of learning. The agent may for instance provide information in the form of instruction or demonstrations, informative feedback about what's right or wrong and what to do instead, approachable but challenging tasks, encouragement, scaffolding of the learner's performance as it unfolds with tips and hints, and so on. The exact forms such learning systems take on vary of course: A skilled individual tutor can tune the learning system much more finely to a particular individual than a classroom teacher can to a room full of individuals.

A team studying together can elaborate on a member's attempts to solve something the individual could not do on his or her own. But such differences aside, the broad idea is the same: Create a better learning system for the primary learner by bringing in a facilitating social agent to help meet the critical conditions of learning. Loosely speaking, socially mediated individual learning might be considered the same as instruction, and the point no more than that instruction inevitably involves some social mediation. But far more is at stake than this. Instruction, in its prototypical forms involving lecturing or question and answer sessions, may be considered a special case, albeit not a very interesting one, of social learning. However, as a learning system it often does not meet the critical conditions of learning very well. And when regular instruction does, the processes involved may not be very socially mediated, as for instance when skilled students learn effectively from lectures because of their own autoregulation skills, but rarely from each other.

2. *Social mediation as participatory knowledge construction*: In the version of active social mediation sketched so far, there is a clear distinction between individuals and the learning products they carry away as their solo, transferable cognitive possession, on the one hand, and the social agents facilitating that learning, on the other. But there is second version of social mediation that deserves recognition, the *socio-cultural* version which sees learning less as the socially-facilitated acquisition of

knowledge and skill and more as a matter of participation in a social process of knowledge construction. Although the illustrative phenomena are the same—individual tutoring, team problem-solving, collaborative and cooperative learning, and so on—the way they are understood by this second version of active social mediation is very different. Social mediation of learning and the individual involved are seen as an integrated and highly situated system in which the interaction serves as the socially shared vehicles of thought. Accordingly, the learning products of this system, jointly constructed as they are, are distributed over the whole social system rather than possessed by the participating individual.

3. *Social mediation by cultural scaffolding*: Even when a learner does not receive direct help from another agent actively adjusting to the learner's needs—the first case of social mediation mentioned above—the learner may enter into some kind of intellectual partnership, or at least be greatly helped by cultural artifacts in the form of tools and information sources. Such artifacts can range from books and videotapes which tacitly embody shared cultural understandings, to statistical tools and socially shared symbol systems embodying, for instance, a "language of thinking" that includes such finely distinguished terms as hypothesis, conjecture, theory, and guess.

Computer-based learning environments offer students "problem spaces" in which they can work through their understandings of challenging concepts.Seen from the point of view of social mediation of an individual's learning, in such learning systems, the cultural surrounds helps meet the conditions of learning in certain ways. It can be a rich information source. It can provide diverse opportunities to act, so that the learner can select approachable but challenging opportunities. It can offer feedback as the learner tries things and sees .them succeed or fail in various ways. From a socio-cultural point of view, cultural artifacts are seen to serve as social mediators of learning in a far more important way. Since artifacts are themselves culturally and historically situated, carrying the wisdom and hidden assumptions that went into their design, they reorganize action, determining what can be carried out when, where and in what form, and for what purpose.

4. *The social entity as a learning system*: Another very different meaning of social learning occurs when people speak of teams or organizations or cultures or other collectives learning. Here it is not necessarily the case that one agent is helping another to learn. Rather, the focus falls on a collective agency that as a collective acquires more knowledge, understanding, or skill, a different climate or culture. A sports team attains patterns of coordination among the individuals that might be quite useless for any one of those individuals functioning alone, meaningless without the context of the team.

A business organization develops internal procedures, based on some commonly held tacit assumptions, that meet customer demands better and more quickly. In such cases, the agreements are not stated, the procedures are not executed, and perhaps not even overseen, by any one individual, but they advance the performance of the organization. In summary, the group constitutes a collective learning system, a system that will function better or worse as a learner depending on how well its structures address critical conditions of learning.

5. *Learning to be a social learner*: Still another sense of social learning concerns a special case of learning—learning to learn. Contemporary cognitive science recognizes that learning to learn is a fundamental aspect of learning. Youngsters acquire not only knowledge, understanding, and skill in particular areas such as language use, soccer, or algebra, they also acquire knowledge, understanding, and skill about learning itself. For instance, the field of "metamemory" concerns children's developing understanding of their own memories and how to manage memory. Of course, all this applies to the learner functioning solo. However, an important dimension of learning to learn involves learning to learn in ways that participate in

and capitalize on the social milieu. One simple aspect is learning when and how to ask questions or to ask for help. Another is learning how to enter into reciprocal learning relationships: I'll help you with this if you help me with that, or we will both help one another with this particularly difficult idea. Here, the individual learner's learning system extends its capacity to deal with the critical conditions of learning by acquiring new ways to capitalize upon the social surround.

6. *Learning social content*: The foregoing categories all concern social factors in the service of learning. Solely for the sake of logical completeness, another possible meaning of social learning needs to be acknowledged: the learning of social content. Social content includes such matters as how to get along with others, how to maintain reasonable assertiveness, how to collaborate in reaching decisions and taking collective actions, and so on. This sense of social learning is quite different from those considered previously. To speak of the learning of social *content* is not to introduce any new kind of learning system into the picture, as the other categories have done.

Here, the learning system would be one of those already discussed, operating on social content. With six meanings of social learning in view, the first four provide the natural focus for development. All four deal with what might be called the dynamics of learning, in contrast with the last two, which deal more with what is learned. The first, social mediation by an active agent (social mediation for short), reflects a range of major figures and lines of inquiry in such areas as cognitive development, tutoring, peer tutoring, collaborative, cooperative and reciprocal learning, and more. The second treats a major stream of contemporary thinking that emphasizes participatory learning and "distributed, situated cognition."

The third deals with the mediating role that tools and cultural artifacts, embodying accumulated social wisdom, play in the process of learning. And the fourth reflects a tide of interest in team and organizational learning, sustained by practical interests in the worlds of business, government, and sports, and by the inquiries of psychologists, sociologists, and anthropologists into the workings of collectives of various kinds and sizes.

THE SOCIAL MEDIATION OF INDIVIDUAL LEARNING

The simplest and most familiar modes of social mediation are configurations of one-to-one (tutor, parent, teacher to learner), one-to-many (teacher to a group), or many-to-one (a pair, trio, or other group of collaborative learners which has the learner as a participant). In all these cases the interactions between the learner and the "other(s)" are expected, and often found, to enhance the individual's learning. Two distinguishable entities are involved in the learning system–the learner and the "other," entities sometimes in complementary relations, as, for example, when a knowledgeable adult tutors a remedial student, and sometimes in more symmetrical relations, as when classroom peers work well together, each facilitating the individual learning of the other.

How does this version of social mediation work and what does it yield? When does the social context facilitate learning and when does it fail to do so? The theoretical underpinnings of the socially mediated learning of the individual were greatly influenced by Vygotsky's conception of the zone of proximal development. According to this conception, external social processes become internalized to serve in a mental capacity, thereby raising the level of individuals' cognitive performance, which they could not have reached on their own. Whether directly inspired by Vygotskian thinking, or by more current constructivist sources, social "scaffolding" entails two critical processes: *internalization* and *active construction of knowledge* in the form of active solutions to problems or formulation of designs, with the help of explicit guidance, modeling, encouragement, mirroring and feedback.

The importance of active, constructive participation is underscored by an interesting difference between tutoring and peer problem solving. Whereas adult tutors aim to facilitate the learning of their tutees, peers working together often aim just to accomplish the task. Consequently, the individual learner often gets more of a chance to participate actively in critical planning and decision making when interacting with an expert tutor than with peers. This highlights an important aspect of social mediation of individuals' learning: Mediation is effective not necessarily as a function of simple "internalization, with modeled information being transferred across a barrier from a social partner to the inside of a child, or with information being transmitted".

Rather, mediation is effective through active, participation whereby learners "transform their understanding and skill in solving the problem". Thus, according to this view, it is active construction that is so crucial to learning, not some social guidance going underground. It becomes clear why social learning and a constructivist approach to learning have become close allies. Lepper and his colleagues emphasize this theme in their analyses of expert tutors, who routinely attain impressive progress in mathematics with remedial, failure prone, and math-phobic students within a single session. Many of the features that distinguish such expert tutors from their less effective colleagues are those that characterize social facilitation of individuals' learning in general: intensive interaction, rapid feedback, highly personalized and situationally contingent guidance, encouragement, and the elicitation of responses from the student in the form of explanations, suggestions, reflections, and considerations, rather than offering them ready-made information, directions, error corrections, or answers.

Effective social facilitation through team work, although it occurs less reliably, appears to share the same characteristics. As these points make plain, this perspective on social learning involves the critical conditions for an effective learning system mentioned earlier. Most importantly, social mediation of learning by tutors or peers, when well conducted, can meet these conditions far more effectively than its solo learning alternative.

In fact, some of the conditions mentioned by necessity socially-based and cannot be easily met by most learners without the facilitating social context: informative feedback, challenge, guidance, encouragement.

There are further characteristics that distinguish socially mediated learning from solo learning to the advantage of the former. One such condition has to do with the "objectivization" of one's thoughts, still to-be-formulated ideas, and considerations which, when communicated and shared, can be discussed, examined and elaborated upon as if they were external objects. Such is quite impossible to do outside the social context. Slavin points to two additional conditions for social mediation to be effective: shared group goals and personal accountability. In his review of the research literature he finds that in their absence, no significant enhancement of learning takes place as members of the learning system might work in incongruent directions and as one may become a "social loafer", not expending the needed mental effort.

Social learning in the present sense of mediating the learning of the individual entails the two interacting poles – learner and "other(s)" – who need to function in complementary ways to be effective. As for the individual, *active participation* and *personal accountability* appear to be of great importance. Together these two underscore the importance of the individual's contribution through the role played by motivated, intentional learning activity accompanied by the expenditure of mental effort. As to the socially facilitating agent, its special functions are the affordance of something to act upon (e.g., information) that can be usefully internalized or constructed, and the socially shared perceptions and goals. The interaction between these poles is what makes the learning system effective.

The account of social mediation reviewed so far has two features that some would view with suspicion. First of all, the notion that cognitive processes can be socially mediated suggests that these same processes, under the right conditions, might proceed without such mediation. Second, by and large the focus has fallen on the learner's learning, without recognizing that the facilitating social agent also may learn. These concerns have led to a different conceptualization of social mediation, influenced by the more qualitative, holistic way of anthropological thinking, the neo-Vygotskian socio-cultural school of thought, and a sharp critique of typical laboratory learning studies as too removed from the social context of real life.

Especially motivating were systematic findings about the non-systematicity of human performance, so highly dependent on particular cultural and social situations. Such factors led to the development of a new paradigm for the study of learning in social contexts. The basic assumption of this socio-cultural paradigm is, as stated by Wertch: Human mental functioning is inherently situated in social interactional, cultural, institutional, and historical context. Such a tenet contrasts with approaches that assume, implicitly or explicitly, that it is possible to examine mental processes such as thinking or memory independently of the sociocultural setting in which individuals and groups function.

Given the relative novelty of the socio-cultural approach, much of its vocabulary and many of its basic constructs are still somewhat vague, it is not easy "to refer to them as a mature scientific paradigm with generally accepted theoretical foundations, a methodology, and a well-delineated set of prescriptions for relating theory to practice". Nevertheless, the basic ideas are pretty clear: It becomes unreasonable to separate cognition or motivation from the socially mediating context, or for that matter, individuals from their activities and the contexts in which they take place. As stated by Resnick: "We seem to be in the midst of multiple efforts to merge the social and cognitive, treating them as essential aspects of one another rather than as dimly sketched background or context."

Indeed, new composite units of analysis have emerged for study and design. Cognitive activity, goal, social interactions and learning materials are seen as a merged unit uniquely situated in a particular context. The base paradigm is the historical event where events and contexts are necessarily and inevitably interwoven. The unit of analysis is the interpsychological functional *system* comprised of interacting individuals, situation, activities, contents and meanings. As phrased by Sfard (in press), "the identity of an individual...is a function of her being (or becoming) a part of a greater entity. Thus, talk about stand-alone learner and decontextualized learning become as pointless as the attempts to define lungs and muscles without a reference to the living body within which they both exist and function". Despite these contrasts with social mediation of individual learning, the notion of learning systems as information processing systems that must meet critical conditions of information provision, feedback, and so on, still makes sense.

However, the description of a learning system changes. Knowledge, rather than being transmitted or internalized, becomes jointly constructed ("appropriated") in the sense that it is neither handed down ready-made, nor something one constructs on his or her own. Rather, knowledge, understandings, and meanings gradually emerge through interaction and become distributed among those interacting rather than individually constructed or possessed. And if knowledge is distributed among participants in a specific activity context, it is necessarily *situated* as well, that is, intimately welded to the context and the activity in which and by means of which it is constructed. Importantly. therefore, *participation* becomes the key concept here, as contrasted with *acquisition*, conceptual change, serving as both the process and the goal of learning (Sfard, in press).

Greeno asks whether we should "consider the major goals and outcomes of learning primarily as collections of sub-skills or as successful participation in socially organized activity and the development of students' identities as learners?" The answer to this question from socio-cultural point of view clearly favors the latter: The name of the game is participation and it stands in stark contrast to the Piagetian-based emphasis on the decontextualizable cognitive attainments of the individual. Whereas accounts of learning offered from Piagetian or information-processing perspectives emphasize *individuals' (solo) knowledge construction,* which can and should be facilitated by social scaffolding, the socio-culturally inspired one emphasizes the *socially-based participatory construction of knowledge.* And whereas the former sees learning and knowledge as pertaining mainly to individuals' transferable cognitive *attainments*, the latter sees learning more as a highly situated activity of *participation*.

These differences between the situative and the cognitive approaches can perhaps be best illustrated by the differences in the instructional design implications that follow from each. In the situative approach, social knowledge construction develops distributed knowledge, skills, and understandings around the target activity system. What is acquired is rather "holistic" and the hoped-for transfer is to other similar activity systems. In the cognitive approach, social knowledge construction serves individual knowledge construction. To illustrate, one might work with a team on joint problem solving activities to improve their collective problem solving *activity*.

The aim is an effect *with*—improved problem solving activity *while* working with one another, or as part of a similar group. Alternatively, one might work with a team on joint problem solving activities to improve individual problem solving *abilities*. The aim is an effect *of*—enhanced individual problem solving as a consequence of and apart from the team. Of course, the *with* initiative might have some *of* effects and the *of* initiative some *with* effects. Even so, one would organize the activities somewhat differently, depending on which purpose was paramount. Emphasis on the former, participatory design, raises serious questions about what in fact should be "taught" in school, what role do the subject matter disciplines ought to play, and what criteria for evaluation ought to be employed.

Social Mediation by Cultural Artifacts

The role of tools and symbol systems as both reflecting and affecting the human psyche has long been recognized. But it is mainly due to the Russian sociocultural tradition of Vygotsky, Luria, and Leont'ev, and their Western interpreters, that scholarly attention has focused on tools as social mediators of learning. A system formed by a person or persons using tools is not usually first and foremost a learning system. It is a system for doing something else, accomplishing some task like digging a ditch or having a conversation across an ocean. Nonetheless, any such system is secondarily a learning system.

The combination of person and tool creates a new cognitive entity with an enriched cultural legacy and extended capabilities. The person may learn to use the tool better, the tool and the objects to which it is applied thereby supplying information and feedback to that end, providing important conditions of learning, helping to teach the user about a better way of accomplishing the task through the tool. Moreover, some tools mediate learning about a wide array of other matters. They may do so simply as information sources, as in the case of books or films, functioning as vehicles for symbolic communications. But more than that, they may do so as implements of information-handling, as with the student's notebook and pencil (or, today, laptop computer), a flexible platform for organizing ideas expressed in the symbolic tools of text, formula, and diagram.

Tools characteristically play a double role, as means to act upon the world and as cognitive scaffolds that facilitate such action. Some tools not only enrich one's cognition but actually *transform* it. Memory is just not the same any more once certain language structures and writing have been acquired. The same applies to acquired ways of reasoning and to socially shared theories which constrain, color, and direct one's thinking and interpretation. For example, statistical tools are said to have become psychological models for the interpretation of human conduct, such as the ANOVA model serving to explain human interaction.

The cognitive transformations triggered by tools have two sides, paralleling the kinds of effects discussed above. One side is learning effects *with* the tool. This recognizes the changed functioning and expanded capability that takes place as the user uses and gets used to particular tools. Impact occurs through the redistribution of a task's cognitive load between persons and devices, including symbol-handling devices (e.g,. a spell checker) or across persons, mediated by devices and symbol systems (telephones, fax machines). As these examples suggest, such tools are all around us, but their possibility also invites the design of special-purpose tools for supporting various cognitive functions.

For instance, experiments have shown that a computerized Reading Partner that provides ongoing metacognitive-like guidance improves students' comprehension of texts while they read *with* the tool. Besides effects *with,* there are effects *of* the tool. This concerns the more lasting ripple effects of using the tool beyond actual occasions of use–the impact on one's cognitive arsenal of skills, perspectives, and ways of representing the world. Thus, for example, students who read texts with the Reading Partner mentioned above became better readers of novel, print-based texts and also better essay writers, apparently as a result of having learned to be more self-regulating, following the tool's model. Recall that the contrast between *of* and *with* parallels in some ways the contrast between a cognitive, acquisition-oriented view of learning and a situative, participatory view.

The acquisition stance emphasizes how tools can affect cognition in a relatively lasting and generalizable way even when people function without the tool. Thus, for example, Scribner and Cole studied the cognitive effects of literacy without schooling in the African tribe of the Vai, and Salomon studied the way elements of media's symbol systems can become cognitive tools. On the other hand, as Olson, Torrance and

Hildyard have argued with respect to literacy, "It is misleading to think of literacy in terms of consequences. What matters is what people do with literacy, not what literacy does to people".

Thus, the "lessons" taught by tools involve not just the immediacies of changed performances while the tools are available, but aspects of a culture's accumulated wisdom and intellectual history. One cannot wield a screwdriver or write down an equation in a historically blank and culturally neutral way. Rather, "the history of a culture–an inherently social history is carried into each individual act of cognition". As argued by Cole and Wertch, Higher mental functions are, by definition, culturally mediated. They involve not a direct action on the world, but an indirect action, one that takes a bit of material matter used previously and incorporates it as an aspect of action.

Insofar as that matter itself has been shaped by prior human practice (e.g., it is an artifact), current action incorporates the mental work that produced the particular form of that matter. A case in point is the introduction of computers into the schools. Whereas computers were initially used as electronic workbooks for drill and practice purposes, it became apparent that in fact they–very much like Trojan Horses–tend to carry with them a whole educational philosophy of knowledge construction, symbol manipulation, design, exploration and discovery. Although often assimilated to business-as-usual, in trend they serve as subversive instruments, their introduction promoting the restructuring of classroom learning environments, changes in teachers' way of functioning, redefinition of curricula, and new ways of assessment.

Widely adopted tools often send certain "messages" about priorities through their presence. For instance, the ubiquitous use of the typewriter and today keyboards and printers signals the priority of legibility and speed over the personal touch of calligraphic style. The Macintosh interface in contrast with the pre-Windows IBM interface has been said to express a more human and "analog" view of how one might relate to computers. The spread of pasta machines, spell checkers, hand calculators, and computer aided design programs sends the message that now, unlike the past, "everybody can do it without much learning." Learning was required for those skills, sometimes even within a privileged guild, but no more. Such circumstances create a tension between, and sometimes heated debates about, the risks and losses of "deskilling" a practice versus the gains of convenience and accessibility.

The Social Entity as a Learner

The core notion of the social entity as a learner says that collective entities can learn. Such entities might include families, high-performance teams, health organizations, business organizations, and more. Close attention to the social entity as a learner might strike some as odd in this overview of social learning with educational issues and agendas in mind. After all, the principal learners in schools are not groups but individuals, even if team-learning techniques are sometimes used. However, such a reaction mistakes both the scope of learning and that of education as developed here.

Not only does a great deal of individual learning and education occur outside of schools, but also, just as families, teams, corporations, and other organizations can be said to learn, so one can speak of educating them. Family therapy sessions or pre-birth child care sessions educate families, not just the individuals involved. Coaches and trainers educate teams of athletes. Corporate consultants concerned with organizational learning might reasonably be said to educate the corporations whose practices they improve. It is within the compass of this broad view of learning and education that the inquiry proceeds. The scholars concerned with the learning of social entities by and large constitute a camp of their own. A number of other shifts are notable.

The social entity typically, although not always, has to learn on its own, subject to its own autoregulation. Where there is a "teacher," usually the relationship is not one-to-many as in a classroom, but one-to-one, as with a coach and team or a consultant addressing the needs of an organization. Whereas a common problem with individual learning is its desituated character, most learning of social entities is well-situated. Sports teams, for example, do not study and practice for years before starting true play. Corporations do not apprentice to other corporations for years before trying it on their own. Finally, at a conceptual level, concepts such as learning, memory, models and modeling, reinforcement, trial-and-error, and so on need to be reinterpreted in the context of social entities.

With such differences in mind, three questions are particularly apt for a brief analysis of the learning of social entities: What is learned? How is it learned? And how can it be learned better? For all three questions, it is also important to examine whether the answers involve any distinctively social characteristics or amount to straightforward extrapolations from the case of the solo learner. As to what is learned, Huber suggests that learning consists in knowledge, in a broad sense, acquired by any unit of an organization and available for acting upon. Superior learning lies in knowledge more widely distributed across units, with common rather than disparate interpretations. Huber, following Morgan and Ramirez, writes of such knowledge as "holographic," in that each unit carries at least a rough picture of the whole.

Levitt and March advance organizational routines as the stuff of organizational learning, including policies and practices and their underlying belief systems. By definition, acquiring new routines means a change in overt behavior, a requirement Huber does not make. Weick points to emerging agreements about standard operating procedures, what's right or wrong in the organizational conduct, and the meanings to be assigned to whatever the organization does. Trying to define an orchestra, he writes: If we then ask where the orchestra is, the answer is that the orchestra is in the minds of the musicians. It exists in the minds of the musicians in the form of the variables they routinely look for and the connections they routinely infer among these variables.

Similarly, Argyris and Schon focus on stable changes in organizational behavior. Cole and Engestrom offer an analysis of activity systems that specifies several loci within which organizational learning can occur, for instance the prevailing rules, the division of labor, the mediating artifacts physical and conceptual, the aims of the enterprise, and of course individual learners. While some differences are apparent among such views, they are by and large compatible. It is also clear that all entail distributions of knowledge only partly analogous to those in the mind of an individual. As noted earlier, knowledge possessed by individuals or larger units about how to coordinate with other units in a particular organization is a distinctively social kind of knowledge.

A second question was how learning occurs. Here it is useful to turn back to the notion of a learning system. One function of a learning system is generation of new representations and behaviors. Within collectives, this can certainly occur by individuals or groups evaluating current practices and goals, reflecting, and devising new plans. It can also occur by "grafting," as an organization acquires new personnel or purchases datasets. Imitation of various kinds is a commonplace mechanism of learning in groups as in individuals. In groups, collective patterns of behavior may be imitated, for instance a new pattern of division of labor.

Productive variation may be stimulated by "organizational slack" that makes room for accidental variations and casual experiments. Feedback on old or new structures and practices commonly takes the form of assessment of performance against such distal goals as bottom-line profit and such proximal goals as people's happiness or divisional efficiencies. Comparison with the performance of other departments within an organization or other organizations can generate feedback, and almost inevitably does so in competitive situations. Levitt and March argue that an organization's history wields a much more powerful selective influence than speculative feedback based on exploration of conjectural scenarios. Another source of feedback derives from comparison of current structures and practices with conceptual models promulgated by the literature and consultants.

While other aspects of a learning system could be examined, these examples of generation of alternatives and of feedback suffice to point up some characteristics of organizational learning and make the case that it involves distinctive features. Grafting, for example, has no straightforward analog in the solo learner, nor do processes of the social distribution of knowledge across various units and individuals. If organizations can learn, this does not mean that they learn very well. A strong theme in the literature on organizational learning is the weakness of the learning system involved. The learning of the collective suffers from a startling range of limitations. Some of these are equally characteristic of solo and collective learning entities.

For instance, rare high-stakes events—marriage decisions in an individual or major shifts of direction in a business—are difficult learning targets because they do not occur often to disambiguate the lessons of experience, and because by the time they occur again circumstances may have changed substantially. Other problems of learning are exacerbated by the specifically organizational character of the learning. For example, different individuals and units within an organization may hold somewhat different criteria of success. Also, advocates of a policy are likely to interpret any difficulties with it as reflecting an insufficiently vigorous pursuit of the policy, while opponents interpret the same data as signifying a bad policy.

Feedback about the results of organizational actions may be distorted or suppressed as people rush to protect their turf or to maintain a positive climate. Argyris and Schon argue that self-sealing systems of beliefs arise in organizations because individuals behave toward one another in ways that pursue agendas while concealing them, as well as aiming unilaterally to protect both the self and others against the distress of negative feedback. Under such circumstances, "single-loop learning" can still occur, accomplishing refinements in conduct without change in the underlying belief systems, but not "double-loop learning," which involves making explicit and reconsidering tacit theories-in-use.

One broad systemic characteristic amplifies many of these problems: Organizational learning systems tend to take the "low road". Learning occurs without any strong intention or coordination or long view, willy-nilly as one or another problem gets identified and a plan adopted, one or another individual gains more influence, one or another practice gets reinforced as much by accidental circumstances as by any reliable consequences. This low-road character of organizational learning should not come as a surprise. After all, first and foremost organizations are designed as performance systems, not learning systems. In consequence, much of the contemporary literature on organizational learning focuses on how to make organizational learning function better.

Broadly speaking, the aim is to introduce more of a high-road learning process, where learning becomes a conscious and deliberate agenda of the organization alongside other more traditionally identified organizational functions. For example, Argyris and Schon focus on helping organizations to solve problems and take opportunities in ways that yield double-loop rather than single-loop learning. This involves helping individuals to air and test tacit assumptions publicly, avoid unilateral protection of self or others, and come together in collective problem-solving processes that deal with large-scale tacit issues, not just surface technical issues. Epistemology is a strong theme in such initiatives.

Both leaders and followers in organization tend to harbor broad impressionistic beliefs about what has happened or how to get things done that thrive on mechanisms of self-fulfilling prophecy but have at best a limited foundation in reality. Accordingly, interventions commonly foreground varieties of belief-testing that look to hard data or a finer grain of informal observation. Still another theme is that people attempting to guide organizations commonly do not understanding organizational dynamics and need better mental models. Thus, interventions often try to introduce new conceptions of organizational dynamics. Senge foregrounds systemic aspects of organizational dynamics, introducing a range of "system archetypes" that capture typical but neglected patterns of interaction, such as repairs that backfire in the long run or the tragedy of the commons.

Stacey emphasizes chaotic characteristics of organizational dynamics and urges anchoring thinking in the here and now, avoiding too uniform an organizational culture, and developing a constantly evolving agenda rather than a long-term stable vision. Argyris and Schon aspire to raise awareness of self-sealing interactions and shift an organization's models of learning toward double-loop practices that allow regular re-examination of underlying concepts and commitments as a part of problem-solving and opportunity-taking. In summary, organizations, like individuals, can learn. Many of the fundamental phenomena of learning are the same for organizations. Not only the general characteristics inherent to any learning system but particular phenomena like the troublesomeness of high-stakes rare events are common to both.

However, organizational learning also has distinctive characteristics with reference to what is learned, how it is learned, and the adjustments called for to enhance learning. These derive from the fact that any organization by definition is a collective, with individuals and larger units in different roles that involve different perspectives and values, passing information through their own filters, and with noisy and loss-prone information channels connecting them. Under such circumstances, it is hardly surprising that organizational learning would have a number of characteristic emergent features.

In contrast with the mixed character of individual learning discussed earlier, the learning of social entities tends strongly to be low road and situated. "Teaching" occurs much less frequently than in the individual case. Autoregulation is often virtually absent. Finally, the social entity can often be divided against itself, with different tacit beliefs and concealed agendas harbored by different subgroups or individuals. Of course, none of these phenomena are entirely absent from the individual case. For instance, one of the great lessons from Freud was that an individual mind can be divided against itself. Nonetheless, a number of contrasts in trend are conspicuous.

How Individual and Social Learning Relate

Whether social learning was a meaningful concept, sufficiently distinct from solo learning to warrant attention? The answer is an emphatic yes. As elaborated above, there is ample evidence to show that individuals' learning is facilitated by others, that meaning is often socially constructed, that tools serve as mediators, and that social systems as organic entities can engage in learning much as individuals do. With the reality of social learning acknowledged, it is tempting to say that the tables have been turned on the notion of individual learning. Far from social learning being a questionable appendix to solo learning, solo learning itself is a suspect phenomenon. Thus, as some would argue, in reality there is no solo learning to speak of.

Virtually anything one learns, according to the socio-cultural view, comes deeply embedded in a cultural context, involves culturally informed and laden tools, and figures as part of a range of highly social activity systems, however alone the learner may be at particular moments. All this may be true enough, but dismissing the notion of solo learning altogether would be to throw out the baby with the bath water by blurring important distinctions. Solo learning is most sensibly viewed not as learning utterly naked of social contexts, influences, and participations but rather learning where the factors discussed earlier have relatively lesser rather than greater presence. Matters of degree and level of analysis are involved. Thus, the anthropologist Sperber, discussing the relationships between culture and cognition, compared them to the relationships between epidemiology and cell biology, respectively. One of his main points was that epidemiology can neither be reduced to cell biology nor vice versa. Rather, each of these needs to be considered as an entity or process on its own right. In Sperber's spirit, we need to ask how solo and social learning relate to one another. The answer takes the form of three propositions.

1.*Individual and social learning mark the ends of a continuum of degrees of social mediation*: While almost all individual learning is social in some sense, the degree of active social mediation may vary considerably from situation to situation. The young basketball player practicing foul shots for hours solo enjoys relatively little social mediation during that period, although of course the activity occurs within the larger context of a highly social endeavor. The same basketball player practicing with team members and a coach functions in a highly socially mediated setting. The same point can be expressed from the perspective of situated or participatory learning. The basketball player's activities are always situated within the larger activity system of basketball, even during solo practice. But during solo practice, that larger system only impinges through the player's memories and the physical structure of the court, not through the immediate words and actions of the other players and coach.

Moreover, if at the individual end of the spectrum social factors still figure, it is likewise so that at the social end of the spectrum, in contexts of active social mediation, the learner remains, and should remain, an individual learner in significant ways. Perkins, while arguing generally for the distributed character of cognition, notes that regulative functions need to be managed by the learner to some extent, else the learner will not develop autoregulative cognitions. Learners who are all the time scaffolded in the management of their learning are less likely to develop such capacities. Bereiter (in press) argues that some learners take the opportunity to engage in more intentional and deeper learning, above and beyond the affordances of the situation and what it calls for.

As pointed out by Damon: Even when learning is fostered through processes of social communication, individual activity and reflection still play a critical role. Sometimes...individual activity may build on collective questions and insights. Other times, however, individual activity actually may need to resist the collective illusions created by a group... Any paradigm that assumes a one-way, deterministic relation between the collective and individual knowledge construction is overly simplistic.

Finally, it is worth noting that while the social end of the continuum may have been neglected in many earlier developmental, cognitive, and behaviorist studies, and important phenomena passed over, those studies proved fruitful in other ways. Many valuable insights about cognition and learning have emerged from laboratory investigations of individuals learning as individuals. For some purposes, such as the focused examination of particular learning processes of self-regulation, the detailed study of misconceptions in science, or the analysis of basic neuropsychological processes of learning, this may be a better approach than a more socially-oriented one.

2. *Individual learning and social learning mark the ends of a continuum from individuals learning for themselves through individuals also learning in behalf of collective entities to collective entities learning with knowledge distributed throughout the participants*: A further sense of social learning is the learning of social entities. This sense generates another relationship between individual and social learning. To return to the case of the basketball player, the individual player even during solo practice is not only learning in his or her own behalf but acquiring skills that strengthen the team. At moments of practicing together or planning together, the team learns

collective skills such as rapid coordination, many of which cannot be reduced to the skills of any one individual but have to do with the way they work together. By hiring a star player, the team may learn through "grafting,", where no individual involved acquires new knowledge and skill, but the team does. Note that the learning of a team or other collective entity, like the learning of an individual, can itself be more or less mediated by social factors outside the entity. In other words, the first continuum applies to both. In the case of the basketball team, a mediating "other" might be a coach, or another team against which the team is playing.

3. *Solo and social aspects of learning in both senses (1) and (2) can interact over time to strengthen one another, in what might be called a "reciprocal spiral relationship"*: A third answer to the question of how solo and social learning interrelate suggests that the two complement each other in a spiraling dynamic of reciprocal influences. Individual and social causes became influenced by their own consequences, sometimes even defined by them. This notion extends Sfard's (in press) suggestion that individual and social conceptions of learning be considered side-by-side to exploit the advantages of each and as a protection against theoretical excesses. To sharpen the idea, let us trace a couple of these spiral reciprocities.

A student experiencing difficulties with mathematics may benefit from joint problem solving sessions with a group of peers (active social mediation of learning), with student and peers reaching through negotiations several understandings concerning the way they want to proceed (the social entity learning to function), which leads to a certain division of labor concerning homework to be done by each member (but with mediation by cultural artifacts like textbooks); the student then returns the next day to the group of peers to compare notes with her partners and jointly solve new and more demanding problems (further active social mediation of a different sort, with the team members having progressed in their math understanding).

In other words, the student learns through different learning systems with varying degrees of social mediation and collectivity at different moments, with their characteristic ways of providing information, generating feedback, and so forth. For the student—indeed for all participants—these different learning systems are symbiotic. They benefit one another. Students may learn better and thus reach deeper understanding of the subject matter at hand, an achievement they will walk away with as their solo achievements, while the team may learn to learn better as a team through participation in such spirals.

A further example turns from the world of schools to the world of business. A manufacturing company's sales slump raises a general readiness for changes in the company's business practices. With such a readiness "in the air," a member of a financial planning team for the company collaborates in discussions mapping likely sales changes for the upcoming year (learning of a social entity), accepts the assignment of investigating the projected cost of key materials and begins by consulting a range of sources in books and on the internet (solo learning supported by cultural artifacts), discusses some puzzles with a professional consultant (social mediation of individual learning), and returns to the group to meld the insights gained into the collective understanding of the group. The suggested changes, now shared by the management, filter down through the organizational grape vine, triggering excitement and gradually becoming a new kind of standard operating procedure (learning of a social entity again).

As in the case of the student, the different learning systems with their different ways of meeting the critical conditions of learning are symbiotic. The spiral through them benefits the individual and the collective alike. A further large-scale characteristic of individual and social learning deserves note here. It is not just that learners learn better through the reciprocities between different learning systems. More than that, *the patterns of reciprocity themselves evolve*—the reciprocity itself "learns," so to speak. When individuals enter a social learning situation they not only take away from it knowledge about the topic at hand but knowledge about how to manage such situations. Likewise, the team, group, classroom, teacher or tutor change as well, affected by the other members of the interaction.

Or consider the example of a research team. While its members enter the team's planning meeting with their own knowledge, dispositions, preferences, attitudes and preconceived notions about the research question and methodology, the team's deliberations might well result in some agreed upon agenda, focused questions, division of labor and even a team's uplifting spirit. Now each member goes home and broods over the deliberations, reconsiders his or her position, and way of relating to the others. One of them might, for example, take notice of the fact that another member tends to dominate the discussions and hence decides to introduce some turn taking procedures. Each change taking place on one occasion colors the interactions on subsequent occasions, thus allowing for developmental continuity. Hence, the reciprocal relationship is all the more a spiral one.

Spiral reciprocity is less evident in the sociocultural approach to social learning where the learning system is a social system without a clear demarcation between individual learner and social agent. The argument made is that cognitions, themselves socially distributed, are inseparable from the socially based activity and from the tools used. As stated by Cobb, "there is no need to equip individuals with tools or to place them in social context for the simple reason that individuals do not act apart from tools and contexts".

Implications for the Design of Instruction

A great deal of learning occurs without instruction. The toddler struggling to climb onto a couch, the car shopper sizing up competing vehicles, the newly formed management team getting to know one another, are all in the midst of learning, but no teacher or instructional plan shapes their learning. Broadly speaking, instruction is designed learning, learning mediated not by fortunate circumstances but by intentional design. When a parent helps the toddler just barely enough, an article advises the car shopper, a book or workshop provides the members of the management team with good initial steps to follow, then we have instruction. When the design of instruction is guided by systematic and validated principles and theories, instruction becomes a design science.

The present analysis of solo and social learning argues that this design science needs to be conceived on a wider scale. If collectives like teams and corporations can learn, it makes sense to speak of instructing them–of establishing carefully designed conditions that favor their learning. Instruction is for collectives as well as solo learners. Moreover, the present analysis of social learning also informs the kinds of designs that would serve best. Earlier we emphasized that effective learning of any scope involves not one learning system but several functioning together in spirals of reciprocity.

Well-designed instruction therefore involves different learning systems at different moments in synergistic interaction. Admittedly, this formula is broad. Its concrete implications become plainer when one looks to the rather impoverished spirals characteristic of many school settings, for example, the routine see-saw system between the teacher interacting didactically with many students or the system of lone student in front of a textbook or worksheet. Innovative instruction of virtually any sort involves a dramatic enrichment of this see-saw model with more varied and intricate spirals of reciprocity.

Another implication of the discussion is that good learning, individual or collective, depends greatly on self-mediation or mediation by other agents – in other words, on high-road (intentional, conceptually-oriented) rather than low-road (practice and automaticity-oriented) learning. Typical school settings do not offer nearly the opportunities they might for the development of self-regulated, high-road learning. If anything, the problem is even more acute for the learning of large collective entities like corporations, which characteristically have hardly any "metacognitive" awareness of their own learning. The collective that worries about mediating its own learning and the learning of individuals within it is far more likely to learn better and foster individual learning. Relatedly, the development of autoregulation of learning in individuals and collectives needs to include attention to the social nature of learning. It is not enough to learn to direct one's own learning as a solo learner abetted by artifacts like textbooks.

Learning to learn in an expanded sense fundamentally involves learning to learn *from* others, learning to learn *with* others, learning to draw the most from cultural artifacts besides books, learning to mediate others' learning not only for their sake but for what that will teach oneself, and learning to contribute to the learning of a collective. For if the reciprocal spiral described earlier has any validity, then one's contribution to the learning of the collective is likely to benefit the individual as well. If all of this seems like a celebration of the potentials of social learning, it is–up to a point. The synergies that can occur between solo and social are powerful. However, the dark side of such interactions also has to be recognized. What is learned by an individual may upset or even subvert rather than abet collective ends, as with the corporate climber more interested in personal advancement than the overall success of the organization.

What is learned by the collective does not necessarily benefit the individual learners, as when a teacher forms a tacit contract with students: "I won't ask too much if you do the little I ask" or a limited conception about learning takes sufficient hold in particular populations: A team of students reaches an agreement to pretend to work but in fact gangs up on the teacher to do as little as possible. In such cases the collective has "learned," but what it has learned happens to be profoundly limiting, both for itself and for the participating individuals. The remedy for such pitfalls, writ broad, lies in the concept of instruction as designed learning. Cautionary examples like the foregoing occur along the "low road," where the goals and processes of learning receive no autoregulative attention from the agencies involved.

DIMENSIONS OF LEARNING AND LEARNER PREFERENCE

When preparing to teach childbirth education classes to adults, the instructor should not fail to address the needs of the learners and the process of learning. As illustrated below, there are four dimensions to the learning process and four basic preferences for learning. As the childbirth educator prepares her curriculum, she must examine her teaching strategies along with the content of the curriculum. With properly chosen strategies, the instructor can ensure the greatest retention level from the participants.

Dimensions of Learning

In order to explain the dimensions of learning, we will take a sample subject (deep breathing) and walk through the various dimensions.

— *Concrete Experience*: when the instructor demonstrates the deep breathing technique to the class and the class, in turn, returns the demonstration.

— *Observations and Reflections*: each learner then interprets the experience doing the deep breathing exercise.

— *Abstract Conceptualization*: the learner may conclude that with adequate practice of the deep breathing technique, the body will be more relaxed and more capable of working with the contractions of labor.

— *Active Experimentation in New Situations*: the learner adapts the deep breathing technique during actual labor and may use the deep breathing in other non-birth related situations.

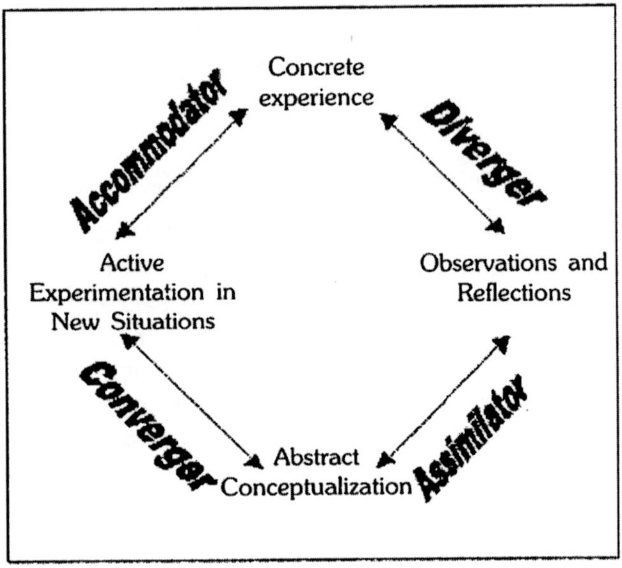

Understanding Learner Preferences

Once you understand the pathway of learning, then you must address the individual's preferences for learning. Each individual learner usually prefers teaching strategies that reflect one or two of the dimensions of learning. Below are the types of learner preferences and appropriate teaching strategies for each:

— *Accommodators*: Like to experience situations and prefer feedback, are planners and doers, they adapt well to situations, and may be known as risk takers.

— *Suggested teaching strategies*: role play, return demonstration, audiovisual materials.

— *Divergers*: Prefer less detail oriented curriculum, are very imaginative, do not focus on details but the end product, need time to process the information given, and explores feelings by watching and listening.

— *Suggested teaching strategies*: Reading, discussion, brainstorming, and small group work.

— *Assimilators*: Choose to draw their own inferences, create their own theories without regard to practicality, prefer information given in an organized manner, and learn from watching others.

— *Suggested teaching strategies*: reading, lecture, charts, graphs, models, and working alone.

— *Convergers*: Need structure and order, are task-oriented and not emotional, prefer a linear view of material, and prefer technical tasks.

— *Suggested teaching strategies*: practical reading, group reports, and discussion.

Since childbirth education classes are made up of several individuals each with their own learner styles and preferences, it becomes imperative that the childbirth educator addresses each class member's needs throughout the childbirth class series. This will improve the effectiveness of the instructor as well as the impact of the birthing class on each participant.

Utilizing individual resources

Learners will utilize their understanding of individual resources gained from the previous learning activity to determine the individual resources that people in scenarios presented by the instructor have to use in problem solving. Learners then apply their own list of individual resources to problem solve scenarios of their own creation.

— *Learning Objective*: Learners will identify and utilize personal resources in solving practical, everyday problems that might arise in the workplace and/or in their family and home. They will be better prepared to approach problems with strategies for problem solving.

— *Primary Skill*: Personal qualities

— *Secondary Skills*: Solve problems and make decisions

— *Learner Needs & Goals*: Some of the learners in this class want to improve basic skills so that they can qualify for a job that does not require a GED, but requires basic math and/or literacy skills. Most of the learners are working for GED certification so they can qualify for a job that requires a GED or so they can advance in their present job or obtain a better job. This activity will help all learners recognize their resources, their potential, and their abilities, and will encourage them in self-management and problem solving.

— *Learning Activity Description*: This activity will be part II of a larger project, and should be undertaken after the activity entitled "Understanding and identifying individual resources" has been successfully completed by all learners. Learners will use their Individual Resource List that they completed in the initial activity.

1. *Reviewing*: Learners will begin this activity by reviewing a clean copy of the Individual Resource List that they used to list their own individual resources in the previous lesson. The resource checklist will be discussed in detail. When this is completed, each learner will be given a copy of a Scenario (attachment). The scenario will be read aloud and discussed by the group. The learners will then utilize the resource checklist as follows: Put a "Y" next to the resources that are available to the individual(s) in the scenario; put an "N" next to any resource that is not available; put a question mark where the resource is uncertain. (Note: there are numerous scenarios in the book A Framework for Understanding and Working with Students and Adults from Poverty by Ruby K. Payne. These could be used, or the facilitator can create his/her own scenarios. Be sure to include scenarios that illustrate different types and amounts of resources available to individuals.)

2. *Analyzing*: Upon completion of this whole group activity, the class will be divided into small groups and each group will be given two different scenarios to analyze. All groups will be given the same two scenarios and each group will complete

one Resource Checklist for each scenario. The groups will read each scenario as a group, discuss the resources available to the individuals in the scenario, and then cooperatively come to a decision regarding the solution to the problem(s) presented in the scenario. After all groups have completed their Resource Checklists, the class as a whole will discuss the problem or situation in the scenario.

3. *Personal Application*: Learners will then review their Individual Resource Lists which list each resource available to him/her for use in everyday problem solving. If they think of additional resources they can add under any of the categories, they should go ahead and add them. Each learner will then write a scenario demonstrating a problem or situation for consideration. Learners will be encouraged to base the scenarios on personal experience; however, the scenario could be based on the experience of a friend or family member, or could be purely fictional. After the scenario is completed, the learner will identify which resources from their personal resource checklist could be utilized to solve the problem in the scenaric.

Learners may need extra time to complete the scenario writing and the resource checklists. The activity could be extended to the next class meeting, giving the learners the opportunity to read their scenarios to the class, followed by group discussion. No learner should be compelled to share their scenario and the solution however, as these may be pretty personal. Upon completion of this activity, learners will have a better understanding of the importance of individual resources in problem solving, and will have developed experience in recognizing and utilizing resources to solve problems.

5

Understanding the Learner in the Light of Differences

LEARNER-CENTERED PSYCHOLOGICAL PRINCIPLES

Throughout its history, psychology has provided vital information for the design of schooling based on theory and research on human learning, development, and motivation. Research in psychology relevant to education has been particularly informative during the past decade. Advances in our understanding of thinking, memory, and cognitive and motivational processes can contribute directly to improvements in teaching, learning, and the whole enterprise of schooling. At the same time, educators concerned with the growing problems of school dropout, low levels of academic achievement, and other indicators of school failure are arguing for more learner-centered models of schooling. Such models attend to the diversity among students, and use this diversity to enrich learning and to produce results within the context of current school reform.

The following principles, which are consistent with more than a century of research on teaching and learning, are widely shared and implicitly recognized in many excellent programs found in today's schools. They also integrate research and practice in various areas of psychology, including developmental, educational, experimental, social, clinical, organizational, community, and school psychology. In addition, these principles reflect conventional and scientific wisdom. They comprise not only systematically researched and evolving learner-centered principles that can lead to effective schooling but also principles that can lead to positive mental health and productivity of our nation`s children, their teachers, and the systems that serve them.

Learner-centered psychological principles provide a framework for developing and incorporating the components of new designs for schooling. These principles emphasize the active and reflective nature of learning and learners. From this perspective, educational practice will be most likely to improve when the educational system is redesigned with the primary focus on the learner. Psychologists, in collaboration with educators, can help decide how best to apply sound psychological principles in the redesign of America's schools. A new and exciting vision of schooling, and psychology's role in this vision, can then emerge. The immediate goal in offering these learner-centered psychological principles is to provide a framework that can contribute to current educational reform and school redesign efforts.

Through dialogue with concerned groups of educators, researchers, and policy makers, these learner-centered principles can evolve further to contribute not only to a new design for America's schools, but also to a society committed to lifelong learning, healthy human development, and productivity. In developing these principles, psychology -- together with other disciplines -- can contribute to the betterment of America's schools and the enhancement of the nation's vital human resources.

LEARNER-CENTERED PSYCHOLOGICAL PRINCIPLES

The 14 Learner-centered psychological principles are:

— *Cognitive and Metacognitive Factors*

1. Nature of the learning process
2. Goals of the learning process
3. Construction of knowledge
4. Strategic thinking
5. Thinking about thinking
6. Context of learning

— *Motivational and Affective Factors*

7. Motivational and emotional influences on learning
8. Intrinsic motivation to learn
9. Effects of motivation on effort

— *Developmental and Social*

10. Developmental influences on learning
11. Social influences on learning

— *Individual Differences*

12. Individual difference in learning
13. Learning and diversity
14. Standards and assessment

The above 14 psychological principles pertain to the learner and the learning process. They focus on psychological factors that are primarily internal to and under the control of the learner rather than conditioned habits or physiological factors. However, the principles also attempt to acknowledge external environment or contextual factors that interact with these internal factors. The principles are intended to deal holistically with learners in the context of real-world learning situations. Thus, they are best understood as an organized set of principles; no principle should be viewed in isolation. The 14 principles are divided into those referring to cognitive and metacognitive, motivational and affective, developmental and social, and individual difference factors influencing learners and learning. Finally, the principles are intended to apply to all learners -- from children, to teachers, to administrators, to parents, and to community members involved in the educational system.

Cognitive and Metacognitive Factors

1. *Nature of the learning process*: The learning of complex subject matter is most effective when it is an intentional process of constructing meaning from information and experience. There are different types of learning processes, for example, habit formation in motor learning; and learning that involves the generation of knowledge, or cognitive skills and learning strategies. Learning in schools emphasizes the use of intentional processes that students can use to construct meaning from information, experiences, and their own thoughts and beliefs. Successful learners are active, goal-directed, self-regulating, and assume personal responsibility for contributing to their own learning. The principles set forth in this document focus on this type of learning.

2. *Goals of the learning process*: The successful learner, over time and with support and instructional guidance, can create meaningful, coherent representations of knowledge. The strategic nature of learning requires students to be goal directed. To construct useful representations of knowledge and to acquire the thinking and learning strategies necessary for continued learning success across the life span, students must generate and pursue personally relevant goals. Initially, students' short-term goals and learning may be sketchy in an area, but over time their understanding can be refined by filling gaps, resolving inconsistencies, and deepening their understanding of the subject matter so that they can reach longer-term goals. Educators can assist learners in creating meaningful learning goals that are consistent with both personal and educational aspirations and interests.

3. *Construction of knowledge*: The successful learner can link new information with existing knowledge in meaningful

ways. Knowledge widens and deepens as students continue to build links between new information and experiences and their existing knowledge base. The nature of these links can take a variety of forms, such as adding to, modifying, or reorganizing existing knowledge or skills. How these links are made or develop may vary in different subject areas, and among students with varying talents, interests, and abilities. However, unless new knowledge becomes integrated with the learner's prior knowledge and understanding, this new knowledge remains isolated, cannot be used most effectively in new tasks, and does not transfer readily to new situations. Educators can assist learners in acquiring and integrating knowledge by a number of strategies that have been shown to be effective with learners of varying abilities, such as concept mapping and thematic organization or categorizing.

4. *Strategic thinking*: The successful learner can create and use a repertoire of thinking and reasoning strategies to achieve complex learning goals. Successful learners use strategic thinking in their approach to learning, reasoning, problem solving, and concept learning. They understand and can use a variety of strategies to help them reach learning and performance goals, and to apply their knowledge in novel situations. They also continue to expand their repertoire of strategies by reflecting on the methods they use to see which work well for them, by receiving guided instruction and feedback, and by observing or interacting with appropriate models. Learning outcomes can be enhanced if educators assist learners in developing, applying, and assessing their strategic learning skills.

5. *Thinking about thinking*: Higher order strategies for selecting and monitoring mental operations facilitate creative and critical thinking. Successful learners can reflect on how they think and learn, set reasonable learning or performance goals, select potentially appropriate learning strategies or methods, and monitor their progress toward these goals. In addition, successful learners know what to do if a problem occurs or if they are not making sufficient or timely progress toward a goal. They

can generate alternative methods to reach their goal (or reassess the appropriateness and utility of the goal). Instructional methods that focus on helping learners develop these higher order (metacognitive) strategies can enhance student learning and personal responsibility for learning.

6. *Context of learning*: Learning is influenced by environmental factors, including culture, technology, and instructional practices. Learning does not occur in a vacuum. Teachers play a major interactive role with both the learner and the learning environment. Cultural or group influences on students can impact many educationally relevant variables, such as motivation, orientation toward learning, and ways of thinking. Technologies and instructional practices must be appropriate for learners' level of prior knowledge, cognitive abilities, and their learning and thinking strategies. The classroom environment, particularly the degree to which it is nurturing or not, can also have significant impacts on student learning.

Motivational and Affective Factors

7. *Motivational and emotional influences on learning*: What and how much is learned is influenced by the learner's motivation. Motivation to learn, in turn, is influenced by the individual's emotional states, beliefs, interests and goals, and habits of thinking. The rich internal world of thoughts, beliefs, goals, and expectations for success or failure can enhance or interfere with the learner's quality of thinking and information processing. Students' beliefs about themselves as learners and the nature of learning have a marked influence on motivation. Motivational and emotional factors also influence both the quality of thinking and information processing as well as an individual's motivation to learn. Positive emotions, such as curiosity, generally enhance motivation and facilitate learning and performance. Mild anxiety can also enhance learning and performance by focusing the learner's attention on a particular task. However, intense negative emotions (e.g., anxiety, panic, rage, insecurity) and

related thoughts (e.g., worrying about competence, ruminating about failure, fearing punishment, ridicule, or stigmatizing labels) generally detract from motivation, interfere with learning, and contribute to low performance.

8. *Intrinsic motivation to learn*: The learner's creativity, higher order thinking, and natural curiosity all contribute to motivation to learn. Intrinsic motivation is stimulated by tasks of optimal novelty and difficulty, relevant to personal interests, and providing for personal choice and control. Curiosity, flexible and insightful thinking, and creativity are major indicators of the learners' intrinsic motivation to learn, which is in large part a function of meeting basic needs to be competent and to exercise personal control. Intrinsic motivation is facilitated on tasks that learners perceive as interesting and personally relevant and meaningful, appropriate in complexity and difficulty to the learners' abilities, and on which they believe they can succeed. Intrinsic motivation is also facilitated on tasks that are comparable to real-world situations and meet needs for choice and control. Educators can encourage and support learners' natural curiosity and motivation to learn by attending to individual differences in learners' perceptions of optimal novelty and difficulty, relevance, and personal choice and control.

9. *Effects of motivation on effort*: Acquisition of complex knowledge and skills requires extended learner effort and guided practice. Without learners' motivation to learn, the willingness to exert this effort is unlikely without coercion. Effort is another major indicator of motivation to learn. The acquisition of complex knowledge and skills demands the investment of considerable learner energy and strategic effort, along with persistence over time. Educators need to be concerned with facilitating motivation by strategies that enhance learner effort and commitment to learning and to achieving high standards of comprehension and understanding. Effective strategies include purposeful learning activities, guided by practices that enhance positive emotions and intrinsic motivation to learn, and methods that increase learners' perceptions that a task is interesting and personally relevant.

Developmental and Social

10. *Developmental influences on learning*: As individuals develop, there are different opportunities and constraints for learning. Learning is most effective when differential development within and across physical, intellectual, emotional, and social domains is taken into account. Individuals learn best when material is appropriate to their developmental level and is presented in an enjoyable and interesting way. Because individual development varies across intellectual, social, emotional, and physical domains, achievement in different instructional domains may also vary. Overemphasis on one type of developmental readiness--such as reading readiness, for example--may preclude learners from demonstrating that they are more capable in other areas of performance.

The cognitive, emotional, and social development of individual learners and how they interpret life experiences are affected by prior schooling, home, culture, and community factors. Early and continuing parental involvement in schooling, and the quality of language interactions and two-way communications between adults and children can influence these developmental areas. Awareness and understanding of developmental differences among children with and without emotional, physical, or intellectual disabilities, can facilitate the creation of optimal learning contexts.

11. *Social influences on learning*: Learning is influenced by social interactions, interpersonal relations, and communication with others.Learning can be enhanced when the learner has an opportunity to interact and to collaborate with others on instructional tasks. Learning settings that allow for social interactions, and that respect diversity, encourage flexible thinking and social competence. In interactive and collaborative instructional contexts, individuals have an opportunity for perspective taking and reflective thinking that may lead to higher levels of cognitive, social, and moral development, as well as self-esteem. Quality personal

relationships that provide stability, trust, and caring can increase learners' sense of belonging, self-respect and self-acceptance, and provide a positive climate for learning.

Family influences, positive interpersonal support and instruction in self-motivation strategies can offset factors that interfere with optimal learning such as negative beliefs about competence in a particular subject, high levels of test anxiety, negative sex role expectations, and undue pressure to perform well. Positive learning climates can also help to establish the context for healthier levels of thinking, feeling, and behaving. Such contexts help learners feel safe to share ideas, actively participate in the learning process, and create a learning community.

Individual Differences

12. *Individual differences in learning*: Learners have different strategies, approaches, and capabilities for learning that are a function of prior experience and heredity. Individuals are born with and develop their own capabilities and talents. In addition, through learning and social acculturation, they have acquired their own preferences for how they like to learn and the pace at which they learn. However, these preferences are not always useful in helping learners reach their learning goals. Educators need to help students examine their learning preferences and expand or modify them, if necessary. The interaction between learner differences and curricular and environmental conditions is another key factor affecting learning outcomes. Educators need to be sensitive to individual differences, in general. They also need to attend to learner perceptions of the degree to which these differences are accepted and adapted to by varying instructional methods and materials.

13. *Learning and diversity*: Learning is most effective when differences in learners' linguistic, cultural, and social backgrounds are taken into account. The same basic principles of learning, motivation, and effective instruction apply to all learners.

However, language, ethnicity, race, beliefs, and socioeconomic status all can influence learning. Careful attention to these factors in the instructional setting enhances the possibilities for designing and implementing appropriate learning environments. When learners perceive that their individual differences in abilities, backgrounds, cultures, and experiences are valued, respected, and accommodated in learning tasks and contexts, levels of motivation and achievement are enhanced.

14. *Standards and assessment*: Setting appropriately high and challenging standards and assessing the learner as well as learning progress -- including diagnostic, process, and outcome assessment -- are integral parts of the learning process. Assessment provides important information to both the learner and teacher at all stages of the learning process. Effective learning takes place when learners feel challenged to work towards appropriately high goals; therefore, appraisal of the learner's cognitive strengths and weaknesses, as well as current knowledge and skills, is important for the selection of instructional materials of an optimal degree of difficulty.

Ongoing assessment of the learner's understanding of the curricular material can provide valuable feedback to both learners and teachers about progress toward the learning goals. Standardized assessment of learner progress and outcomes assessment provides one type of information about achievement levels both within and across individuals that can inform various types of programmatic decisions. Performance assessments can provide other sources of information about the attainment of learning outcomes. Self-assessments of learning progress can also improve students self appraisal skills and enhance motivation and self-directed learning.

USERS, USERS AS LEARNERS

Current theories of learning, broadly labeled constructivism, tell us that learning is not about getting content into a student's head, or imprinting a procedure in a student's cognitive structure by extensive practice. Rather, learning is a process of constructing understanding by grappling with problems, seeking solutions, and organizing knowledge for oneself. The process of learning takes on major significance, because the desired outcome is no longer limited to knowing a set of facts or procedures, but rather encompasses understanding and being able to use a range of content.

Many educators and policy makers argue that computer technology can and should be a major player in this reformed teaching and learning because computers offer unique possibilities for providing individualized interactions with multiple representations of content, and more. Students can, at least theoretically, engage with computers in processes which offer the possibility of understanding content and constructing knowledge in ways previously unimaginable. And yet, much software available for schools fails to live up to the expectations and hopes of educators, reformers, and technologists. From Web browsers to Math Blaster, software misses the mark of engaging students in throughtful interaction with appropriate content.

Why is this so? There are, of course, many reasons for these shortcomings, from commercial pressures to rapidly changing technology to school budgets. But, from the point of view of HCI methods, current design methods may be inadequte for successful design of software for learners. By learners, we mean students who are using software to learn about something other than the software itself. The fundamental problem is easy to state: User-centered design focuses on goals of the user, goals which have to do with getting a task done, or creating something. This focus misses the most important aspect of software use for learners, the process of using the software. What a student does during the time she uses a computer becomes the site for and source of constructivist learning. The focus of the design must be to enable a process through which the learner can confront and grapple with appropriate ideas, content, and procedures. The process is the thing.

As conceived by Norman, human-computer interaction can be modeled as a process with seven stages which include both physical and mental actions. The user's goal is of primary importance, and the problem for designers is to bridge the gaps which exist between the user's ability to express his goals and intentions through actions and the computers interpretation of those actions - the "gulf of execution"; and the user's understanding of the system's response – the "gulf of evaluation." User-centered design methods regularly take Norman's theory as given and suggest strategies for proceeding with actual design – task analysis, iterative design, user involvement and feedback, etc. These strategies aim to help designers understand user goals and provide user input to decisions about usability.

In these methods, the gulfs of execution and evaluation mark the big leverage points for designers. All of this is placed in the framework of getting to the end result: completing a task or creating a product. To take learners into account, more is needed. First, the goals of learners themselves in most cases don't resemble the goals of users. For example, software for search and retrieval of information is written with the goal of optimizing returns, getting the best possible results for a user whose goal is to find what he's looking for. A student may not have as a goal to find anything in particular, or he may not know enough to know what to look for. He may have much to learn before he can begin to act like a novice user. His reasons for searching may be entirely at odds with user goals envisioned by system designers: he may search because he has to (it's an assignment), to stay busy-looking during a class, or to get a good grade.

At the same time, the teacher may have students search for information to help them learn about a particular topic, or to teach them the research process, to name two possibilities. How can these three often divergent sets of goals come together – the goals the software designers impute to users, the actual goals of students, and the goals the teacher has for her students?

Second, a perennial problem in schools is motivation: students may not want to do what the teacher wants them to do. Unlike the prototypical user, who, it is assumed, intends to do a task and do it successfully, a student may actually intend not to do any more than she must do to get what she wants from the class (e.g, a passing grade for some, an A for others.) This isn't cynicism. Rather, it is a real and justifiable problem of teaching: how does a teacher go about keeping students motivated to learn, not just to go through the motions of school?

User-centered design simply does not deal with the affirmative aspects of motivation, with how to capture and retain the user's interest. (It does make the assumption that poor usability can cause users motivation to flag, what one might call the negative aspects of motivation, or motivation not to use the software.) Third, the point of software for learners is for them to learn, and thus change their state of knowledge and understanding. Yet user-centered design assumes a static target of design, a fixed product or task which does not change over time.

A goal of much design effort is to make it possible for a novice user to effectively use the exact same product an expert would use. This is not how software for learning should operate: as the student learns, the software should be able to provide ever growing challenges. (This is not to imply here that the software needs to intelligently or automatically provide these challenges, but rather that design take into account a teaching and learning process through which the software can be used at varying stages of student progress.)

The learner must be able to use the software in ever more complex ways as his knowledge and expertise in the domain increase. Using the example of searching again, a learner new to a given field might benefit from software-provided support for generating keywords, or summaries of documents retrieved or a place to keep notes about what he finds, while a student with knowledge in the domain might shun all those supports and make effective use of his background knowledge, behaving more like the prototypical user. Finally, design of software for use in schools needs to consider the contexts for and practices of teaching. In K-12 classrooms, and especially in classrooms which are taking calls for reform seriously, learning is a social activity, intimately connected with teaching.

The image of computer-as-tutor, in a one-on-one dialog with a student doesn't work in many different ways including its failure to fit with current conceptions of learning as well as the realities of life in classrooms. Contexts and practices of teaching include grouping students to share limited computer resources; ways in which the teacher can interact with students working at a computer to help them learn and to assess their learning; ways that the whole class can benefit from the separate actions of individuals or smaller groups of students; and ways that the teacher can manage the disparate activites of small groups of students (or individual students). User-centered design is undertaken with consideration for only the user-computer dyad, a simplicity not usually realistic or, some would argue, desirable, in a school setting.

How do these issues relate to Norman' model of User-centered design? First, user goals seems to be the wrong place to start: learners have some gaps to bridge before they can even begin to act like users. These gulfs can really be though of as two major issues: knowledge and intentions. The learner lacks knowledge which designers must assume the prototypical user has. This may include background knowledge of the domain of study, knowledge of strategies for learning in the domain, and knowledge about how to evaluate their own progress. This "Gulf of Knowledge" is a problem which design for learners – learner-centered design or LCD – needs to address. Learners also lack the assumed coherent intentions – e.g., accomplishing the goals established for use of the software.

For learners, motivation to work toward an established goal can not be assumed. This constitutes a "Gulf of Intention" which also should be addressed through LCD methods. Briefly, the methods of learner-centered design build on and expand user-centered design. Task analysis is expanded to include three types of analysis: learning analysis which investigates what should be learned through use of the software and what is known about learning those things in the given domain; task analysis of the task(s) as done by a prototypical user; and teaching analysis which investigates contexts and practices of teaching which surround learning with this software. The big questions are:

— What do we want students to learn through the use of this software?

— How would an expert engage in the activities or use the knowledge we want students to learn?

— How can a teacher teach students to learn these things through use of the software?

These analyses need to be intertwined and recursive, with decisions about software feeding into the teacher analysis, and that feeding back to design decisions. User objects are exanded to include objects for learning and teaching. Scaffolding, for example, may be included as a learning object and a teaching object. Feedback is obtained in real classroom settings, perhaps in the mode of "design experiments" in which teachers, students, and designers are participants.

Principles and methods of LCD have been used extensively in the hi-ce design group, and many of these principles are evident in projects undertaken at other educational research institutions. Commercial success has been elusive for even the very best of the carefully designed, research-based educational software perhaps because of the very ambitious domains in which they have worked. However, with the remarkable spread of Internet access in schools, possibilities for dissemination and use of software in schools is changing drastically, and it is time for the broader HCI community to recognize the unique problems of designing for K-12 learners.

DIFFERENCE BETWEEN TRAINING, LEARNING AND PERFORMANCE ENHANCEMENT

A simple starting point of discussion is the difference in their orientation. While training is trainer-centered and learning is learner-centered, performance is outcome-centered or focused. 'Trainer-centered' tends to direct the trainer's attention and efforts in solving the trainer's problems and achieving training effectiveness. A training cycle such as 'tell — show — do' becomes a normal procedure or sequence in a typical training session. In terms of training evaluation, the 'smile sheet' is used to assess the trainee's thoughts on the usefulness of the training and effectiveness of the trainer. Issues like presentation skill, time management, keeping the class in control, etc. are emphasised.

Compared to 'learner-centered', the trainer is expected to take a stronger leadership role and then more responsibility in ensuring training results. 'Learner-centered' tends to begin with 'start where the learner is' including learning objectives, motivation, knowledge level, preference of learning modes, etc. The trainer is positioned as a resource person or catalyst among all other resources and means of learning such as the library, internet, self-paced learning, peer support group, mentor system, on-the-job training, etc. An adult learning cycle such as 'gaining experience — reviewing experience — conceptualisation — experimentation' is followed in designing and delivering a learning event. Much effort is spent on pre-course preparation in understanding the learner profiles and the underlying problems or challenges they face. In case more time is required to share and solve common problems, the 'learner-centered' trainer or facilitator is more flexible and comfortable to do so.

As a result the facilitator may be regarded as too loose, poor time manager, insufficient input, etc. 'Performance-focused' will go beyond the 'knowledge-skill-attitude' factors affecting individual performance. While training and learning efforts can help with the so-called 'commitment' and 'competence' factors, performance enhancement efforts will look at the 'conditions' factors as well. The 'commitment' factor addresses the question 'Does he/she want to perform?' The 'competence' factor answers 'Can he/she perform?' The 'condition' factor looks at 'Is it possible for him/her to perform?' Can you think of some examples affecting your own performance or that of the whole organisation?

A performance enhancement practitioner will look at performance issues or factors at individual, team and organisational level. While educational efforts may be partial solutions, other non-educational efforts such as systems review, process re-engineering, performance management, culture change, incentives programs, technological advancement, etc. may be adopted. The 7S model of organisational performance advocates a holistic or systems view of organisational performance and the interplay of the 7S factors: strategy, systems, structure, shared value, skills, staffing and style in affecting individual and organisational performance. Any performance enhancement efforts will take into account the current and desirable states of the 7S factors, the gaps identified, change priorities, resources and options available.

WHAT BRAIN RESEARCH TELLS US ABOUT LEARNER DIFFERENCES

Learning is distributed across three interconnected networks: the recognitionnetworks are specialized to receive and analyze information (the "what" of learning);the strategic networks are specialized to plan and execute actions(the "how" of learning); and the affective networks are specialized to evaluate and set priorities (the "why" of learning). Learners cannot be reduced to simple categories such as "disabled" or "bright." They differ within and across all three brain networks, showing shades of strength and weakness that make each of them unique.

The brain, the most powerful learning tool that a student brings to the classroom, is highly complex and something of a mystery. In recent years, scientists have made unprecedented progress toward unlocking the secrets of how our brains learn, driven in part by remarkable new technologies and techniques for imaging the brain'sactivity. Even when scientists explore learning directly, the educational significance of scientific research is rarely self-evident.

UNDERSTANDING THE LEARNING BRAIN

Most pictures of the brain show only the tissue visible on the surface—the deeply fissured and folded gray matter called the *cortex*. The complex organization and unique structure of this tissue gives it a central role in learning. Cortical tissue features astonishing connectivity: The approximately 1 trillion neurons in the cortex are linked by approximately 10 trillion connections, creating an incredibly dense network. Similar to a telephone or computer network, these multifaceted connections help individual parts of the brain communicate flexibly and along multiple pathways, regardless of whether they are close to each other or on opposite sides of the brain.

Within this large network, many smaller networks are specialized for performing particular kinds of processing and managing particular learning tasks. Three primary networks, structurally and functionally distinguishable but closely connected and functioning together, are equally essential to learning. These networks by terms that reflect their functions: the *recognition*, *strategic*, and *affective* networks. The activities of these networks parallel the three prerequisites for learning described by the Russian psychologist Lev Vygotsky: recognition of the information to be learned; application of strategies to process that information; and engagement with the learning task. In brief:

— *Recognition networks* are specialized to sense and assign meaning to patterns we see; they enable us to identify and understand information, ideas, and concepts.

— *Strategic networks* are specialized to generate and oversee mental and motor patterns. They enable us to plan, execute, and monitor actions and skills.

— *Affective networks* are specialized to evaluate patterns and assign them emotional significance; they enable us to engage with tasks and learning and with the world around us.

These three neural networks work together to coordinate even simple acts like signing a birthday card for a friend. Through recognition networks, we understand the concept of a birthday and identify the card, the pen, our hands as we write, and our signature. Through strategic networks, we set our goal of signing the card, form a plan for picking up the pen and moving it to produce our signature, monitor our progress, and make small course corrections, such as reducing the size of the letters if we begin to run out of space. Affective networks connect us to our feelings for our friend, motivate us to sign the card, and keep us on task.

These three networks share two common characteristics that have particular significance for learning:

1. Processing is *distributed* laterally across many brain regions operating in parallel (enabling, for example, simultaneous processing of color and shape); and
2. Processing is *hierarchical*,enabling simultaneous processing of sensory information entering low in the hierarchy("bottom-up") and contextual influences entering high in the hierarchy("top-down").

Although all brains share these general characteristics, individual brains differ substantially—a point that bears critical implications for teaching. Understanding the specialized functions of the recognition, strategic, and affective networks can help us appreciate the unique strengths and weaknesses of individual students. Let's take a closer look at each of the networks.

RECOGNITION NETWORKS

Recognition Processes

The general task of recognition is distributed across different areas, each specialized to handle a different component of recognition. (From this point on, we will refer to these specialized areas of the brain as "modules.") Distributed processing is not limited to differences between distinct sensory modalities, such as vision and hearing. The subprocesses within each sense modality are also distributed. For example, visual recognition is distributed across at least 30 different modules, so that elements like vertical lines, diagonal lines, color, and motion are all processed in physically discrete areas of the brain. An analogy may clarify how distributed modular specialization works. Think of the brain as a kitchen full of food processors.

Imagine that all the processors are the same basic make and model, but each comes with a specialized attachment for blending dough, shredding cabbage, or performing another specialized task. Although each processor performs the same general function, their *output* is as different as piecrust is from coleslaw. By keeping a kitchen full of processors, a chef needn't switch the blade for each new task or worry about getting cabbage in the piecrust! In the brain, distributed processing provides a similar advantage. All the modules have the same basic structure, but the tissue in each region is fine-tuned to process one type of input extremely efficiently. This works more effectively than would "all-purpose" brain tissue that would have to adapt to each new task.

Recognition is quick and efficient because all the modules are working in parallel. Through parallel processing—the simultaneous performance of multiple tasks by interconnected modules—our brains process and pool information that is distributed throughout our recognition networks, all in less than half a second. The brain's modules are interconnected through multiple pathways, enabling visual, auditory, olfactory, and tactile recognition to influence one another. This accounts for the interesting observation that an auditory or tactile stimulus can bias our interpretation of a visual pattern. The distributed nature of recognition has profound implications for individual differences.

If recognition were the product of one homogeneous area of brain tissue, recognition abilities would vary from person to person in only a limited number of ways. Differences in recognition would have global effects. For example, if an entire modality, like vision, were the product of one sub network, any difference would affect vision as a whole. But because recognition is actually a coordinated act of many different modules, each very small component of recognition has the potential to exhibit person-to-person differences. The differences between us may affect one module, and therefore one aspect of recognition, or many modules, and therefore many aspects of recognition.

Bottom-Up and Top-Down Processing

We have learned that individual aspects of patterns, such as color, shape, orientation, and motion, are processed in parallel by separate pathways within the recognition networks. Each of these pathways is organized into a hierarchical continuum, containing some brain regions that are highly complex, some that are comparatively simple, and others that are somewhere in between. Let's continue to use vision as an example. As visual sensory information we take in though our eyes departs from our retinas, it travels up through an increasingly complex hierarchical network, eventually reaching the visual cortex. This is called "bottom-up" processing, and it is part of the way we extract visual details from an image such as "The Unexpected Visitor." This type of processing is responsible for identifications based on particular sensory features, meaning the quality of sensory input is very important.

Poor lighting, low-quality photocopies, or mumbled speech can all impede bottom-up processing and make everyday recognition tasks difficult. Just as important as the information flowing up the hierarchy of recognition structures is the information that travels down the hierarchy. To facilitate the recognition of details, our brains make use of higher-order information, such as background knowledge, context, and the overall pattern. When examining "The Unexpected Visitor," you applied knowledge about the kind of room the scene is set in (gleaned from bottom-up recognition of the room's more visible objects) to help you identify other objects that are difficult to recognize based on visual detail alone. Bottom-up and top-down recognition processing both play critical roles in learning.

Consider learning to read: The common assumption used to be that reading was mainly a bottom-up activity, wherein letters are recognized by their features, synthesized into words and sounds, and then analyzed for meaning. But research has shown that it is easier and faster to recognize letters in the context of words than it is to recognize them in isolation. This phenomenon, termed the *word superiority effect*, occurs because familiarity with the larger pattern (the word) constrains the bottom-up process of individual letter recognition and leads a reader to rely more on his or her expectation of what letters will come next and less on the actual visual features of those letters. That's why proofreading is so difficult. We miss errors because our word expectations are so powerful that they influence how we see the individual letters. Use of context and meaning to predict what is coming next is another familiar example of the top-down processing used in reading.

Individual Differences in Recognition Networks

Although human brains all share the same basic recognition architecture and recognize things in roughly the same way, our recognition networks come in many shapes, sizes, and patterns. In anatomy, connectivity, physiology, and chemistry, each of us has a brain that is slightly different from everyone else's.

PET scan images usually represent averages across individuals. These averages highlight commonalities between individuals but obscure the fact that each individual brain actually reveals a unique pattern of activity. For example, most people, when they recognize an object visually, show increased activity in the back part of their brains; however, the exact magnitude, location, and distribution of that increased activity varies quite a bit. The active area of the cortex may be larger or smaller, more localized to the right or left hemisphere, or more widely or closely distributed.

These variations undoubtedly manifest in the way people recognize things in the world—their recognition strengths, weaknesses, and preferences. The distributed nature of processing in the brain leads to myriad subtle differences in recognition between individual learners. Unlike the global notion of ability suggested, for example, in a Stanford-Binet IQ score, learners' abilities are multifaceted. When two students perform the same academic task, the patterns of activity in their brains are as unique as their fingerprints. The uniqueness may not be visible in the overall level of brain activity, but rather lies in the pattern of activation: how the activity is distributed across different brain regions. For this reason, no one measure of brain activity—and no one learning score or variable—differentiates or describes individual learners in any meaningful way.

Traditional views of disability, also based on an implied assumption of unitary brain functioning, suggest that a person either does or does not belong to the category "disabled." New understanding about the distributed nature of neural processing shows that abilities in many domains fall along a very large number of continua. Further, the importance of a particular strength or weakness depends upon what is being asked of the learner. This is why, for example, a youngster with perfect pitch who has difficulty recognizing letters is seen as disabled, but a child who is tone deaf but can read words easily is not. Specific differences in the recognition networks of individual learners range from the subtle to the profound.

The recognition cortex in Albert Einstein's brain was disproportionately allocated to spatial cognition. He had difficulty recognizing the letter patterns and sound-to-symbol connections required for reading, but he was a genius at visualizing the deepest fundamentals of physics. Awareness of these differences across his recognition networks could have helped Einstein's teachers shape instruction that would both capitalize on his spatial genius *and* support his areas of weakness.

Although all three brain networks—recognition, strategic, and affective—are involved in learning any task, curricular teaching goals and methods tend to cluster into broad types that coincide with each network. For example, subject-verb agreement, the causes of The War of 1812, the structure of the atom, and the nuances of Dostoyevsky's style are all *patterns* to be recognized; these things are the "what" of learning. Traditionally, when teachers teach these kinds of patterns, they tend to present them in one way for the entire class. But the overt and subtle differences in how students best recognize patterns suggest that more varied means of presentation can reach more students.

Being aware of the distributed nature of recognition processes and the combination of top-down and bottom-up processing can help teachers understand individual learners better and shape instruction and assessment accordingly. The power, flexibility, and speed of recognition networks are critical to how humans experience the world and are thus worthy of the attention of teachers and curriculum designers.

As teachers, understanding the pattern of strengths and weaknesses within a learner's recognition networks can help us individualize the kind of challenge and support we provide, thus maximizing every student's opportunity to learn. Recognition represents one way of "knowing" the world: building factual knowledge and relating new information we encounter to what we already know. Traditional curricula focus primarily on recognition, at times overlooking the other kinds of "knowing" served by strategic and affective networks. And yet these networks are no less important to effective learning.

STRATEGIC NETWORKS

It is through strategic networks, execute, and monitor our internally generated mental and motor patterns—actions and skills as diverse as sweeping the floor, deciding a chess move, or choosing a college. During some activities, such as playing sports, orchestrating an April Fool's joke, or composing an essay, we maybe conscious of applying strategy. What most of us do not realize is that conscious or not, strategy is involved in essentially *everything* we do. The strategic components of everyday tasks serve to illustrate the centrality of strategy for cognition and learning.

Most likely you glanced at the image and had no trouble determining that it shows a living room or a parlor. Without being aware of it, you relied on your strategic networks to figure this out. You identified the goal of the task, came up with a plan to achieve it, executed that plan, and evaluated its outcome, all the while avoiding distractions that might carry you off track. The neural networks responsible for generating patterns of mental and motor action occupy their own unique territory, located primarily in the part of the brain called the frontal lobes. Research into the effects of selective damage to the frontal lobes has revealed that like recognition, the ability to think and act strategically is distributed across specialized modules

Neurological and brain imaging studies tell us that within the frontal lobes, the prefrontal cortex oversees complex strategic capacities and is critical for identifying goals, selecting appropriate plans, and self-monitoring. The pattern of activity distributed across the modules of the frontal lobes shapes how we plan and execute actions. These modules function in parallel, enabling us to perform highly complex actions with ease. Consider, for example, what's involved in playing the organ. If it were not for parallel processing within strategic networks, organists would never be able to simultaneously coordinate not one but several different keyboards and numerous pedals and switches!

Strategic modules, although operating in parallel, are also interdependent. The connections between modules enable modules doing different things to influence one another. In fact, elements of our plans-of-action that come later in a series can influence those that come before. This is why, for example, you will pick up a bowling ball one way if you intend to bowl the ball yourself and another way if you intend to hand it to a friend. Similarly, when we speak, separate but connected modules process syllables and words simultaneously, so that the pronunciation of any syllable or word is highly influenced by those that follow it. That's why prerecorded "voices" like the automated flight-arrival information broadcast in airports sound so odd to us: Both the words and sentences are spliced together from prerecorded individual sounds, and each sound is articulated the same way regardless of the linguistic context.

Cursive writing provides yet another example: When we write, we form individual letters differently depending on which letters precede and follow them. As teachers, being mindful of the parallel nature of strategic processing can help us better understand individual learners and design optimal supports for each. For example, school requires students to learn discrete strategic skills (such as listening, extracting relevant information, and writing down the information) and to execute these skills simultaneously (as when taking notes in class). From what we know about strategic networks, we can appreciate that these patterns of actions are not "built" by putting together a step-by-step sequence.

Different layers of an action are added on at the same time and mutually influence one another. For this reason, skill instruction is often more effective when the various components of the process are learned simultaneously rather than one at a time. Thus, a tennis instructor may model the whole serve and encourage the learner to try it out, only analyzing individual steps (ball toss, backswing, step forward, swing, and follow-through) when particular aspects must be corrected. Likewise, each subcomponent of a task like writing an essay makes the most sense to our students if it is taught in the context of the whole task.

Like recognition modules, strategic modules form part of a two-way hierarchical pathway. Neural signals travel from higher-order regions in the cortex down to the spinal cord, where the neurons that innervate muscles are found, enabling internally driven strategies("I will pick up this pencil") to influence how we act on—and in—the world (picking up the pencil). Modules specialized to carry out different steps within a skills sequence reside at different levels along that path. The top of the hierarchy orders the steps, "commands" our muscles to act, and keeps track of whether or not the goal is reached, modifying the plan as needed. As actions are practiced and perfected, they require decreasing amounts of monitoring from the top. Anyone who knows how to touch-type will remember that as a beginner, you had to rely heavily on conscious monitoring capacities to check finger placement and letter sequence.

With practice, though, the pattern of movements necessary to hit the right keys became automated, requiring little if any conscious monitoring. The top-down flow of information in strategic networks makes intuitive sense. We can understand that top-down processing enables us to carry out a plan formed high up in the neural hierarchy. When we as teachers express goals clearly, give verbal instructions, or offer models for students to work from, we are supporting students' top-down processing by stressing the importance of strategic skills and encouraging students to be guided by clear goals and plans. Within strategic networks, information travels not only down from the cortex to the muscles, but also up from the muscles to the cortex.

One source of bottom-up strategic pathways is the cerebellum, the cauliflower-shaped structure located at the back and base of the brain, overlaying the brainstem. Pathways from the cerebellum to strategic modules in the cortex serve an important role in learning skills and strategies. The cerebellum takes sensory feedback, which clues it in to how actions are being executed, and compares it to other signals that convey the actions we intended. Then, through these bottom-up projections, the cerebellum informs our strategic networks about whether our actions are "on target." Although this is best described for motor patterns, bottom-up processing operates in a similar way to refine mental patterns. It works much like a thermostat, but regulating skills and strategies rather than temperature. Thus, to acquire skills, students need support for both top-down and bottom-up strategic processing. They learn best when they have not only good instruction and good models but also plenty of opportunities to practice and to receive ongoing, relevant feedback. The kinds of models and supports most suitable for individual learners depend on the students' particular strategic strengths and weaknesses.

Individual Differences in Strategic Networks

The distributed organization of strategic networks introduces a level of complexity that would not exist in a homogeneous network in which all tissue looks and acts the same and a deficit in one part of the network has the same effect as a deficit in another. In reality, deficits and strengths can affect very specific aspects of strategic skills. For example, a student may be skilled at making a plan but have difficulty self-monitoring when executing the plan. Another student might be an expert at finding information, but have difficulty organizing and keeping track of that information. Recent brain imaging experiments provide a novel illustration of individual differences in strategy. When two people are confronted with the same problem but solve it using different cognitive strategies, the brain images reveal two very different patterns of activity.

Differences in strategic networks manifest themselves in various ways in the classroom. For example, learners differ dramatically in their abilities to acquire and automate pattern-based routines such as forming letters, typing, spelling, and multiplying. Learners also differ in their ability to enact higher-level strategies such as planning, organizing, monitoring progress, devising alternative approaches, and seeking help when they need it. For example, students with executive-function disorders (disorders affecting reasoning, logic, hypothesis-testing, and similar high-level abilities) can have difficulty at all levels of reading. When decoding words, they may make impulsive guesses rather than apply their phonics knowledge or search for context cues. When reading a paragraph, they may fail to use organizing strategies to help them focus on the key points.

Variation within students' strategic networks also influences their abilities to use different kinds of learning tools. Students with motor difficulties may be marginally able or unable to use a keyboard or a mouse, to scan a line of text, or to turn the pages of a book. Speech difficulties may impede oral presentations, and students with language and learning difficulties may find that they expend so much energy attending to the mechanics of producing written text that they have difficulty communicating effectively in that medium. These are just a few of the obvious examples; often the strengths and weaknesses in strategic networks are more subtle. Variations in the degree of bottom-up and top-down processing influence how students acquire skills. We have all seen students with the uncanny ability to watch someone else do something and then do it almost perfectly the first time; this is an indication of strong top-down strategic processing.

On the other hand, students who seem to learn best by doing; these are the students who achieve expertise only after lots of practice and feedback—an indication of strong bottom-up strategic processing. Awareness of these subtle differences can help teachers design optimal strategic teaching for different kinds of learners.

Differences in Strategy

Understanding the way strategic networks function and the differences in students' strategic networks is a useful guide when teaching skills and strategies such as predicting, summarizing, and determining the steps needed to solve a problem or write an essay. Differences in strategic skills manifest as preferences, proclivities, or significant strengths and weaknesses. The following set of classroom examples illustrates some of these differences. These classroom examples illustrate the multiple and varied influences of strategic networks on students' performance. Understanding the many facets of strategic learning, the approaches most suited to supporting strategic networks, and the patterns of strength and weakness in different students can help shape instruction to support every learner's unique needs.

AFFECTIVE NETWORKS

Learning requires interaction with the external world-with varied materials, tools, people, and contexts. But different students experience the same situations in very different ways.

Affective Processes Are Distributed

Intuitively, emotion seems to be a more complex and elusive phenomenon than recognition or strategy. However, the neural processing of emotion occurs in a very similar way. Affective networks are made up of many specialized modules, located predominantly at the core of the brain and associated with the limbic system.

Evidence of the distributed nature of affective networks comes from the selective deficits that result from disease or damage in specific locations within the brain. Some patients can express emotion but cannot recognize emotion in other people's faces or voices. Others show the reverse deficit: They can read emotional responses of others but they cannot express emotion themselves. These two types of deficits are linked to brain damage in different, specific locations. What this research tells us is that we use different parts of our affective networks to recognize emotion and to express emotion. Further, the subprocesses involved in recognizing emotion, like being able to interpret facial expressions and speech for emotional content, are each handled by different areas. It should come as no surprise that affective networks operate in parallel.

They process different kinds of emotional information simultaneously and communicate closely though myriad interconnections to create a whole affective impression. When students watch a teacher during a lecture, they process the expression on her face and the emotion in her voice at the same time. Further, because the brain modules are interconnected, the teacher's facial expressions influence how the students interpret her voice.

Affect Involves Bottom-Up and Top-Down Processing

As with the other two networks, the modules that make up affective networks are hierarchically organized, and the information travels in both bottom-up and top-down directions. Bottom-up connections in affective networks ensure that we are emotionally responsive to the outside world. Information travels from the sensory organs (such as the eyes and ears) up the hierarchical continuum. When it reaches the apex of the pathway—the limbic cortex—we "feel" emotional reactions.

We respond to emotionally reactive stimuli, such as scary faces, even when we are not consciously aware of them. Before we even identify a sound or shape, our nervous system may initiate physiological responses such as an adrenaline rush, muscular contractions, and increased blood pressure—our bodies' physical manifestations of fear. This purely unconscious emotion reflects a second type of bottom-up processing, in which information travels only partway up the hierarchy, stopping short of the cortex. This type of processing gives rise to a cruder emotional response, one that may or may not be appropriate to the given situation. Here's an everyday example that illustrates bottom-up affective processing. Suppose you are walking in unfamiliar woods and detect a sudden movement in your peripheral vision. Almost before you become aware of the disturbance, your eyes leap to focus on the source, and your body prepares for fight or flight.

Seconds later, you identify the source of the sound: a harmless robin. Your initial responses to the noise—the physiological changes, the protective hunching of your body, and covering your head with your arms—are part of a crude defensive instinct mediated by rapid bottom-up processing. A full second may pass before your conscious awareness of fear coincides with a more analytical look at the source of the noise, so that you can decide what to do. In this case, you probably chuckle over your reaction and walk on. Of course, instinctual emotional responses can be counterproductive. Extreme nervousness before a presentation, a recital, or an athletic competition can overwhelm and distract us, diminishing the effectiveness of our performance.

Affective top-down processing helps us consciously calm ourselves through a variety of techniques such as breathing, refocusing attention, and visualizing success. Without top-down emotional processing, we would be vulnerable to intense, overblown emotions of all kinds and unable to practice the self-restraint needed to keep ourselves on task. Teachers can take advantage of top-down processing to help alleviate the negative emotion students may have learned to associate with schoolwork.

Individual Differences in Affective Networks

Because affective networks work in roughly similar ways across many individuals, we can make some fairly solid generalizations about how people respond to particular situations. Upon the death of a loved one we become sad; startled by a sudden loud noise or dangerous animal we become surprised and scared. However, human beings are not emotional clones. When confronted with the same life event, different people exhibit different kinds and intensities of emotion. In study after study, scientists have shown that people can be sorted into "high" and "low" emotional responders based on their patterns of self-reported emotion, changes in facial expression, or autonomic reflexes. Even animals display this variabil.

It is easy to spot the outcomes of affective variability. The next time you find yourself in a doctor's office waiting room, take note of the other patients. Some will start to show signs of agitation the minute their appointment time has come and gone. Others will simply sit back and sigh; they might become upset only if the wait continues for an extended period. Still others will appear to simply accept the situation; they will remain relaxed and calm no matter how long the delay persists. We might like to think that our emotional tendencies are acquired traits and therefore entirely controllable. However, brain research has revealed that some affective characteristics are strongly associated with measurable neurological differences. For example, functional brain imaging techniques have revealed that people suffering from clinical depression exhibit a characteristic asymmetry in the brain.

Depressives tend to have abnormally high resting brain activity in right-hemisphere affective networks. People suffering from panic disorder also show increased resting activity on the right side of the brain, but in different affective modules from those who are depressed. Affective differences exert powerful influences on learners' ability to engage with learning and to progress. In studies of highly successful adult dyslexics, Rosalie Fink conclusively demonstrated the very significant positive impact affect can have on learning. The individuals in her study overcame severe deficits in recognition and strategic skills by virtue of their deep engagement with and interest in particular subject matter. Strong positive affect made the critical difference in their learning outcomes.

Conversely, and as more commonly noted, affective problems also interfere with learning in various ways. One of the reasons students with severe affective disorders related to childhood depression or abuse are often vulnerable to reading failure is because strong affective influences can derail the work of recognition and strategic networks. Students preoccupied with emotional concerns may have little attention left over for schoolwork. In addition, students with a history of learning problems often become discouraged about their own abilities and withdraw effort from learning tasks. Still others may learn to associate negative feelings with certain subjects or media.

Understanding affective issues can help teachers support all learners more appropriately. Of the three learning networks, affective networks are perhaps intuitively the most essential for learning, yet they are given the least formal emphasis in the curriculum. All teachers know how important it is to engage students in the learning process, to help them to love learning, to enjoy challenges, to connect with subject matter, and to persist when things get tough. When students withdraw their effort and engagement, it is tempting to consider this a problem outside the core enterprise of teaching. We believe this is a mistake. Attending to affective issues when considering students' needs is an integral component of instruction, and it can increase teaching effectiveness significantly.

Consider these differences: Some students prefer to read in a quiet environment; others are comfortable reading in the middle of noisy activity. Some like the predictability of reading familiar stories multiple times, whereas others find rereading boring. Some students like the structure of being told what books to read and when to read them; others thrive on choice and independence. In addition, of course, there is huge variation in the type of content that interests different learners. All these preferences factor in to why students whose skills and achievement levels appear very similar on a test may react—and perform—very differently to particular assignments.

Implications for Educators

Brain imaging technologies and neural networks are certainly not the first things that jump into most teachers' minds on the way to school each morning. But you do not need to have a degree in neuroscience to reap the benefits of understanding the learning brain. The fundamental nature of the recognition, strategic, and affective networks form a framework we can use to analyze our students' individual strengths and weaknesses and understand their individual differences. One of the clearest and most important revelations stemming from brain research is that there are no "regular" students. The notion of broad categories of learners—smart, not smart, disabled, not disabled, regular, not regular—is a gross oversimplification that does not reflect reality. By categorizing students in this way, we miss many subtle and important qualities and focus instead on a single characteristic.

The modular organization of learning networks and the highly specialized subprocesses within networks mean that each student brings a unique assortment of strengths, weaknesses, and preferences to school. Patterns of strength and weakness across all three networks interact with the teaching and learning environment in ways that can either bring about progress or frustration. Sometimes a problem in one area can receive so much attention that other issues are missed. For example, students with learning disabilities are often mistakenly thought to have problems only with recognizing words.

6

Personality Development with a Special Reference of Freud's Theory

When discussing any type of development, most theorist break it down into specific stages. These stages are typically progressive. In other words, you must pass through one stage before you can get to the next. Think about how you learned to run; first you had to learn to crawl, then you could learn to walk, and finally you could develop the skills needed to run. Without the first two stages, running would be an impossibility. Most infants develop motor abilities in the same order and at approximately the same age. in this sense, most agree that these abilities are genetically preprogrammed within all infants. The environment does play a role in the development, with an enriched environment often reducing the learning time and an impoverished one doing the opposite.

COGNITIVE DEVELOPMENT IN CHILDREN

Probably the most cited theory in the cognitive development in children is Jean Piaget . As with all stage theories, *Piaget's Theory of Cognitive Development* maintains that children go through specific stages as their intellect and ability to see relationships matures. These stages are completed in a fixed children, even those in other countries. The age range, however can vary from child to child.

Sensorimotor Stage: This stage occurs between the ages of birth and two years of age, as infants begin to understand the information entering their sense and their ability to interact with the world. During this stage, the child learns to manipulate objects although they fail to understand the permanency of these objects if they are not within their current sensory perception. In other words, once an object is removed from the child's view, he or she is unable to understand that the object still exists. The major achievement during this stage is that of *Object Permanency*, or the ability to understand that these objects do in fact continue to exist. This includes his ability to understand that when mom leaves the room, she will eventually return, resulting in an increased sense of safety and security. Object Permanency occurs during the end of this stage and represents the child's ability to maintain a mental image of the object (or person) without the actual perception.

Preoperational Stage: The second stage begins after Object Permanency is achieved and occurs between the ages of two to seven years of age. During this stage, the development of language occurs at a rapid pace. Children learn how to interact with their environment in a more complex manner through the use of words and images. This stage is marked by Egocentrism. or the child's belief that everyone sees the world the same way that she does. The fail to understand the differences in perception and believe that inanimate objects have the same perceptions they do, such as seeing things, feeling, hearing and their sense of touch.

A second important factor in this stage is that of Conservation, which is the ability to understand that quantity does not change if the shape changes. In other words, if a short and wide glass of water is poured into a tall and thin glass. Children in this stage will perceive the taller glass as having more water due only because of it's height. This is due to the children's inability to understand *reversibility* and to focus on only one aspect of a stimulus (called *centration*), such as height, as opposed to understanding other aspects, such as glass width.

Concrete Operations Stage: Occurring between ages 7 and about 12, the third stage of cognitive development is marked by a gradual decrease in centristic thought and the increased ability to focus on more than one aspect of a stimulus. They can understand the concept of grouping, knowing that a small dog and a large dog are still both dogs, or that pennies, quarters, and dollar bills are part of the bigger concept of money. They can only apply this new understanding to concrete objects (those they have actually experienced). In other words, imagined objects or those they have not seen, heard, or touched, continue to remain somewhat mystical to these children, and abstract thinking has yet to develop.

Formal Operations Stage: In the final stage of cognitive development (from age 12 and beyond), children begin to develop a more abstract view of the world. They are able to apply reversibility and conservation to both real and imagined situations. They also develop an increased understanding of the world and the idea of cause and effect. By the teenage years, they are able to develop their own theories about the world. This stage is achieved by most children, although failure to do so has been associated with lower intelligence.

Erikson's Stages of Psychosocial Development

Like Piaget, Erik Erikson maintained that children develop in a predetermined order. Instead of focusing on cognitive development, however, he was interested in how children socialize and how this affects their sense of self. *Erikson's Theory of Psychosocial Development* has eight distinct stage, each with two possible outcomes. According to the theory, successful completion of each stage results in a healthy personality and successful interactions with others. Failure to successfully complete a stage can result in a reduced ability to complete further stages and therefore a more unhealthy personality and sense of self. These stages, however, can be resolved successfully at a later time.

Trust Versus Mistrust: From ages birth to one year, children begin to learn the ability to trust others based upon the consistency of their caregiver(s). If trust develops successfully, the child gains confidence and security in the world around him and is able to feel secure even when threatened. Unsuccessful completion of this stage can result in an inability to trust, and therefore an sense of fear about the inconsistent world. It may result in anxiety, heightened insecurities, and an over feeling of mistrust in the world around them.

Autonomy vs. Shame and Doubt: Between the ages of one and three, children begin to assert their independence, by walking away from their mother, picking which toy to play with, and making choices about what they like to wear, to eat, etc. If children in this stage are encouraged and supported in their increased independence, they become more confident and secure in their own ability to survive in the world. If children are criticized, overly controlled, or not given the opportunity to assert themselves, they begin to feel inadequate in their ability to survive, and may then become overly dependent upon others. lack self-esteem, and feel a sense of shame or doubt in their own abilities.

Initiative vs. Guilt: Around age three and continuing to age six, children assert themselves more frequently. They begin to plan activities, make up games, and initiate activities with others. If given this opportunity, children develop a sense of initiative, and feel secure in their ability to lead others and make decisions. Conversely, if this tendency is squelched, either through criticism or control, children develop a sense of guilt. They may feel like a nuisance to others and will therefore remain followers, lacking in self-initiative.

Industry vs. Inferiority: From age six years to puberty, children begin to develop a sense of pride in their accomplishments. They initiate projects, see them through to completion, and feel good about what they have achieved. During this time, teachers play an increased role in the child's development. If children are encouraged and reinforced for their initiative, they begin to feel industrious and feel confident in their ability to achieve goals. If this initiative is not encouraged, if it is restricted by parents or teacher, then the child begins to feel inferior, doubting his own abilities and therefore may not reach his potential.

Identity vs. Role Confusion: During adolescence, the transition from childhood to adulthood is most important. Children are becoming more independent, and begin to look at the future in terms of career, relationships, families, housing, etc. During this period, they explore possibilities and begin to form their own identity based upon the outcome of their explorations. This sense of who they are can be hindered, which results in a sense of confusion ("I don't know what I want to be when I grow up") about themselves and their role in the world.

Intimacy vs. Isolation: Occurring in Young adulthood, we begin to share ourselves more intimately with others. We explore relationships leading toward longer term commitments with someone other than a family member. Successful completion can lead to comfortable relationships and a sense of commitment, safety, and care within a relationship. Avoiding intimacy, fearing commitment and relationships can lead to isolation, loneliness, and sometimes depression.

Generativity vs. Stagnation: During middle adulthood, we establish our careers, settle down within a relationship, begin our own families and develop a sense of being a part of the bigger picture. We give back to society through raising our children, being productive at work, and becoming involved in community activities and organizations. By failing to achieve these objectives, we become stagnant and feel unproductive.

Ego Integrity vs. Despair: As we grow older and become senior citizens, we tend to slow down our productivity, and explore life as a retired person. It is during this time that we contemplate our accomplishments and are able to develop integrity if we see ourselves as leading a successful life. If we see our lives as unproductive, feel guilt about our pasts, or feel that we did not accomplish our life goals, we become dissatisfied with life and develop despair, often leading to depression and hopelessness.

PERSONALITY DEVELOPMANT THROUGH INTERACTION DURING EARLY LIFE

During infancy, childhood, adolescence, and young adulthood, new needs and tensions arise in the individual. In attempt to seek ways of adapting to these newfound stresses, people develop different kinds of intimate relationships that ultimately form their personality. Relationships formed during each stage of life serve as a prototype for interactions in later stages. For this reason, there exists a continuum of relationships formed throughout a lifetime that shape and mold specific personality traits. Neither intimacy nor individual development can exist alone. The birth of a child initiates a human being into a life-long process of mutual adaptation between the child, his or her intimate relationship partners and the broader social environment.

Intimate interactions and relationships affect adaptations to the changing needs and stresses that evolve with each stage of development throughout one's lifetime. Intimate interactions from early life serve as the basis upon which relationships later in life are formed. Environmental contingencies to which individuals must adapt are rooted in these relationships. In an attempt to adapt to other people's styles of relating, one must adjust his or her own behaviors. Based on the fact that human development is a product of complex interplay of forces that reside within the individual human being and the environment by which he or she is surrounded, it can be proposed that interpersonal interactions and relationships shape individual personality and coping styles. Psychological maturity involves integrating intimacy into a life framework that encompasses all parts of the self.

From the time of birth, every individual is biologically predisposed to approach the world with his or her own personal style. Studies of infants suggest that some variability in human behavior may result directly or indirectly from genetic differences. Developmental psychologists term these differences as dimensions of temperament. Based on chemical, biological, experiential, interpersonal. and social factors, different dimensions of temperament manifest themselves over time and across different situations. Psychologists Buss and Plomin have proposed the existence of four basic temperament dimensions present in human beings:

1. *Emotionality* is the tendency to express negative emotions such as anger and fear frequently and vigorously.
2. *Activity* is the degree of physical movement that a person characteristically shows.
3. *Impulsivity* is the degree to which a person acts quickly without deliberation, moves from one activity to the next, and finds it difficult to practice self-control.
4. *Sociability* is the tendency to be outgoing and friendly and to enjoy the company of others.

According to this theory, persons are inherently born with tendencies to develop these four temperaments to different levels. These dimensions are present in infancy and continue to grow throughout childhood and adulthood. The social environment reacts to these tendencies, modifying and shaping them in different ways. Such modifications are the results of interpersonal relationships that begin to form during early life. The development of a unique interpersonal style is a function of temperament.

MOTHER-CHILD RELATIONSHIP

A human being's first intimate relationship is the mother-child relationship. According to Freud, a human being's first encounter with intimate behavior is with his or her mother during the act of breast-feeding. "The act of sucking is the most primitive manner of knowing the innermost self of another, and to suck the other into one's innermost". During infancy, the baby obtains nourishment and pleasure from sucking at the mother's breast, thus reducing tension caused by the hunger drive. Engagement in such a tension-relieving activity during this early stage serves as the prototype for relationships that develop later on in life. Life-stage-related changes in stress, tension, and needs are based on the outcome of such coping attempts formed during infancy. The need for security and comfort play an important role in shaping the interactions with caregivers.

According to the Bowlby and Ainsworth, the love between a mother and an infant is the result of an attachment bond formed during the first year of life. Interactions between a child and his or her mother form behavioral patters that are reflected in later relationships. An example of the development of personality as a result of this bond can be seen in the securely attached infant. As a result of sensitivity and responsiveness on the part of the caregiver, an infant may develop a "secure" attachment style. Infants who develop "secure" personality types feel confident and at ease when relating to others. They learn how to take turns, how to lead and follow, and how to express and receive. The attachment bond serves as a prototype and provides the earliest pattern for warm and close relationships.

Interactions With Peers

During preschool years, a child's need for autonomy and individuation influences his or her intimate interactions with peers. Children look to share and communicate while enjoying the company of their peers. These interactions are based on the quest for coexistence between their newfound independence and the love they experienced during infancy. Aspects of the parent-child relationship affect the efficacy of children's adaptations. Competencies acquired through interactions with parents are reflected in children's interactions with peers. In laboratory studies, children who show more self-reliance and control are found to have parents who are nurturing. In contrast, children who are less autonomous are found to have parents who are more permissive.

In nursery school and kindergarten, children who had developed a secure attachment bond during infancy are described by their teachers as more socially competent and popular. They are observed to show more dominance and initiative. Such peer interactions characterized by autonomy, sensitivity, empathetic concern, and ability to verbalize emotions reflect the formation of intimate friendships later on. It is thus apparent that behavioral patterns resulting from relationships formed during infancy are reflected in peer interactions. In turn, these interactions serve as a basis for relationships that develop in the next stage of life.

Relationships in Adolescence and Early Adulthood

Children entering adolescence must begin to adapt to the adult world and its institutions while coming to terms with emerging parts of themselves. They discover themselves as having new emotional and sexual needs. As they make these discoveries, adolescents begin to realize the limitations of their parents. Taking responsibility for aspects of their own character requires distancing from authoritative figures.

Over the course of social development, the role of friends and parents changes significantly. During early adolescence, the amount of time that North American children spend with their family drops roughly in half. As an adolescent undergoes physical and emotional changes, he or she seeks out relationships that enhance efforts to adapt to new needs and stresses. Adolescents seek to share their thoughts and feelings with those who are experiencing similar changes. Intimate interactions increase between friends during this stage in life because they provide teens with opportunities for self-clarification.

Through the formation of coconstructive dialogues between friends, teens can participate together in exploring and constructing selves. Referring back to the example of the securely attached infant, it can be inferred that the ability to construct such dialogues directly stems from earlier interactions. The secure infant's sensitive and autonomous personality traits were reflected in relationships with peers. These traits reappear in the dialogues formed with friends during adolescence. The egalitarian authority structure of friendship lends itself to such exchanges and relieves the pressure adolescents might feel to yield to the views of adult supremacy.

During late adolescence, one must first confront the problem of multiple selves. For the first time, an adolescent realizes that his or her personality changes from one situation to the next. This is the stage of life during which one looks to craft a narrative of the self that provides a sense of sameness and continuity. The desire to discover how one is the same from one situation to the next dominates the desire to discover how one is the same as other people. The importance of intimate friendship and romance formed during early adulthood stems from the valuable and adaptive contribution dialogues made with friends during adolescence. Personality differences can be identified by capacities to form intimate relationships characterized by commitment, depth, and partner individuation based on interactions of early life.

During the transformation from adolescence to early adulthood, a person seeks to discover the self through story in historical and biographical terms. Whereas the child views his or her past as a simple series of factual events, a curiosity is invoked in a young adult who seeks to uncover the meaning and the validity of these facts. For the first time, one does not search for oneself in others, but rather confronts the other as a separate person with whom one longs to connect. The ability of an individual to combine his or her multiple selves and to create a well-articulated life story results in the ability to guide one's actions, emotions, and personality traits.

FREUD'S STAGES OF PSYCHOSEXUAL DEVELOPMENT

Sigmund Freud is probably the most well known theorist when it comes to the development of personality. Freud's Stages of Psychosexual Development are, like other stage theories, completed in a predetermined sequence and can result in either successful completion or a healthy personality or can result in failure, leading to an unhealthy personality. This theory is probably the most well known as well as the most controversial, as Freud believed that we develop through stages based upon a particular erogenous zone. During each stage, an unsuccessful completion means that a child becomes fixated on that particular erogenous zone and either over– or under-indulges once he or she becomes an adult.

Oral Stage (Birth to 18 months): During the oral stage, the child if focused on oral pleasures (sucking). Too much or too little gratification can result in an Oral Fixation or Oral Personality which is evidenced by a preoccupation with oral activities. This type of personality may have a stronger tendency to smoke, drink alcohol, over eat, or bite his or her nails. Personality wise, these individuals may become overly dependent upon others, gullible, and perpetual followers. On the other hand, they may also fight these urges and develop pessimism and aggression toward others.

Anal Stage (18 months to three years): The child's focus of pleasure in this stage is on eliminating and retaining feces. Through society's pressure, mainly via parents, the child has to learn to control anal stimulation. In terms of personality, after effects of an anal fixation during this stage can result in an obsession with cleanliness, perfection, and control (anal retentive). On the opposite end of the spectrum, they may become messy and disorganized (anal expulsive).

Phallic Stage (ages three to six): The pleasure zone switches to the genitals. Freud believed that during this stage boy develop unconscious sexual desires for their mother. Because of this, he becomes rivals with his father and sees him as competition for the mother's affection. During this time, boys also develop a fear that their father will punish them for these feelings, such as by castrating them. This group of feelings is known as Oedipus Complex (after the Greek Mythology figure who accidentally killed his father and married his mother).

Later it was added that girls go through a similar situation, developing unconscious sexual attraction to their father. Although Freud Strongly disagreed with this, it has been termed the Electra Complex by more recent psychoanalysts. According to Freud, out of fear of castration and due to the strong competition of his father, boys eventually decide to identify with him rather than fight him. By identifying with his father, the boy develops masculine characteristics and identifies himself as a male, and represses his sexual feelings toward his mother. A fixation at this stage could result in sexual deviancies (both overindulging and avoidance) and weak or confused sexual identity according to psychoanalysts.

Latency Stage (age six to puberty): It's during this stage that sexual urges remain repressed and children interact and play mostly with same sex peers.

Genital Stage (puberty on): The final stage of psychosexual development begins at the start of puberty when sexual urges are once again awakened. Through the lessons learned during the previous stages, adolescents direct their sexual urges onto opposite sex peers, with the primary focus of pleasure is the genitals.

Freud's Structural and Topographical Models of Personality

Sigmund Freud's Theory is quite complex and although his writings on psychosexual development set the groundwork for how our personalities developed, it was only one of five parts to his overall theory of personality. He also believed that different driving forces develop during these stages which play an important role in how we interact with the world. Structural Model (id, ego, superego) According to Freud, we are born with our Id. The id is an important part of our personality because as newborns, it allows us to get our basic needs met. Freud believed that the id is based on our pleasure principle. In other words, the id wants whatever feels good at the time, with no consideration for the reality of the situation. When a child is hungry, the id wants food, and therefore the child cries.

When the child needs to be changed, the id cries. When the child is uncomfortable, in pain, too hot, too cold, or just wants attention, the id speaks up until his or her needs are met. The id doesn't care about reality, about the needs of anyone else, only its own satisfaction. If you think about it, babies are not real considerate of their parents' wishes. They have no care for time, whether their parents are sleeping, relaxing, eating dinner, or bathing. When the id wants something, nothing else is important. Within the next three years, as the child interacts more and more with the world, the second part of the personality begins to develop. Freud called this part the Ego. The ego is based on the reality principle.

The ego understands that other people have needs and desires and that sometimes being impulsive or selfish can hurt us in the long run. Its the ego's job to meet the needs of the id, while taking into consideration the reality of the situation. By the age of five, or the end of the phallic stage of development, the Superego develops. The Superego is the moral part of us and develops due to the moral and ethical restraints placed on us by our caregivers. Many equate the superego with the conscience as it dictates our belief of right and wrong. In a healthy person, according to Freud, the ego is the strongest so that it can satisfy the needs of the id, not upset the superego, and still take into consideration the reality of every situation. Not an easy job by any means, but if the id gets too strong, impulses and self gratification take over the person's life. If the superego becomes to strong, the person would be driven by rigid morals, would be judgmental and unbending in his or her interactions with the world. You'll learn how the ego maintains control as you continue to read.

Topographical Model Freud believed that the majority of what we experience in our lives, the underlying emotions, beliefs, feelings, and impulses are not available to us at a conscious level. He believed that most of what drives us is buried in our unconscious. If you remember the Oedipus and Electra Complex, they were both pushed down into the unconscious, out of our awareness due to the extreme anxiety they caused. While buried there, however, they continue to impact us dramatically according to Freud.

The role of the unconscious is only one part of the model. Freud also believed that everything we are aware of is stored in our conscious. Our conscious makes up a very small part of who we are. In other words, at any given time, we are only aware of a very small part of what makes up our personality; most of what we are is buried and inaccessible. The final part is the preconscious or subconscious. This is the part of us that we can access if prompted, but is not in our active conscious. Its right below the surface, but still buried somewhat unless we search for it. Information such as our telephone number, some childhood memories, or the name of your best childhood friend is stored in the preconscious. Because the unconscious is so large, and because we are only aware of the very small conscious at any given time, this theory has been likened to an iceberg, where the vast majority is buried beneath the water's surface. The water, by the way, would represent everything that we are not aware of, have not experienced, and that has not been integrated into our personalities, referred to as the nonconscious.

Ego Defense Mechanisms

The ego's job was to satisfy the id's impulses, not offend the moralistic character of the superego, while still taking into consideration the reality of the situation. This was not an easy job. Think of the id as the 'devil on your shoulder' and the superego as the 'angel of your shoulder.' We don't want either one to get too strong so we talk to both of them, hear their perspective and then make a decision. This decision is the ego talking, the one looking for that healthy balance. According to Freud, we only have two drives; sex and aggression. In other words, everything we do is motivated by one of these two drives. Sex, also called Eros or the Life force, represents our drive to live, prosper, and produce offspring.

Aggression, also called Thanatos or our Death force, represents our need to stay alive and stave off threats to our existence, our power, and our prosperity. Now the ego has a difficult time satisfying both the id and the superego, but it doesn't have to do so without help. The ego has some tools it can use in its job as the mediator, tools that help defend the ego. These are called *Ego Defense Mechanisms* or Defenses. When the ego has a difficult time making both the id and the superego happy, it will employ one or more of these defenses:

Kohlberg's Stages of Moral Development

Although it has been questioned as to whether it applied equally to different genders and different cultures, Kohlberg's stages of moral development is the most widely cited. It breaks our development of morality into three levels, each of which is divided further into two stages:

Preconventional Level:

— *Self focused morality*

1. Morality is defined as obeying rules and avoiding negative consequences. Children in this stage see rules set, typically by parents, as defining moral law.
2. That which satisfies the child's needs is seen as good and moral.

Conventional Level (age nine to adolescence):

— *Other Focused Morality*

3. Children begin to understand what is expected of them by their parents, teacher, etc. Morality is seen as achieving these expectations.

4. Fulfilling obligations as well as following expectations are seen as moral law for children in this stage.

Postconventional Level (adulthood):

— *Higher Focused Morality*

5. As adults, people have different opinions about morality and that rules and laws vary from group to group and culture to culture. Morality is seen as upholding the values of your group or culture.

6. Understanding your own personal beliefs allow adults to judge themselves and others based upon higher levels of morality. In this stage what is right and wrong is based upon the circumstances surrounding an action. Basics of morality are the foundation with independent thought playing an important role.

CORE OF PERSONALITY

Core Characteristics:

A. *Id* - a "cauldron of seething expectations", it contains the instincts. From the German das Es ("it"). The German phrase for "I am hungry" is "Es hungert mich" or, in direct translation, "It hungers me" - a recipient of actions initiated in me, but not by me. Freud believed that instincts are experienced as foreign rather than part of ourselves. From German "das Trieb" - impulse; not "der Instinkt".

1. *Instincts* - the original contents of the mind, or the mental representation of a somatic process.

a. Two types:

— Life - Sex (Eros) & self-preservation

— Death - Thanatos

b. Four Characteristics:

— Source - somatic process in body

— Energy - rooted in somatic deprivation; libido = "fluid-like substance of biological origin".

— Aim - satisfaction, tension-reduction

— Object -objects in external world that make satisfaction possible.

2. *Pleasure Principle*: to maximize instinctual gratification (feel good) without regard to external reality.
3. *Primary Process Thinking*: where imagined objects give hallucinatory (and thus only partial) satisfaction. - Autism & magical thinking.
4. *Death Instinct (Thanatos)*: developed after WWI to explain aggression, war, why people engage in self-destructive behaviors. Never well developed.

B. *Ego* - from German das Ich ("I"). Famous quote: "Where the id ("it") was, there shall become ego ("I").

1. *Reality Principle*: the ego derives from the id and tends to maximize instinctual gratification while minimizing punishment & guile (the core tendency).
2. *Secondary Process Thinking*: is logical, rational, & deals with the external world.
3. *Two functions*:

   a. Deal effectively with external world

   b. Behave defensively (it's major function) - to translate instinctual demands into expressions not inconsistent with the demands of the superego.

4. *Defensive Behavior*:
    a. Anxiety - a signal the some instinctual wish might bring punishment and/or guilt - triggers a defense mechanism
    b. Defense Mechanism - strikes a compromise between demands of instincts & society. Some (denial) distort reality more than others (sublimation).
5. *Implication of defensive behavior*: Without much introspection and/or psychoanalysis, most people are not fully aware of their true wishes, feelings, or desires. "The ego knows how, not why".

C. *Superego*:from German das Uberich ("over-I"). It is differentiated from the ego, & is partially unconscious

1. The part of the mind containing the traditional values & taboos of society as interpreted by the parents.
2. *Makes guilt possible*: the internal version of punishment. Get depression if it is too strong.
3. *Two parts*:
    a. Conscience - cultural bans (the don'ts)
    b. Ego ideal - positive acts (the do's)
4. *Is the heir of the Oedipus Complex*: men have more fully developed superego than women.

Development (Psychosexual Stages)

Freud viewed development as the process of the transference of libidinal energy from one erogenous zone to another. If things go well, the energy will move forward (like advancing armies). With problems (either frustration or overindulgence), the energy will become fixated (not free to advance) or regress (retreat to earlier outpost).

Oral Stage - first year of life (—> 18 months)

1. *Erogenous zone*: mouth (watch an infant feed) - "He who

sees a satiated child sink back from mother's breast and fall asleep with reddened cheeks and blissful smile will have to admit that this picture remains as typical of the expression of sexual gratification in later life".

2. *Area of Conflict*: feeding
   — *Frustration*- schedule-fed. Fed only on schedule to meet nutrition requirements. Result in tight-lipped people who eat only for nourishment.

   — *Overindulgence*- demand-fed. When "super-mom" feeds the child at the slightest whimper. Gives rise to emphasis on oral pleasures (eating, drinking, smoking, oral sex, etc.)

3. *Primary Activities*- receiving vs taking
   — *oral incorporative (receiving)*- first 6 months.

   — *oral aggressive (taking)*- with teeth, learn to bite.

4. *Love Crisis*: Love vs Indifference. Here, the child is self-absorbed (narcissistic). Needs to recognize external world as necessary for fulfillment of needs. Must go from selfishness to relationships.

5. France could be considered an "oral" culture with it's emphasis on food & wine.

Anal Stage (18 mo —> 3-5)

Parents change an average of 2,200 diapers for first 18-20 months. Then, they expect child to delay gratification.

1. *Erogenous zone*: anus. Comes about with the myelination of nerve fibers and control of muscles.

2. *Area of Conflict*: Toilet training
   — *Frustration*- when parents demand exacting control of bowel habits. (develop strong habits)

   — *Overindulgence*- when parents allow child freedom to develop his/her own control. (become expressive)

3. *Primary Activities*: withholding vs giving
   — *anal retentive*- withholding (controlled, hoarding)
   — *anal expulsive*- giving (uncontrolled, expressive)
4. Love Crisis: Love vs Hate. Here aggression and love can be fused so that there are strong vacillations between love and hate.
5. Switzerland could be considered an anal culture with its emphasis on time, cleanliness, and money/banking.
6. A primitive ego and secondary process thinking starts at the end of this stage.

Phallic Stage (3-5 —> 6-8)

At this stage, language and primitive concepts become important. Gradually, secondary process thinking is being developed. The simple frustration/overindulgence concept does not apply to this stage.

1. *Erogenous zone* - genitals. At this age, children walk around without clothing and explore their genitals (often in front of embarrassed parents). Notice that there is no good term for children playing with their genitals (definitely not masturbation).
2. *Primary Activity*: heterosexualizing interactions. With ego development, become more aware of external world. Must go from nonsocial (narcissistic) to social being. Become aware that they are not the center of the universe and that Mother & Daddy have a relationship independent of themselves. Become jealous of that relationship.
3. *Male Oedipus Complex* (A complex is Carl Jung's term for an unconscious collection of ideas).
   — *Greek mythology*- based on play by Sophocles.
   — *Ontogeny recapitulates phylogeny*- Around 3-5, find a re-enactment of the primordial lusting for the female in the home (mother). The boy wants to become his

mother's lover in such a way as he has divined from his child-like observations & intuitions about sexual life (now from TV and movies). In a general sense, he would like to have mother all to himself.

— *Castration anxiety*- The boy views Dad as the major threat to his desire for Mom and worries about what Dad would do if Dad found out what he wanted. As an aside, many Freudians view death of a father or divorce here as particularly destructive. If the child wishes Dad would disappear and he does, this makes the child forever fearful of his thoughts and desires - called infantile omnipotence.

— *Solution* - drop desire, identify with Dad

a. Develop superego- adopt father's values

b. Give up on sex- move into latency period where boys want nothing to do with girls.

c. Repress the whole event- best evidence is no evidence (what wonderful logic).

4. *Female Oedipus Complex*: Freud never used term Electra Complex. He never fully developed this aspect of his theory.

— *Penis envy*- Girls come to enjoy their sexual organs just like boys. However, notice that they do not have protruding organ. Since "bigger is better", she feels cheated. Since you can't fear losing what you have never had, there is no real equivalent of castration anxiety. Thus, women have weaker developed superegos.

— *Solution*- develop a special relationship with Dad, but keep sexual identity with Mom. Someday may be able to marry and have a son.

— Some modern theorists maintain that the daughter's competition with mother comes later during the preteen/

teen years with clashes over who is "sexy". Also, fathers must pull away from daughter at this age which girls view as a withdrawal of affection.

5. Moral developmental views of Kollberg & Gilliagn

Latency Stage (6-8 —> puberty)

1. Both sexes "forget" (repress) their Oedipal attachments and there is a reduction in sexuality in the child.
2. The development of the reality principle and the learning of skills becomes important.
3. Their identity improves by playing only with members of the same sex. Harry Stack Sullivan called this stage of development the "Chum" stage.

Genital Stage (puberty —> death)

1. *Adolescence*: not much said here. With re-emergence of sexual instinct, sexual conflicts reappear. The first manifestation is usually in the form of an "adolescent crush" on an older person of the opposite sex. Possibilities include:

   — Sublimate sexual energy into emotional commitments to sports, cheerleading, academics, politics, church, or other endeavors.

   — The death instinct reappears in hostility, rebelliousness, or juvenile delinquency.

   — Or the sexual instinct can be repressed "out of sight" with vows of celibacy, or attractions to mystical philosophies, religions, or cults.

2. *Adulthood & Genitality*: not fully reached by many people (without help). Two characteristics:

   — *Ability to love*- including sexual intercourse and ability to have orgasms. Freud said vaginal orgasms are better than clitoral orgasms. Controversial even today.

— *Ability to work*- effectively and diligently add to society without anal compulsiveness or dependence of oral character.

Periphery of Personality

Freud specified various character types which are expressive of the activities and conflicts of the various psychosexual stages of development and the defense mechanisms common to those stages.

Oral Character: due to excessive fixation of libidinal energy during oral stage of development.

A. Primary activities are giving/receiving

B. Major Defense Mechanisms:

1. *Projection*: "blame it" - attribute objectional traits to others. Actually, attempt to convert neurotic or moral anxiety into objective anxiety.

a. *Neurotic anxiety*- clash between id and reality (I am bad student —> He is a bad teacher)

b. *Moral anxiety*- clash of id vs superego (I am unfaithful —> my wife/husband is unfaithful)

2. *Denial*: "Don't see it" - failing to perceive threatening objects in the external world. Main defense mechanism of alcoholics & drug addicts.

3. *Introjection*: "Don't admit where you got it" - the acceptance of other's values & norms as one's own even if they are contrary to one's previous assumptions. Hazing, fraternity initiations

C. *Traits*: remember that oral aggressive are more sarcastic & cynical than destructive.

Oral Incorporative	Oral Aggressive
"swallow anything"	"biting remarks"

overindulged	frustrated
optimistic	pessimistic
gullible	suspicious
passive	manipulative

The public stereotype here is of the Oral Incorporative - affable, chubby & loquacious. Try to conceptualize an anorexic Santa Claus.

D. *Love Crisis*: Love vs. Indifference (narcissistic)

E. *Breakdown* —> schizophrenia (indifference to its illogical extreme, "blunted emotional affect).

Anal Character

A. Primary activities are giving-withholding

B. Defense mechanisms

1. Intellectualization: "redefine it" - dealing with painful situation only on intellectual level. Nuclear bombs are "deterrents"
2. Reaction formation: "reverse it" - concealing a motive by consciously experiencing the opposite. Usually accompanied by much emotion - "The lady doth protest too much".
3. Undoing: "take it back" - engaging in thoughts or acts to atone for immoral desires or acts - Pontious Pilot.

C. Traits:

Anal Retentive	Anal Expulsive
controlled	expressive
frustration	overindulgence
stingy	overly generous
orderly	messy

meticulous	dirty
precise	vague

The typical stereotype is of the anal retentive type who is excessively neat. The "Odd Couple" of Felix Ungar (retentive) vs Oscar Madison (expulsive).

D. Love Crisis: Love vs. Hate. For many anal characters, sex and aggression become fused. Thus adults often vacillate between love and hate.

E. Breakdown —> Obsessive-compulsive

Phallic Character

A. *Primary activity*: heterosexual interactions

B. Defense Mechanism:

  1. *Repression*: "Don't remember it" - active prevention of threatening thoughts from entering consciousness. Solution to Oedipus complex

C. *Traits*: Here the traits are not related to frustration or overindulgence. Basically, sexual identity is formed during the phallic stage and the masculine or feminine pole is determined. Males may become Don Juans or homosexuals. Females may become Southern Belles or castrating females.

  vanity - self-hatred

  pride - humility

  gregariousness - isolated

  promiscuous - chaste

D. *Love Crisis*: Love vs. Being Loved - here one is torn between the active (male) or passive (female) sexuality

  1. *Male*: needs an erection to make love. Thus major fear is impotency & failure

  2. *Female*: is dependent upon male's erection. Thus, major fear is loss of love and being left alone.

E. *Breakdown* —> hysteria in women; homosexuality or perversions in men.

Genital Character

A. Is fully able to love and work.

B. Defense Mechanism:

   1. *Sublimation*: "transform it" - Finding culturally approves outlets for primitive impulses (aggressive green beret becoming a street cop)

Major Problems of Character Types:

A. *Orals*: have problems with dependency needs (theory of ulcer formation)

B. *Anals*: have problems with aggression - either overcontrol or undercontrol.

C. *Phallics*: have problems with sex & sexual identity

Evaluation

Criticisms:

A. Overemphasis on infantile sexuality

B. Overstressed early personality formation

C. Failed to consider adult personality changes

D. Overemphasized the unconscious

E. Artificial division of personality (id, ego, superego)

Contributions- commonly accepted views

A. People are irrational

B. Exploration of the unconscious - never quite so sure of your motives as you were before

C. Animal nature of man - human nature is what we are to rise above

D. Importance of infancy & childhood - Benjamin Spock went through 3 personal psychoanalyses - the first in 1933, the last in the 1980s.

E. Defense Mechanisms - Behavior is not always what it seems.

F. Physical symptoms can have psychological causes - Psychosomatic medicine & Psychophysiology

G. Psychoanalysis - still popular if money is no object

Personal growth movement

Evolving from the influence of Freudian theory, this area has multiplied rapidly. In 1945 there were approximately 9,000 such professionals. In 1992 it was estimated that there were about approximately 200,000 - 40,000 psychiatrists, 70,000 psychologists, and 80,000 social workers - a 22-fold increase during the years in which the population of the nation did not quite double.

7

LEARNING IN A NEW ERA

The process of global restructuring is underway. Accompanying this reordering of the world economy are ripples and repercussions that touch every man, woman, and child in both industrialized and developing nations. Technology profoundly alters the ways in which people are expected to work for those who employ them. And, when such expectation goes unmet, jobs (as well as workers) migrate. Indeed, the fluidity of work— in terms of both *content* and *setting*—may be the primary characteristic that distinguishes 21st Century economic reality from that of the past. Fluidity of workers and jobs is logically the byproduct of a technology revolution that places all planet dwellers within close proximity of one another.

Computers, communications satellites and mass transport facilitate an endless flow of information among individuals and groups. The definition of community is expanded to embrace "virtual groupings" of like-minded, culturally compatible individuals working together to pursue common interests and goals. No matter that they are physically far flung and unlikely to ever meet face to face. It has been suggested that low-income nations could use "wireless" technology to bypass an entire phase of communications development. Such "leapfrogging" would enable these countries to participate more cost-effectively in the development of a communications infrastructure.

In an information-driven employment environment, it is the appearance of such infrastructure that sets the stage for a transformed set of relationships between worker and workplace. *Mobility*, both of jobs and workers, is at the heart of this transformation. But, what does it mean to be part of an information-based society? The answer is found in an examination of its means of production. If production is dependent upon the use of information to increase wealth and improve living standards, then that society is information-based. Reich suggests that living in such an information-driven society means that one's capacity to command both tangible and intangible wealth is determined by the value that the global economy places on one's skills and insights.

Hence, one aspect of workplace fluidity is the rapidly evolving set of skills workers need to possess. In addition to the ability to make greater use of information technologies, members of the next generation's labor force will also have to show greater dexterity in the management of complexity. The latter is particularly critical as more and more *batches of jobs* get folded into single positions. What an individual worker brings to the job in terms of education, skills, attitude and self-reliance will assume ever greater importance as organizations increasingly view their employees more as assets and less as fixed costs. If the first aspect of workplace fluidity relates to the *content* of jobs, then the second aspect surely is the *setting* in which these jobs will be performed. The goal of the new global manager will be to maximize profits by locating production activities around the world in order to achieve the highest returns on investment.

Jobs will be exported to wherever it is most efficient and profitable to do business. For example, routine fabrication and assembly will occur wherever workers are available for the lowest cost. When jobs become mobile, workers must adapt to this change either by relocating (if they can find appropriate work) or by meeting the expectations that their employers hold for them. Already, millions of rural workers are flocking to the cities.

At the same time, the lowering of trade barriers diminishes protection for some of the most vulnerable individuals employed in these urban manufacturing belts. While job fluidity and mobility pose severe challenges for citizens of low-income countries, demographic trends also favor them.

As the population in industrialized countries grows older, the younger, more recently educated populations of the developing world have the opportunity to play a larger role in the global economy. By the year 2000, fewer than 40 percent of the workers in industrialized nations will be under 34, compared with 59 percent in Pakistan, 55 percent in Thailand and 53 percent in China. When demographic differences are combined with different rates of economic growth, the likely result is a redefinition of the labor market. Countries and companies largely populated with older workers may have greater difficulty adapting to new technologies or changes in markets, compared to those nations with large pools of younger workers.

As the world's employers reach across borders to find the younger workers they need, an unparalleled opportunity will present itself to those nations that can develop the capacities of their citizens effectively. Already a profound shift has occurred as tasks once reserved for white collar workers in developed countries are now performed in such developing nations as Mexico, Brazil, India, the Philippines and China. The exponential growth in world trade and the internationalization of finance are, of course, the outgrowth (as well as the cause) of an increasingly unimpeded information flow. As one business publication recently observed, "Just as Westerners learned in the 1970s and 1980s that manufacturing could be moved virtually anywhere, today it is getting easier to shift knowledge-based labor as well".

National, regional, and village-level economies are now intertwined in highly complex networks which are as geographically extensive as they are inherently delicate. Such fragility is exacerbated by the surge of deregulation and persistent recessions which took place in most countries over the last two decades (United Nations Research Institute for Social Development, 1994). Indeed, recession and indebtedness may well have been important catalysts for the rapid elimination of longstanding economic barriers among nations and peoples. While these changes undeniably create new opportunities, they also impose new pressures. For example, in many developing countries, small farmers who have long produced for the export market suddenly find themselves competing with larger numbers of similar producers in other parts of the world.

Correspondingly, their urban compatriots, if unskilled, are also unprecedentedly thrust into greater competition from an emerging global pool of cheap, increasingly fungible laborers. This competition is heightened by the Soviet Bloc's collapse (itself another manifestation of the forces of global integration) and, with it, the unfettering of vast numbers of low-wage, high-skill workers. Perhaps compounding this economic volatility is the uncertainty created by recent developments in science and technology. The shrinking of industrial employment is altering the demand curve for unskilled labor. Even if current recessionary trends give way to high growth in the future, the long-term result is not likely to be a significant upswing in the number of low-skill factory jobs throughout the world.

The trend in modern manufacturing is toward smaller, more flexible, less labor-intensive operations that are situated near customers. Such technology diminishes the need for unskilled labor. Hence, for many marginalized, illiterate workers, the future holds little promise of a *job* at all. Instead, they will search out *diverse and multiple livelihood activities* (e.g., small-scale gardening, hawking, food processing, and casual labor) which collectively furnish the wherewithal to survive.

FOUR PILLARS OF EDUCATION FOR THE 21ST CENTURY

The idea about the four pillars of education wa expressed in *Learning: the Treasure Within,* the report to UNESCO of the

International Commission on Education for the Twenty-first Century. Simply speaking, the Commission felt that education throughout life is based upon four pillars: learning to know, learning to do, learning to live together and learning to be.

These four pillars of knowledge cannot be anchored solely in one phase in a person's life or in a single place. There is a need to re-think when in people's lives education should be provided, and the fields that such education should cover. The periods and fields should complement each other and be interrelated in such a way that all people can get the most out of their own specific educational environment all through their lives.

Learning to know

This type of learning is concerned less with the acquisition of structured knowledge than with the mastery of learning tools. It may be regarded as both a means and an end of human existence. Looking at it as a means, people have to learn to understand the world around them, at least as much as is necessary for them to lead their lives with some dignity, develop their occupational skills and communicate with other people. Regarded as an end, it is underpinned by the pleasure that can be derived from understanding, knowledge and discovery. That aspect of learning is typically enjoyed by researchers, but good teaching can help everyone to enjoy it.

Even if study for its own sake is a dying pursuit with so much emphasis now being put on the acquisition of marketable skills, the raising of the school-leaving age and an increase in leisure time should provide more and more adults with opportunities for private study. The broader our knowledge, the better we can understand the many different aspects of our environment. Such study encourages greater intellectual curiosity, sharpens the critical faculties and enables people to develop their own independent judgements on the world around them. From that point of view, all children - no matter where they live - must have a chance to receive an appropriate science education and become friends of science throughout their lives.

However, since knowledge is multifarious and capable of virtually infinite development, any attempt to know everything becomes more and more pointless. In fact, after the basic education stage, the idea of being a multi-subject specialist is simply an illusion. The initial secondary and university curricula are therefore partly designed around scientific disciplines with the aim of giving students the tools, ideas and reference methods which are the product of leading-edge science and the contemporary paradigms.

Such specialization must not exclude general education - not even for future researchers who will work in specialized laboratories. A truly educated person nowadays needs a broad general education and the opportunity to study a small number of subjects in depth. This two-pronged approach should be applied right through education. The reason is that general education, which gives pupils a chance to learn other languages and become familiar with other subjects, first and foremost provides a way of communicating with other people. If specialists rarely set foot outside their own scientific circle, they are likely to lose interest in what other people are doing.

Regardless of the circumstances, they will find working with others a problem. On the other hand, general education, which forges spatial and temporal links between societies, tends to make people more receptive to other branches of knowledge. While the history of science is written by historians, scientists find it useful. By the same token, lawyers, sociologists and political scientists increasingly need basic economics. Lastly, some breakthroughs in the advancement of human knowledge occur at the interface of different specializations.

Learning to know implies learning how to learn by developing one's concentration, memory skills and ability to think. From infancy, young people must learn how to concentrate - on objects and on other people. This process of improving concentration skills can take different forms and can be aided by the many different learning opportunities that arise in the course of people's lives (games, work experience programmes, travel, practical science activities, etc.).

The development of memory skills is an excellent tool for countering the overpowering stream of instant information put out by the media. It would be dangerous to conclude that there is no point in people's improving their memory skills because of the vast amount of information storage and distribution capacity available. While some selectivity is undoubtedly required when choosing facts to be "learned by heart", there are numerous examples of the human memory's ability to outperform computers when it comes to establishing connections between memorized facts that apparently have very little to do with each other. The specifically human ability of associative memorization is not something that can be reduced to an automatic process; it has to be carefully cultivated. Furthermore, specialists in this field agree that memory skills have to be developed from infancy and that it is dangerous to discontinue various traditional exercises in schools simply because they are considered to be boring.

Thinking is something children learn first from their parents and then from their teachers. The process should encompass both practical problem-solving and abstract thought. Both education and research should therefore combine deductive and inductive reasoning, which are often claimed to be opposing processes. While one form of reasoning may be more appropriate than the other, depending on the subjects being taught, it is generally impossible to pursue a logical train of thought without combining the two. The process of learning to think is a lifelong one and can be enhanced by every kind of human experience. In this respect, as people's work becomes less routine, they will find that their thinking skills are increasingly being challenged at their place of work.

Learning to do

This question is closely associated with the issue of occupational training: how do we adapt education so that it can equip people to do the types of work needed in the future? Here we should draw a distinction between industrial economies, where most people are wage-earners, and other economies where self-employment or casual work are still the norm.

In societies where most people are in paid employment, which have developed throughout the Twentieth century based on the industrial model, automation is making this model increasingly "intangible". It emphasizes the knowledge component of tasks, even in industry, as well as the importance of services in the economy. The future of these economies hinges on their ability to turn advances in knowledge into innovations that will generate new businesses and new jobs. "Learning to do" can no longer mean what it did when people were trained to perform a very specific physical task in a manufacturing process. Skill training therefore has to evolve and become more than just a means of imparting the knowledge needed to do a more or less routine job.

From certified skills to personal competence

The major part played by knowledge and information in manufacturing industry renders obsolete the notion of specialist skills on the part of the workforce. The key concept now is one of "personal competence". Technological progress inevitably changes the job skills required by the new production processes. Purely physical tasks are being replaced by tasks with a greater intellectual or cerebral content such as the operation, maintenance and monitoring of machines and design and organizational tasks, as the machines themselves become more intelligent.

There are several reasons for this increase in skill requirements at all levels. Instead of being organized to perform specified tasks in juxtaposition in accordance with Taylor's principles of scientific labour organization, manufacturing workers are often divided into work teams or project groups on the Japanese model. This approach represents a departure from the idea of dividing labour into similar physical tasks which are essentially learned by repetition. Furthermore, the idea of personalized tasks is taking over from that of employee interchangeability. There is a growing trend among employers to evaluate potential employees in terms of their personal competence rather than certified skills which they see as merely demonstrating the ability to perform specific physical tasks. This personal competence is assessed by looking at a mix of skills and talents, combining certified skills acquired through technical and vocational training, social behaviour, personal initiative and a willingness to take risks.

If we add a demand for personal commitment on the part of employees in their role as change agents, it is clear that this kind of personal competence involves highly subjective innate or acquired qualities, often referred to as "people skills" or "interpersonal skills" by employers, combined with knowledge and other job skills. Of these qualities, communication, team and problem-solving skills are assuming greater importance. The growth of the service industries has resulted in an increase in this trend.

The shift away from physical work - the service industries

In advanced economies there is a shift away from physical work. The implications of this trend for education are even clearer if we look at the development of the service industries in both quantitative and qualitative terms. Most of the active population (60 - 80 per cent) of the industrialized countries is employed in the service sector. The main defining characteristic of this extremely broad category is that it covers activities which are neither industrial nor agricultural and which, despite their diversity, do not involve any tangible product.

Many services are defined primarily in terms of the interpersonal relationship involved. Examples of this are found both in the rapidly expanding private service sector which is benefiting from the growing complexity of economies (every kind of expertise imaginable, security services or high-tech consultancy services, financial, accounting and management services) and in the more traditional public sector (social services, health and education services, etc.). In both these cases, information and communication play a vital role. The key aspect here is the personalized acquisition and processing of specific data for a clearly defined project. In this type of service, both the provider and the user influence the quality of the relationship between them. Clearly, people can no longer be trained for this sort of work in the same way as they learned how to plough the land or make a sheet of steel. These new jobs are about interpersonal relationships; workers' relationships with the materials and processes they are using are secondary. The growing service sector needs people with good social and communication skills - skills that are not necessarily taught at school or university.

Lastly, in the ultra high-tech organizations of the future, where relational inadequacies might cause serious dysfunctions, new types of skills will be required, with an interpersonal rather than intellectual basis. This may provide an opportunity for people with few or no formal educational qualifications. Intuition, common sense, judgement and leadership skills are not confined to highly qualified people. How and where are these more or less innate skills to be taught? The problem is akin to that raised by the idea of vocational training in developing countries. Educational content simply cannot be inferred from a statement of the skills or abilities required for specific tasks.

Work in the informal economy

The nature of work is very different in the economies of

developing countries where most people are not wage-earners. In many sub-Saharan African countries and some Latin American and Asian countries, only a small proportion of the population is in paid employment. The vast majority works in the traditional subsistence economy, where specific job qualifications are not required and where know-how is the fruit of tacit knowledge. For this reason, education cannot simply be modelled on the types of education that seem to fit the bill in post-industrial societies. Besides, the function of learning is not confined to work; it should meet the wider aim of achieving formal or informal participation in development. This often involves social skills as much as occupational skills.

In other developing countries, a thriving unofficial modern economy based on trade and finance may exist alongside a small official economic sector and agriculture. This parallel economy indicates the existence of business communities capable of meeting local requirements. In both these cases, there is no point in providing the population with high-cost training (since the teachers and the educational resources have to come from abroad) either in conventional industrial skills or in advanced technology. On the contrary, education should be brought into endogenous development by strengthening local potential and the spirit of empowerment. We then have to address a question that applies to both developed and developing countries: how do people learn to act appropriately in an uncertain situation, how do they become involved in shaping the future?

How can people be prepared to innovate?

This question is being asked in developing and developed countries. It basically comes down to knowing how to develop personal initiative. Paradoxically, the richest countries are sometimes restrained in this respect by the excessively coded and formal way they are organized, particularly as regards their educational systems, and by a certain fear of risk-taking which may be engendered by the rationalization of their economic model. Undoubtedly, sport, club membership and artistic and cultural activities are more successful than the traditional school systems at providing this kind of training. The discovery of other societies through study and travel may encourage such behaviour. From this point of view in particular, a great deal may be learned by observing the economies of developing countries.

In all countries, lastly, the growing importance of small groups, networking and partnerships highlights the likelihood that excellent interpersonal skills will be an essential job requirement from now on. What is more, the new working patterns, whether in industry or in the service sector, will call for the intensive application of information, knowledge and creativity. All things considered, the new forms of personal competence are based on a body of theoretical and practical knowledge combined with personal dynamism and good problem-solving, decision-making, innovative and team skills.

Learning to live together

Violence all too often dominates life in the contemporary world, forming a depressing contrast with the hope which some people have been able to place in human progress. Human history has constantly been scarred by conflicts, but the risk is heightened by two new elements. Firstly, there is the extraordinary potential for self- destruction created by humans in the twentieth century. Then, we have the ability of the new media to provide the entire world with information and unverifiable reports on ongoing conflicts. Public opinion becomes a helpless observer or even a hostage of those who initiate or keep up the conflicts. Until now education has been unable to do much to mitigate this situation. Can we do better? Can we educate ourselves to avoid conflict or peacefully resolve it?

While the idea of teaching non-violence in schools is certainly praiseworthy, it seems quite inadequate if we look at what is really involved. The challenge is a difficult one since people have a natural tendency to overestimate their own abilities or those of the group to which they belong and to entertain prejudices against other people. Moreover, the general climate of competition that prevails in both domestic and international economies tends to turn competitiveness and personal success into modern values. In fact, this competitiveness is nowadays translated into a relentless economic war and a tension between rich and poor that breaks apart nations and the world and exacerbates historic rivalries. Regrettably, with its incorrect interpretation of what is meant by competition, education sometimes helps to sustain this state of affairs.

How can we do better? Experience shows that it is not enough to set up contacts and communication between people who are liable to come into conflict to reduce this risk (for example, in inter-racial or inter-denominational schools). If the different groups are rivals or if they do not have the same status in the same geographical area, such contact may have the opposite effect to that desired - it may bring out hidden tensions and degenerate into an opportunity for conflict. If, on the other hand, this kind of contact is organized in an egalitarian setting and common aims and projects are pursued, the prejudices and latent hostility may give way to a more relaxed form of co-operation, or even friendship.

The conclusion would seem to be that education should adopt two complementary approaches. From early childhood, it should focus on the discovery of other people in the first stage of education. In the second stage of education and in lifelong education, it should encourage involvement in common projects. This seems to be an effective way of avoiding conflict or resolving latent conflicts.

Discovering other people

One of education's tasks is both to teach pupils and students about human diversity and to instil in them an awareness of the similarities and interdependence of all people. From early childhood, the school should seize every opportunity to pursue this two-pronged approach. Some subjects lend themselves to this - human geography in basic education, foreign languages and literature later on.

Moreover, whether education is provided by the family, the community or the school, children should be taught to understand other people's reactions by looking at things from their point of view. Where this spirit of empathy is encouraged in schools, it has a positive effect on young persons' social behaviour for the rest of their lives. For example, teaching youngsters to look at the world through the eyes of other ethnic or religious groups is a way of avoiding some of the misunderstandings that give rise to hatred and violence among adults. Thus, teaching the history of religions or customs can provide a useful reference tool for moulding future behaviour.

Lastly, recognition of the rights of other people should not be jeopardized by the way children and young people are taught. Teachers who are so dogmatic that they stifle curiosity or healthy criticism instead of teaching their pupils how to engage in lively debate can do more harm than good. Forgetting that they are putting themselves across as models, they may, because of their attitude, inflict lifelong harm on their pupils in terms of the latter's openness to other people and their ability to face up to the inevitable tensions between individuals, groups and nations. One of the essential tools for education in the twenty-first century will be a suitable forum for dialogue and discussion.

Towards common goals

When people work together on exciting projects which involve them in unaccustomed forms of action, differences and even conflicts between individuals tend to pale and sometimes disappear. A new form of identity is created by these projects which enable people to transcend the routines of their personal lives and attach value to what they have in common as against what divides them. In sport, for example, the tensions between social classes or nationalities can eventually be welded into a spirit of solidarity by the commitment to a common cause. In the world of work, too, so many achievements would not have been possible if people had not successfully moved beyond the conflicts that generally arise in hierarchical organizations through their involvement in a common project.

Formal education should therefore set aside sufficient time and opportunity in its curricula to introduce young people to collaborative projects from an early age as part of their sports or cultural activities. But this approach should also get them involved in social activities: the renovation of slum areas, help for disadvantaged people, humanitarian action, senior citizen help schemes and so on. Other educational organizations should take over these activities from the schools. Another point is that, in everyday school life, the involvement of teachers and pupils in common projects can help to teach a method for resolving conflicts and provide a valuable source of reference for pupils in later life.

Learning to be

At its very first meeting, the Commission powerfully re-asserted a fundamental principle: education should contribute to every person's complete development - mind and body, intelligence, sensitivity, aesthetic appreciation and spirituality. All people should receive in their childhood and youth an education that equips them to develop their own independent, critical way of thinking and judgement so that they can make up their own minds on the best courses of action in the different circumstances in their lives.

In this respect, the Commission embraces one of the basic assumptions stated in the report Learning to Be:. the aim of development is the complete fulfilment of man, in all the richness of his personality, the complexity of his forms of expression and his various commitments - as individual, member of a family and of a community, citizen and producer, inventor of techniques and creative dreamer'.

This human development, which begins at birth and continues all through a person's life, is a dialectic process which is based both on self-knowledge and on relationships with other people. It also presupposes successful personal experience. As a means of personality training, education should be a highly individualized process and at the same time an interactive social experience.

In its Preamble, the report Learning to Be expressed the fear of dehumanization of the world, associated with technical progress and one of its main messages was that education should enable each person >to be able to solve his own problems, make his own decisions and shoulder his own responsibilities.' Since then, all progress in different societies, particularly the staggering increase in media power, has intensified those fears and made the imperative that they underpin even more legitimate. This dehumanization may increase in the twenty-first century. Rather than educating children for a given society, the challenge will be to ensure that everyone always has the personal resources and intellectual tools needed to understand the world and behave as a fair-minded, responsible human being. More than ever before, the essential task of education seems to be to make sure that all people enjoy the freedom of thought, judgement, feeling and imagination to develop their talents and keep control of as much of their lives as they can.

This is not simply a cry for individualism. Recent experience has shown that what could appear merely as a personal defence mechanism against an alienating system or a system perceived to be hostile, also offered the best opportunity for making social progress. Personality differences, independence and personal initiative or even a task for upsetting the established order are the best guarantees of creativity and innovation. The rejection of imported high-tech models, the harnessing of traditional implied forms of knowledge and empowerment are effective factors in endogenous development. New methods have evolved from experiments at local community level. Their effectiveness in reducing violence or combating various social problems is widely recognized.

In a highly unstable world where one of the main driving forces seems to be economic and social innovation, imagination and creativity must undoubtedly be accorded a special place. As the clearest expressions of human freedom, they may be threatened by the establishment of a certain degree of uniformity in individual behaviour. The twenty-first century will need a varied range of talents and personalities even more than exceptionally gifted individuals, who are equally essential in any society. Both children and young persons should be offered every opportunity for aesthetic, artistic, scientific, cultural and social discovery and experimentation, which will complete the attractive presentation of the achievements of previous generations or their contemporaries in these fields. At school, art and poetry should take a much more important place than they are given in many countries by an education that has become more utilitarian than cultural. Concern with developing the imagination and creativity should also restore the value of oral culture and knowledge drawn from children's or adults' experiences.

NEW SKILLS FOR A NEW WORLD

Globalization, seen from the perspective of the poor, the marginalized, and those who daily struggle to meet their basic human needs, offers not an open-ended opportunity but an ill-defined threat. A skill-poor labor pool encourages global employers to search transnationally for productive people. But with such searches comes the possibility of wrenching dislocations. Migration and increased participation in the informal or illegal economy may be the survival strategy of choice for millions. But such choices do not constitute viable policy options for governments. As Kanter notes, "If security no longer comes automatically with being employed, then it must come from being *employable*.

Employability security rests on the knowledge that competence is growing to meet tomorrow's challenges...." As gaps between experience levels and wages narrow around the world, workers will require a new and different kind of preparation for employment. It is clear from the foregoing that changes in the emerging workplace make the attainment of higher-order skills a *sine qua non* for long-term employment prospects. But can this analysis be extended to cover other kinds of participation opportunities? Have flexibility, collaborativeness, adaptability, and strong problem-solving skills also become critical prerequisites for effective civic participation, community development, environmental responsibility, and the rearing of sound and strong families? In his discussion of the conditions that make for effective civic participation, Boggs makes three salient observations which strongly suggest that at least with respect to citizenship in a democratic society, such cognitive skills are indeed essential to effective behavior.

— First, he argues, meaningful participation is *context specific*. Debates over such issues as taxes, schooling, leadership, reform, and service provision are deeply rooted in the ongoing, changing lives of adult citizens.

— Second, the knowledge that adults need to address or influence these issues is at the same time both *continually expanding* and *incomplete*. Weekly, if not daily, there are developments in key issues that challenge the capacity of citizens to respond with understanding and competence.

— Third, understanding the political environment requires engagement with it. Because the conditions are dynamic, they cannot be fully comprehended until engagement takes place. Civic knowledge comes out of the interplay between reflection and action.

These same observations can be applied readily to the intersection of worker and workplace. There, too, task engagement is essential to mastery. Likewise, workplace skills are becoming increasingly context-specific. And, whether on the job or at the polling place, essential knowledge requirements continue to expand, because technological development remains forever incomplete. In his exploration of what democracy means in an information age, Boyte takes such observations a step further. His thesis is that effective citizenship is predicated upon the ability of individuals to gain access to information of all kinds and to use such information effectively. As information proliferates, it becomes increasingly difficult for the average citizen to both collect and assess all the relevant data.

Unlike those in school or the workplace, interactions among citizens in a democracy are, relatively speaking, transactions among equals. As such, no single individual has binding authority over another. The onus rests on every citizen to draw inferences from and act upon information as an independent agent. In short, as democratic institutions proliferate around the world, citizens must, within the realm of their civic lives, increasingly confront ill-defined and novel problems much as they do in the world of work. The dynamics of participation opportunities related to promoting family development or protecting the environment are similar to those that govern civic and workplace participation. New insights abound about how children grow, develop, and learn.

In turn, these new understandings have given rise to a redefinition of essential parenting skills. And, as anyone who has ever reared a child can attest, parenting wisely is the quintessential and constant art of responding to novel situations with effective problem-solving skills. Likewise, our understanding of the earth's fragility expands exponentially. Fortunately, at the same time that sensitivity to this issue is heightened, so, too, is our understanding of the actions that individuals can take to sustain the earth's bounty. Many of these actions, however, are predicated on sophisticated knowledge, problem diagnosis skills, and an ability to predict the long-term consequences of behaviors.

Thinking to learn, learning to think

If we are willing to accept the notion of human capacity development as *the byproduct of participation opportunities that are both available and accessed* and, if we see such participation opportunities as *productive* interactions which allow individuals to contribute to the development of their nations, communities, and families, then three conclusions are inescapable.

— Accessing existing participation opportunities and creating new ones in an environment of rapid change, information proliferation, and globalization will require that individuals function at higher levels of learning, thinking, and doing.

— The need for these higher-order skills is not just confined to the requirements of the workplace. On the contrary, effective participation in *each* of the four major domains of productive interaction—family life, livelihood, environment, and civic affairs—will increasingly call for these competencies.

— Human capacity development, depends upon enabling large numbers of children, women, and men to acquire

1. specific content in relation to a range of participation opportunities, and
2. specific cognitive strategies for achieving higher levels of thinking and problem solving in these content areas.

Embedded in these conclusions is an important message: *what* one knows as well as *how* one knows are both of paramount importance. Citizens, workers, and parents must rise above rote, factual levels of information processing. Critical, flexible and creative thinking will assume an ever-greater primacy as individuals confront a growing number of problems that are ambiguous, ill structured and unfamiliar. Indeed, the growth of problems that individuals will encounter and for which they have little or no first-hand information is a consequence of globalization which brings us into contact with the hitherto unknown on a regular basis. Preparing citizens—be they children or adults—to develop high-order skills is an unprecedented challenge. No nation has ever tried to educate all its citizens to be higher-order thinkers.

Schools often perform in ways that defeat the development of necessary cognitive competencies for life in a global era. For example, schools teach skills and theoretical principles that are supposed to be generalizable and transferrable. Yet, in the so-called "real world," people generally need situation-specific forms of competence. Schools focus on mastery by the individual. Yet, in the world of work, tasks—both mental and physical—are often shared. Schools promote "tool-less" thought. In contrast, outside school, mental work frequently relies on cognitive tools. Schools emphasize symbolic thinking; real-life mental activity, on the other hand, calls for direct engagement with objects and situations.

This disjuncture between life in and out of school sharply diminishes the transferability of knowledge across environments, settings, and contexts. Yet, such transferability is critical in an era of rapid change. Transfer reflects learning through observation, rule making, and definition. It involves the application of old knowledge in a setting sufficiently novel so that, in effect, it becomes new knowledge. Increasingly, the field of cognitive science is shedding important insights on how knowledge transfer occurs and the conditions that facilitate it. Essentially, the more varied the kinds of problems learners confront, and the more they have to think to solve them, the greater the chances are that when new real-life problems are encountered, transfer of skills or knowledge to the new situation will occur. This insight is the key to a vision of the future in which the development of higher-order skills might become the paramount goal of all schooling and structured learning programs.

In such a future, notions about teaching, guiding, learning, and intelligence would be reshaped, and relationships among learners, the community and its institutions would be reconstituted. Given the potential contribution of cognitive science to human capacity development, it is worth spending a bit of time to understand a few of the field's over-arching concepts.

Cognitive scientists view the world as a series of *task environments*, or problems and settings in which individuals encounter the problem. A *problem* is what happens when a person wants something but does not know immediately what actions must be undertaken to get what is wanted. In each problem there is an *initial state* and a *goal state* (what the person wants). As people solve problems, they determine how to move from the initial state to the goal state. Most problems that occur in ordinary life have many viable solutions. There is no single correct way to perform many jobs (particularly knowledge-based jobs), raise children, bring about community betterment, or ensure the sustainability of planetary resources. Such tasks are called *ill-defined problems* by cognitive scientists. Clarity about what constitutes an adequate solution comes only after problem solving is begun.

The discipline of cognitive science is a promising vehicle for promoting human capacity development in low-income countries. This assertion stems from the major finding associated with cognitive science research: It is possible to facilitate a learner's development by helping that individual build better rules to solve problems. People can be assisted, through explicit instruction, to develop schemas that influence what they notice, recall, and remember. They can learn how to encode information and remember it in appropriate ways. This, in turn, allows them to construct more useful initial representations of problems they seek to solve.

In the 1980s, cognitive science researchers started to observe that there were "intelligent novices," people who learned new fields and solved novel problems more expertly than most, regardless of how much specific knowledge they possessed. These people controlled and monitored their thought processes and made use of general and domain-specific skills in appropriate ways. The conclusion that emerged from this work is that there is more to expert performance than domain-specific knowledge and skills. Indeed, the evidence suggests the existence of thinking skills related to specific domains that can account for differences among individuals in their problem-solving abilities.

Such thinking skills might include ways to organize and evaluate information, techniques for selecting relevant facts, and strategies for comparing and contrasting a concept newly learned to one that is well understood. Since the ability to activate prior knowledge enhances understanding and retention, learners might receive explicit instruction in how to access what they already know and connect it to what they are about to learn (a technique called *elaboration*). Other specific skills that might be taught include planning; possibility mapping; means-ends analysis; fact assembly; problem contextualization; problem representation; and problem definition.

Metacognitive instruction would also address the abilities of learners to plan, classify, think divergently, identify assumptions, recognize misleading information, and generate questions. Metacognition refers to an individual's ability to think about thinking. It involves being consciously aware of one's role as a problem solver and describes an ability to monitor and control one's mental processing. It is distinct from such other cognitive skills as demonstration of effective memory, the ability to perform defined tasks, or the use of generic strategies for solving new problems. The individual who exemplifies strong metacognition is one who easily moves from one high-order function in a particular domain to an understanding of functions in another domain.

Metacognition is qualitatively different from general thinking and problem-solving skills. A metacognitively aware person is one who can monitor comprehension while undertaking a learning project. In contrast, the poor learner is often unaware that there is a mastery problem and, hence, is unable to take steps to overcome it. In addition to the ability to predict the results of one's own problem-solving actions, basic metacognitive development includes skills that enable individuals to check the results of their own actions, to track their progress toward a solution, and to gauge the reasonableness of their actions and solutions against some larger reality. Although learners might first develop these skills in the context of some specific subject matter, once learned, they can be applied to other learning situations.

However, take note of the caveat: such transfer will occur *only* if the learner has also been helped to understand and internalize the notion that the skills may be usefully applied in other learning situations. In other words, explicit teaching is required for general learning or problem-solving skills to be transferred to new domains. With such teaching, transfer occurs. Absent this instruction, little transfer takes place. A key to enabling learners to use metacognitive strategies effectively is helping them select which strategies are most appropriate for specific settings. Learners need to know in a context-rooted way which strategies will work and what makes particular strategies especially effective in specific settings. Research shows that learners will transfer a metacognitive strategy to a new situation if they understand why it works and the circumstances under which it can help them to learn.

In recent years, researchers have begun to combine the teaching of thinking skills with instruction in specific content areas. The results of this combination, the *new synthesis*, have been very encouraging. The term "new synthesis" has been coined to convey the need to fuse mastery of domain-specific subject matter and thinking skills with general thinking skills and techniques for controlling one's own thinking and learning. What is novel about the new synthesis is that it suggests a need to be as concerned with *how* we teach as with *what* we teach. As Bruer notes, "... if we can apply the new synthesis in the classroom, we should be able to teach school subjects as high-order cognitive skills and help [students] become intelligent novices and expert learners."

The "new synthesis" suggests that domain-specific skills and knowledge, along with an ability to think about one's own thinking and general learning strategies, are all elements of expert performance and intelligence. The basis for this conclusion is that in many different studies, it was precisely this combination of high-order skills that intelligent novices used to apply knowledge flexibly and solve ill-structured, novel problems. General programs designed to teach broad-based problem-solving skills are ineffective. It is probably impossible to make people better general-problem solvers. On the other hand, according to the latest work by cognitive scientists, it is possible to teach *general* problem-solving and information-processing skills within the framework of *specific* content and domains.

As Siegler observes, "... much of the task of education in problem solving may be to identify the encoding [strategies] that we would like people to have on specific problems, and then to devise instructional methods to help them attain it." While studies suggest that the teaching of general-thinking and problem-solving skills contributes little to improved student performance, it is also clear that curricula which merely transmit facts are not a better alternative. Research indicates that the transfer of problem-solving strategies to new contexts relates to what the problem is about and how familiar learners are with that content. The more they know about a particular domain, the more likely learners are to use a general memory strategy.

As Bruer notes, "Strategies can help us process knowledge, but first we have to have the knowledge to process,". As we have seen, then, most cognitive scientists believe that domain-specific knowledge and problem-solving methods intimately related to specific domains are the bases of expertise and intelligence. But, how does an individual acquire *new* *knowledge*? Over the last thirty years, there has been a widening acceptance of the notion that learning is the process of knowledge *construction*. Such construction, however, is itself knowledge dependent. In other words, new knowledge is the elaboration and extension of previously acquired knowledge. The acquisition of this knowledge is intimately connected to a *situation* which enables individuals to embed learning in an organizing structure. As individuals actively interpret—rather than record—information, they construct new knowledge for themselves. Such construction occurs within a web of social interactions.

Scaffolding is an important idea derived from Vygotsky's theories. The term conveys the image of an adjustable and temporary support that can be removed when no longer needed by the learner. It refers to the practice of providing learners with ample support during the early stages of learning and then diminishing this assistance as they become competent to take on increased responsibility for task performance. In metacognitive instruction scaffolding occurs as the role of "critic" is transferred in stages from the teacher to the learner. Historically, apprenticeship models of learning adopted similar strategies through modeling, scaffolding, and by making critical skills explicit and overt. Thus, scaffolding evokes the training mechanisms, pedagogical strategies, and instructional techniques that master practitioners use to assist learners in becoming full-fledged members of communities of practice.

Unfortunately, in conventional formal instructional settings, content all too frequently tends to obscure or overwhelm the learning strategy and thus render the scaffolding invisible. In recent years, the cognitive apprenticeship model of learning has begun to influence instructional practice in a number of countries. In settings where the model is used, teaching methods give learners the chance to observe, engage in, and invent or discover expert (as opposed to novice) strategies in context. Modeling, coaching and scaffolding are the core of cognitive apprenticeship; they help learners acquire an integrated set of skills. Guided practice and reflection are methods, within the cognitive apprenticeship framework, that help learners to focus their observations of expert problem solving and to gain conscious access to their own problem-solving strategies.

Exploration, another technique employed within this framework, encourages learner autonomy, not only in carrying out expert problem-solving processes, but also in formulating the problems to be solved. Overall, the approach is intended to help learners make generalizations about new skills and to foster the transfer of such skills to novel contexts. This is done by identifying the processes within a task, making them transparent to learners, and by situating abstract tasks in authentic contexts so that the relevance of the task is apparent. Learners work at problem solving by actively sharing skills and expertise. The cognitive apprenticeship model also thrusts learners into diverse situations where they are helped to articulate common aspects of the specific task setting in order to maximize the transfer of learning to new settings. Transfer of knowledge is accomplished by unbinding it from a single specific context.

Towards Science of Learning for Participation Across the Lifespan

The cognitive apprenticeship framework reflects a growing, research-based understanding that high-order skills require extensive domain knowledge, a grasp of when this knowledge should be used, and the ability to engage in metacognitive monitoring and control. Citizens who achieve these capabilities can solve novel, ambiguous problems. The framework also suggests that when teaching for transfer, the learning facilitator must not only provide many examples of a new concept, but also show how essential features of the concept are reflected in a range of settings. The cognitive apprenticeship model, Vygotsky's theories about the importance of socially constructed knowledge, and our growing understanding of how metacognitive strategies promote learning transfer are all major developments that, if harnessed creatively, can help vulnerable populations flourish in rapidly changing, globalizing, information-based societies.

However, one might well ask, "Do these ideas have any relevance for the kind of lifelong, continuous learning that adults need to pursue? Or, is their applicability limited to the education of children in classroom settings?" To respond meaningfully to these queries we need to examine the skills and knowledge that are essential to accessing those participation opportunities that are at the heart of human capacity development: the opportunity to participate in activities that will yield an adequate income; the opportunity to participate in and exert influence on civic affairs and community development; the opportunity to protect and sustain environmental quality; as well as the opportunity to promote family development. We also need to determine whether models developed primarily to improve the learning of children have any applicability to adults.

Within the adult education literature there is general support for the idea that teaching adults requires different methodological approaches from those used in educational settings that address the needs of children and adolescents. Nevertheless, in the last few years the chasm between adult and non-adult education appears to be narrowing as the *socio-constructivist* theories of education—a fusion of recent developments in cognitive science and the work of such psychologists as Vygotsky—gain currency. Another reason for a crumbling of the walls between the two fields is that the views of Malcolm Knowles, once the most cogent proponent of a distinction between adult and non-adult education, have evolved.

Knowles originally contrasted *andragogical* (learner-centered) methods with *pedagogical* (teacher-centered) ones and held that andragogical approaches were better suited for adults. His assertion rested on the following assumptions:

1. adults are generally self-directing;
2. adults have a rich array of experiences that can serve as learning resources;
3. adult learning is usually influenced by the learner's self-

defined need and intrinsic motivation to acquire knowledge in order to solve specific problems or meet specific needs. In light of this "needs-driven" audience, Knowles concluded that adult education lends itself readily to a problem—rather than a subject matter—orientation.

Since he first proposed these distinctions, Knowles has gradually moderated his position regarding the differences between adult and younger learners. What he once viewed as unique characteristics of older learners, he now acknowledges as innate tendencies in all human beings. Such tendencies, he notes, manifest themselves as individuals mature. This methodological bridging between older and younger learners can also be seen in the more recent literature about how adults can be helped to develop new skills, knowledge, and behaviors. Increasingly, there are references to the notion that adult education should exemplify collaborative and participatory learning. This is characterized by interactions in which both facilitators and adults are active participants in the learning process.

The intent is to eliminate the hierarchy between facilitators and learners while creating a sense of community. In this collaborative model, knowledge is constructed rather than transferred. Furthermore, knowledge is considered to be found within the community rather than in the individual. The basic assumption undergirding collaborative learning is that knowledge is best constructed in a social context by communities of individuals. Furthermore, the shaping and testing of ideas is a process in which anyone can participate. Because learning is significantly enhanced when new knowledge is created, transmitted, and shaped by group activities, the facilitator's role as a source of authority is significantly diminished.

This model involves a departure from the traditional view of learners. In collaborative learning settings, adults function as problem solvers, contributors, and analytic discussants. As participants grow to accept the view that learning should be *interactive*, the emphasis shifts from competition to collaboration with peers. Adults are assisted in developing the skills they need to learn *interdependently* rather than *independently*. A number of theoretical benefits are associated with this collaborative learning approach. The setting is considered to provide an environment for democratic planning, decision making, and risk taking as participants develop insights into the power and potential of groups as well as the interdependence of their members.

As individuals develop better judgment through the exposure and resolution of previously unshared biases, they also develop self-confidence which has long been considered essential to such risk-taking behavior as the adoption of new technologies. Finally, the model enables adults to develop metacognitively by giving them both a framework and encouragement to tap into previous experiences and knowledge. To date, there has been little research regarding the efficacy of the collaborative learning model in adult education settings, despite strong theoretical support for its premises. The view proposed herein is that the essence of such development is an individual's ability to access and create (either directly or indirectly) available participation opportunities. This means that to promote human capacity development we must know a great deal about the specific knowledge and skills needed to access and create participation opportunities *at different stages in an individual's life.*

The distinctions between *pedagogy* and *andragogy* are not helpful to understanding more about human capacity development for two important reasons. Neither term conveys any specifics with regard to the *content* to be acquired by learners. The terms pave the way for establishing a false dichotomy with respect to how individuals become more competent by overstating differences between older and younger learners. As the trends of globalization and information cascade manifest themselves with increasing vigor, the need to help citizens gain the skills required to transfer knowledge and solve novel problems grows. We cannot afford to mislabel processes that will result in a misapplication of resources.

We, therefore, propose the creation of a new learning science, *partagogy*. Its primary focus is to help individuals develop the skills and knowledge they need to access available participation opportunities and create new ones over the course of their lifespans. The participation opportunities with which partagogy concerns itself are related to four core domains of human behavior and national development: family life; livelihood; civic affairs; and environmental stewardship.

Table 1: Partagogy's four core domains

Core domains:	The ability of individuals to...
Family Life	secure the conditions that they and their fellow family members require to realize their innate potential.
Livelihood	create and manage a portfolio of activities which yields adequate income, at a minimum, to meet basic standards.
Civic Affairs	contribute to and meaningfully influence the discussion, debat, and resolution of issues that concern either a local community or some broader unit of civil society.
Environmental Stewardship	protect natural resources and maintain biodiversity by conserving, improving, and properly managing air, water, and soil quality.

Partagogy is inextricably tied to a particular view of human capacity (as opposed to human *resource)* development. This view holds human capacity development to be the byproduct of participation opportunities that are both available and accessed. Available participation opportunities represent the set of inputs that lead to human capacity development. The output of human capacity development can be expressed as the sum of those participation opportunities accessed by individuals; and the new participation opportunities created in the course of such engagements. Partagogy, unlike andragogy or pedagogy, has both a methodological foundation and a content basis.

YOUNG CHILDREN AND THE POTENTIAL TO PARTICIPATE

A country's level of human capacity development is reflected in the predisposition and ability of its citizens to *access* and *create* opportunities for earning a living, promoting family development, protecting the environment, and participating in civic affairs. How and when are such predispositions and abilities developed? A compelling body of research suggests that many of the differences between individuals in terms of their *participation behaviors* can be explained by what happens to them very early in life. Even before birth, factors are already in play that will shape—for better or for worse—an individual's potential to take advantage of existing participation opportunities or create new ones.

Child development is a dynamic and interactive process. Infants and young children who enjoy psychosocial support, adequate nutrition, good health, and cognitive stimulation (the necessary prerequisites for child development) are likely to actively explore their environments and engage their caregivers in developmentally beneficial interactions. Studies of youngsters enrolled in early childhood development programs that provide these necessary ingredients indicate that the effects of such a "package" are both long lasting and profound. The most ambitious of these investigations is the High/Scope Perry Preschool Study which has followed a population of disadvantaged, African-American preschool graduates for over 20 years along with a matched control population that did not have the preschool experience.

The initial treatment consisted of exposure to a cognitive development curriculum as well as home visits designed to improve parenting skills. The latest findings, obtained when the cohort had reached age 27, reveal significant differences between the two groups in three of the four major participation opportunity domains. The graduates had higher employment rates, were less likely to start a family as teenagers, were more likely to enter into marriage, and less likely to commit crimes. Other researchers have found strong and positive relationships between the quality of a child's early development experiences and primary school performance. Participation in comprehensive programs that include health, nutrition, and cognitive stimulation lead to increased primary school enrollment rates, lowered primary school enrollment ages, enhanced academic performance, improved retention, and reduced drop-out and repetition rates.

The evidence continues to mount that, from the time of conception, children are profoundly influenced by their early experiences and environment. Indeed, the degree to which they will reach their full potential as adult members of society is significantly shaped during gestation and the early years of life. As we have seen, exposure to a developmentally facilitative environment is critical to an individual's future behavior vis-à-vis participation opportunities. But what are the characteristics of such an environment? What makes a particular setting facilitative?

In essence, the prerequisites for optimal development are met when attention is given to the child's mental, social, emotional, and physical well-being. Unfortunately, such holistic thinking is often hard to achieve. The boundaries of sectors and disciplines that exist within and among entities concerned with the futures of children all too often operate at cross-purposes with the kind of service integration needed to meet a young child's developmental requirements. The health and nutritional status of a child are, of course, important areas of concern; so, too, is the child's progress in attaining social, psychological and cognitive competence.

The interactive relationship of health and nutritional status on the one hand, and social, emotional and cognitive development on the other hand, frequently go unrecognized. While good health and nutrition undergird psychosocial development, the converse proposition is also true. Social, psychological and cognitive growth contribute to a child's health and nutritional status. The young child's development occurs as a result of many productive *transactions* between child and caregivers. These transactions enable the child to form basic ideas about objects and spatial relations, to develop language abilities, and to acquire a host of interpersonal skills including the ability to interact with and make demands upon caregivers and family members. As with any successful transaction, all parties contribute to and gain something from the exchange.

The infant or young child offers a range of reflexive, auditory, visual and affective capabilities to the caregiver. In turn, the caregiver responds. The product is the growth of love bonds that shape the relationship between the participants and enhance the child's emotional and cognitive development. Such bonds also serve as an impetus to respond to the child's health and nutritional needs. It is difficult to erect neat divisions between a child's physical state and cognitive development. Children who are malnourished or chronically ill are both physically and intellectually disadvantaged. Studies show that young children who suffer from protein-energy malnutrition (PEM) are likely to have impaired physical growth and brain development. Such children often have attentional deficits and are less motivated to respond to and engage in productive transactions with the adults present in their environments.

Similarly, inadequacies of iodine intake (either prenatally or postnatally) have been shown to cause neurological disorders, deafness and reduced intelligence in young children. Other micronutrient deficiencies also impair a child's development. Both iron and vitamin-A deficiencies, for example, impede brain growth and are associated with impaired intellectual abilities. This delicate interplay between the psychosocial and physical aspects of child development can be seen quite clearly in three bodies of research. The first deals with the efficacy of intervention strategies designed to meet the needs of children who are both nutritionally and intellectually vulnerable.

When young malnourished children with developmental deficits are exposed to both nutritional supplementation and intellectual stimulation, they tend to benefit more than when the treatment consists either of supplementation alone or cognitively oriented interventions without nutritional inputs. The second body of studies to illustrate the interplay between physical and psychosocial development relates to the sensory stimulation of infants and young children and the effect it has on physical well-being. Touch deprivation in babies, for example, has been linked to digestive problems, marasmus and even, in cases of severe deprivation, death. Studies on low birth-weight babies show that even a brief regimen of massage (three 15-minute sessions per day over a ten-day period) leads to increased weight gain *without* additional caloric intake.

Finally, research on the effects of breast-feeding also highlights the intimate linkages between physical and psychosocial well-being. Nutritionally, breast milk and colostrum provide all the protein and nutrients infants require. The skin-to-skin contact of breast-feeding as well as the milk itself may transfer immunizing bacteria and antibodies to infants. Furthermore, the act of breast-feeding with its holding, touching, eye-to-eye contact, talking and responding, enhances the infant's emotional resiliency and psychosocial development. As we have seen, the pattern of children's physical, cognitive and emotional maturation is a byproduct of their health, nutrition, and psychosocial status.

Children develop rapidly and in a highly differentiated way. Thus, it is necessary, in attempting to identify the factors that *enable or inhibit* child development, to examine the needs of young children in terms of specific age subgroups and developmental factors. There are four discrete waystations on a child's journey toward maturity: the prenatal period; toddlerhood (which runs from birth through age two); the young child stage (which covers ages three through five); and the optimal period of primary school entrance (ages six through eight). At each of these stages, we will examine how an array of nutritional, health, and environmental factors constitute the chalk that is writing on a virtual *tabula rasa*.

The Prenatal Period

During this period, the mother serves as gatekeeper. Fetal development is entirely dependent on whether she admits into her own system those elements that are essential to a healthy pregnancy. These include adequate nutrition, a relative absence of stress, timely medical care, and sufficient education to make informed choices on behalf of her future son or daughter. Nutrition plays a critical role in fetal development. When nutrition is adequate, the newborn's intellectual capacity is strengthened.

Research in developing countries indicates that when malnourished women receive protein supplements in the last trimester of their pregnancy, their children's cognitive functioning is improved. Such benefits are observed to age six or seven. Furthermore, when maternal supplementation involves both protein and kilocalories and is extended to include the neonate, then effects can be sustained into adolescence and even young adulthood. Maternal malnutrition and inadequate weight gain during pregnancy increase the risk of having a low birth-weight baby. Such infants are more likely than other newborns to have hearing, vision, or learning problems, each of which carries significant implications for limiting individual ability to take advantage of available participation opportunities.

A study undertaken in the US found that 15 percent of *very* low birth-weight children and nearly 5 percent of low birth-weight infants require special education services, compared to 4.3 percent of children born at normal birth weight. Other investigations suggest that low birth weight results in subtle cognitive and language acquisition delays as well as differences in IQ. In one recent study, investigators found that very premature or very low birth-weight infants were at significant risk for grade retention. By age nine, 32 percent of this US sample had already repeated a grade. When maternal malnutrition takes the form of iodine or iron deficiency, the fetus suffers an assault to its well-being. Iodine deficiency leads to stillborn births or newborn deaths at the rate of five to ten children per 1,000. Additionally, one in five maternal deaths is linked to iron deficiency in developing countries.

Iron deficiency during the prenatal period is also associated with premature birth and low birth weight. Infants born too soon or too small often face serious and fatal threats. Indeed, low birth-weight infants die during the neonatal period at a rate 40 times that of other infants. When considering the nutritional status of mothers, one must also consider the beliefs and practices of the culture that affect the quantities and types of food expectant mothers will eat. A number of sociocultural factors play an important role in malnutrition. Such factors go beyond the abundance and availability of food.

For instance, in some countries special food taboos exist for pregnant women. Expectant mothers choose to be malnourished. They realize that if they eat less, they will have a smaller baby. And, if they have a smaller baby, their own chances for survival will be greater, even if their baby dies. This logic is driven by a belief that it is the mother's survival, and not the baby's, that will ensure continuity of the species. Maternal levels of stress also play an important role in fetal development. Where stress is high, labor is often difficult and births are more likely to be premature. Stress increases the secretion of adrenaline and cortisone which pass through the placenta. Researchers hypothesize that such problems are related to the effects of elevated levels of these hormones on the fetus.

Another source of maternal stress during the prenatal period is an unwanted pregnancy. In one study of an international sample of mothers and newborns, difficult labor and premature delivery were markedly present for women experiencing an unwanted pregnancy, even when they had access to adequate prenatal care. The importance of prenatal medical care is highlighted by a growing body of research. Studies undertaken in the US and elsewhere suggest that women who obtain prenatal care have infants with higher birth weight than women without such services. This finding is true regardless of other background characteristics. Adequate prenatal care may well serve as the first critical participation opportunity available in the life cycle. When quality care is available, mothers receive vital nutritional supplements, appropriate information and some of the emotional support needed for a successful pregnancy.

Prenatal care may take many forms. Medical clinics, peer support groups or trained traditional birth attendants can all offer the essential elements of prenatal care if the needed inputs are at their disposal. Environmental variables can work to enable or inhibit mothers' access to prenatal care. Factors such as availability of medical facilities, medication and nutrition supplements; cultural practices or taboos with regard to pregnancy; and the relative isolation of the mother, either help or hinder expectant mothers' access to these vital services.

Fally, an important factor influencing child development during the prenatal period is a mother's schooling. Studies indicate that even modest levels of education (for example, to the level of literacy) equip individuals with the knowledge and skills to use medical resources more efficiently. This suggests a greater propensity on the part of educated expectant mothers to avail themselves of prenatal care including nutritional monitoring. Of course, educational levels also correlate to household incomes which, in turn, confer the economic wherewithal needed to obtain an adequate diet, housing and health care.

From birth through toddlerhood (0-2 years)

Unlike humans in later stages of life, infants begin the learning process with no prior cognitive experience to guide them. What infants lack in experience, however, they make up for in receptivity. Unique physiological wiring allows healthy infants to learn in months the equivalent of what older learners may take years to master. Such receptivity has one caveat, however. Infants are entirely dependent upon their external surroundings for the nourishment, stimulation and "information" they need to thrive and develop. The extent to which infants and young children receive "inputs" from the external environment, therefore, largely determines their later capacity to learn actively and participate fully in the world around them.

A substantial body of research highlights several inputs which significantly affect the development of infants and toddlers. These include adequate nutrition, physical and sensory stimulation, attachment to a stable caregiver, and maternal education. The evidence that nutritional status exerts a powerful influence on how infants and toddlers develop is quite compelling. Iron deficiency in infancy may cause a permanent loss of IQ later in life (ERIC Clearinghouse on Elementary and Early Childhood Education). Additionally, infant anemia is often the cause of impaired motor development; increased fearfulness; inattentiveness; and reduced social responsiveness (Consultative Group on Early Childhood Care and Development).

Protein-energy malnutrition (PEM) in young children also has a deleterious impact on subsequent developmental outcomes. This condition is associated with reduced play and exploration as well as with increased apathy and irritability. The result is impaired cognitive development. PEM affects the formation of infant synapses and dendrites, thereby impinging upon the child's school readiness and ability to concentrate. Studies suggest that a child without *adequate physical and sensory stimulation* will experience high levels of apathy and, overall, stunted development. Babies ignored on a regular basis become listless and introverted. They withdraw from their external environment which, in turn, leads to stunted psychological and physical development. Indeed, touch deprivation in the early years of life has been linked to physical and emotional problems in later years, including digestive problems, difficulty in maintaining relationships, and even, in severe instances, marasmus.

On the other hand, physical and sensory stimulation can enhance a young child's physical growth, emotional security, resistance to disease, cognitive functioning and coordination. The mechanisms that account for these developmental gains are not fully understood although such stimulation is thought to foster neural development which is not complete at childbirth. Attachment to a stable caregiver significantly contributes to an infant or toddler's psychosocial, cognitive and emotional development. Investigators have found a strong emotional bond between infants and specific caregivers beginning in the infant's sixth month. Such attachment is fostered by a caregiver's ability to attend to the infant's signals and respond promptly and appropriately to the infant's needs. In this fashion the infant recognizes that its signals initiated the response.

Secure attachment is associated with positive emotional, social, and cognitive development as children grow older. Not only do shared emotional relationships between caregiver and child elicit vocalizations and accompanying facial expressions from the adult that are attractive to the child, but such exchanges function as the precursors to language learning. Infants and young children use the caregiver's speech and facial expressions to begin to associate objects and events with words. For optimal development of language skills, however, infants must be in contact with "reasonably nurturant talkers" to talk themselves into language.

With respect to *maternal education*, research indicates that a mother's education correlates with decreased infant mortality rates. A study undertaken in Kerala, India, for example, found that this relationship could be explained by a greater use of available medical services on the part of better schooled women. Another investigation determined that each additional year of a mother's education signified a 9 percent decrease in the mortality rates of her very young children and infants.

The young child

The entire process by which a child develops is best understood as a continuum rather than as a series of discrete stages. Junctions rather than disjunctures typify the child's expanding ability to engage in complex transactions and to make sense of chaotic environments. In keeping with this view of developmental continuity, the young child's needs between ages three to five represent an extension of the child's requirements for healthy growth and development during toddlerhood: adequate nutrition, physical and sensory stimulation, attachment to a stable caregiver, and maternal education. Of course, during these years a child's ability to interact with the environment undergoes dramatic changes. Dependence upon adults diminishes, sense of self evolves, and cognitive skills develop.

Among three- to five-year olds, anemia has been found to cause delays in cognitive and motor development (as is the case with infants). Anemia has also been linked to increased apathy and insecurity in social interactions. In general, malnourished children tend to cope with their condition by self-limiting mental and physical activity, which leads to a spiraling of their cognitive deficits. However, some studies have shown that when physical activity was encouraged among malnourished two- to four-year olds, the children became more active and gained more weight than their less active counterparts. In these investigations, the active group received the same caloric intake as the controls, but they expended 30 percent more calories. Since such activity may well contribute to cognitive as well as physical development, this finding suggests the vast potential of interventions that combine attention to the psychosocial as well as nutritional needs of children.

As with infants, positive interactions with adults continue to be very important to the healthy growth and development of children between ages three and five. Research conducted with children in this age range and adults indicates that when adults initiate and explain tasks that are appropriate to children's needs, the young learners will in turn develop and adapt goal-directed behavior, particularly when the tasks involve cognitive function. The children demonstrate a high level of responsiveness to the adult guidance and instruction that they receive (Saxe, et al., 1987). The implications of this work are profound: cognitive development in very young children is linked to the social interactions they encounter in the learning setting.

When productive interactions with adults are absent from the child's environment, the result is often an underestimation of the young child's ability. Frequently, the child experiences high levels of frustration and diminished self-confidence. Often, the naïveté and pre-causal reasoning exhibited by children of this age group lead parents and preschool caregivers to underestimate their capabilities. The strong, pervasive message of Piagetian theory has been to wait for the logical thought that should emerge between the ages of five and seven before presenting tasks that require logical reasoning skills. New research, however, has suggested that if problems are presented to preschoolers in familiar contexts and do not rely solely on verbal skills, they can be solved. In many cases, preschoolers can "show you the answer" but not "tell you the answer".

Cognitive science research indicates that knowledge acquisition and mastery is very domain-specific during these years. The areas of social interaction, musical ability, and mathematical reasoning skills, in particular, are unevenly developed in some three-to-fives. Thus, a child may speak in complex sentences and possess ample vocabulary, yet be unable to recognize that water poured from a tall, thin container to a short, wide container retains the same volume of water. If the development of problem-solving skills and knowledge transfer are important to long-term human capacity development, then it is at this age that many important cognitive strategies can be introduced that foster these outcomes.

In general, interactive learning is particularly important as a vehicle for the development of new cognitive abilities. This view builds on an ever-increasing body of research which demonstrates that learning is the process of knowledge construction. Such construction, however, is itself knowledge dependent, and often the product of domain-specific problem-solving strategies which allow the young learner to elaborate upon and extend what is already known. Interactivity is essential because knowledge acquisition is intimately connected to a situation which enables young children to embed their learning in an organizing structure. As they actively interpret and process information, they construct new knowledge for themselves. Such construction occurs within a web of social interactions.

Key components of the interactive learning process include opportunities for children to derive conclusions and formulate questions independently; to learn through social interactions and play; to acquire knowledge based on individual motivation and interests; and to learn through a repeating cycle of awareness-exploration-inquiry-utilization.

The primary school entrant

The beginning of primary school marks an important transition for young learners. They must, simultaneously, leave the insular world of home and perhaps a child-care program while responding to dramatic new social and cognitive demands that are foisted upon them. As school-aged children begin to develop sophisticated thinking, problem-solving and communications abilities, the prime focus of attention shifts to social relationships and the acquisition of basic life competencies, particularly in the areas of literacy and numeracy.

The emergence of symbolic thought during these years allows children to link abstract numbers and symbols with concrete values and sounds. As their capacity for abstract reasoning grows, children are able to view themselves, their actions, and their own thinking process. The potential for metacognitive activity and emerging new cognitive skills allow children to solve a variety of problems, ranging from the use and counting of money, to the responsible caretaking of younger siblings. At this stage, children's ability to access and create new participation opportunities begins to depend more and more upon their prior access to such crucial inputs as nutrition, sensory stimulation, and positive interactions with adults.

However, research indicates that even if such vital inputs were lacking during early childhood, consistent access to, and use of, nutritional supplements, active learning environments, and supportive adult and peer networks can enable previously deprived children to participate more fully in the world around them. Among children entering primary school, poor health, hunger caused by short-term fasting, poor nutrition and inadequate psychosocial support all constitute significant risk factors. They threaten the development of the youngster's Active Learning Capacity (ALC) which can be defined as the child's propensity and ability to interact with and take optimal advantage of the full complement of resources offered by any formal or informal learning environment.

Such nutritional problems as iron deficiency, for example, are associated with lethargy and impaired intellectual performance. Investigators have found that iron deficiency in school-aged children is correlated with a host of problems such as reduced alertness, attention, concentration, intellectual performance, and interest in the immediate environment. Children with deficient iron stores often display increased irritability, and poor achievement as captured by their performance on tests and promotion rates. Many children in developing countries arrive in school while engaged in short-term fasting. This is particularly common when familial dietary practices include one relatively large meal daily which is offered at midday or late in the afternoon. By the time school begins, the child who has not breakfasted may well be in the midst of a short-term fast which can last from 15 to 20 hours.

The attendant hunger adversely affects attention, interest, and learning. A great number of investigations conclusively demonstrate that social and environmental factors influence intellectual ability. Today, there is an emerging consensus that one such environmental factor is protein-energy malnutrition (PEM) which is estimated to affect 210 million school-aged children worldwide. The presence of PEM has been negatively associated with such indicators as cognitive test scores, school performance, verbal comprehension, and attention span. PEM wields its influence in two ways. When it occurs prior to school enrollment, the condition appears to reduce many basic aptitudes associated with satisfactory schooling outcomes.

Current PEM diminishes a child's ability to concentrate and respond to present-day situations. Activity levels, so essential to exploratory behavior and the construction of knowledge, are reduced. At the same time, irritability, listlessness and distractibility appear to intensify. Studies of children in Kenya and the Philippines showed that good nutritional status was a more important indicator of cognitive ability and school performance than socioeconomic status or academic quality. Health status also exerts significant influence on a child's ALC and, hence on school success. Acute respiratory infection, severe measles, and diarrheal disease (frequently associated with vitamin-A deficiency) are linked to school absenteeism and low rates of school completion. Blindness, which can result from severe vitamin-A deficiency, precludes school participation in many developing countries.

Among school-aged children, parasitic infections are very common. Prevalence data suggest that in some parts of the developing world this condition is virtually universal among school-aged children. A growing body of research on the effects of such infections on the lives of children points to impaired health, stunted growth, diminished nutritional status, and reduced cognitive function. The impact of parasitic infection on schooling outcomes manifests itself through high levels of school absenteeism, under-enrollment, and heightened attrition.

Depending upon the type of parasitic infection, symptoms that have a bearing on the child's schooling experience include growth retardation, chronic colitis, iron deficiency anemia, impaired psychomotor development, fever, weakness, lassitude, muscular pain, nausea, vomiting, diarrhea, and fatigue.

Instructional quality is also a critical factor in any examination of how schools contribute to human capacity development. While there is a vast research literature on how instructional characteristics influence learning, there is also consensus on key points. Task- or problem-oriented instruction, opportunities for individual, small-group and collective work, inquiry-based learning, structured development of metacognitive strategies and integration of several knowledge domains are acknowledged to stimulate active participation in the learning process

These elements enable the learner to construct new knowledge in social contexts. In turn, this lays a foundation for developing the skills needed to solve novel problems, transfer concepts to new settings and construct new knowledge that builds on what the child already knows. These competencies are, of course, the fundamental building blocks of human capacity development. They constitute a citizen's "tools of the trade" for securing a livelihood, promoting family development, and contributing to civic betterment in an era of rapid change.

If human capacity development is the goal, then the major challenge confronting those who make policies that affect the lives of young children is how to *bundle inputs* so that they are affordable, sustainable, and "meaningful" in terms of the influence they exert on a child's ability to both access and create participation opportunities. Inputs that bear on the course of a child's development are present at many different levels of a societal structure. Bronfenbrenner's Ecological Model of Human Development provides a highly useful framework for examining both the web of inputs essential to child development and the policy environment needed to ensure that these necessary inputs will be forthcoming.

The model describes the individual as an interdependent part of a larger ecological system. The developing person resides within nested concentric structures, each interacting with the other. The model identifies four structures in particular:

— The microsystem, or the context in which individuals experience a pattern of activities, roles, and interpersonal relationships. For children this includes their home and relationships with parents, siblings, and other caregivers. As children develop, the microsystem expands to include school and those who teach them.

— The mesosystem comprises the interrelations between two or more settings in which an individual actively participates. For young children, the mesosystem defines the interactions among parents, siblings, other caregivers, and later on, their teachers.

— The exosystem describes settings that do not involve individuals as active participants, but which, nonetheless, influence their development. For the child the exosystem can include the parents' workplace and economic opportunities, the family's network of social support, as well as the policies and practices of local governing bodies.

— The macrosystem refers to the factors that shape or could shape the form and content of the other systems described above. With respect to early childhood development in low-income countries, the macrosystem is the policy framework that offers a blueprint for programming to support the comprehensive development of young children.

As Bronfenbrenner's model suggests, child development may be *endogenous* (i.e., a natural outgrowth of a family or community structure) or *exogenous* (i.e. conceived, implemented or funded by actors outside an individual's immediate family or community circle). An integrated, holistic approach to child development would entail concern for *practices* (primarily in the family setting), *programs* (generally delivered—although not necessarily conceived—in the community setting) and *policies* (usually the product of regional or national strategies and deliberations). The challenge is to build the necessary connective tissue so that practices, programs and policies come together seamlessly in ways that expand the number of participation opportunities a young child is likely to access and create over the course of a lifetime.

One way to promote the necessary articulation among these three spheres of influence on a child's development is to apply a set of criteria to determine the *cohesiveness, efficacy* and *adequacy* of proposed interventions. The Three-C Framework (for continuity, comprehensiveness, and coordination) is such a criterion-based assessment approach.

Continuity: It refers to the importance of planning and implementing specific strategies to sustain the gains a child makes as a result of policies, programs, and practices that are introduced to promote healthy growth and development. Investigators have determined, for example, that long-term benefits to US children who participate in Head Start, a comprehensive early childhood development program, are curtailed if similar interventions are not maintained in later years. Studies now reveal that children's cognitive gains drop off sharply by the time they reach the third grade if the tailored, intensive interventions provided in Head Start are not supported in later years. Unlike inoculations which must be administered only once to build immunity, children need interventions that promote and sustain their development as they move from one stage to another, and from one learning setting to another.

Comprehensiveness: It relates to the mix of services across programs, and the ability of this mix to foster and sustain children's development over time. Comprehensiveness is that aspect of a program that allows it to respond to the needs of children across developmental domains. When a program is comprehensive, attention is given to the child's physical, cognitive and psychosocial development. Children's lives are intertwined with the people and institutions that surround them. Participation opportunities that address the needs of the people and institutions in a child's microsystem—whether parents, siblings, caregivers, or schools—can reflect and support the complex interactions among children, families, and the community. Comprehensiveness reflects the belief that child development cannot be broken up into separate domains.

Coordination: It refers not only to the integration of program activities across domains but also to the integration of a program with respect to the environment in which it operates. In this sense, coordination focuses attention on a program's ecology.

Implications for the Practice of Partagogy

Partagogy is a new science of learning that is essential for optimal human *capacity* (as opposed to human resource) development. Partagogy is relevant throughout the lifespan, since its goal is to help individuals over the course of their lives to develop the skills and knowledge needed to access available participation opportunities and create new ones. The skills and knowledge fostered by partagogy are crucial for the creation of participation opportunities across four separate yet interrelated domains: securing a livelihood; promoting family development; protecting the environment; and contributing to civil society or community development. Partagogy's concern with participation opportunities stems from a view of human capacity development as the byproduct of participation opportunities that are both available and accessed.

Available participation opportunities represent the set of inputs that lead to human capacity development. The output of human capacity development can be expressed as the sum of (1) those participation opportunities accessed by individuals; and (2) the new participation opportunities created in the course of such engagements. Partagogy has both a methodological foundation and a content basis—in contrast to andragogy or pedagogy which are neutral with respect to the knowledge, skills and behaviors they seek to develop in learners. The methodology and content associated with partagogy reflect research findings on the factors that enable or inhibit participation behaviors linked to human capacity development.

In relating the notion of partagogy to the early years of an individual's life, six major conclusions readily emerge. First, the period between conception and age eight is critical in terms of setting the stage for an individual's future participation behaviors. Enrollment in and completion of primary schooling, for example, are tied to experiences that occur in early life. As detailed in the following chapter, schooling, in turn, significantly affects labor force participation, an individual's ability to promote family development, and such outwardly-oriented behaviors as participation in civic affairs or environmental action. Furthermore, secure bonding in a child's early years is essential for the development of self-confidence and the belief that one's actions and behaviors matter. This belief is linked to participation in civic affairs, community development and environmentally responsible actions.

Second, a partagogical approach to early childhood development depends upon creating new competencies, attitudes and behaviors on the part of adults who hold responsibility for programs and policies with the potential to shape a young child's environment. If one were to attempt to coin a catch phrase that best expresses the quintessential imperative for operationalizing the partagogical approach to early childhood development, it might be "facilitation through integration." In other words, the facilitation of a young child's development occurs optimally when there is an integration of services that promote the child's mental, social, emotional and physical well-being. Such integration requires planners and implementors to develop new skills that lead to the intersectoral design and coordination of activities.

New attitudes are also essential in order to willingly forego the comfort of traditional ministerial arrangements and relationships. However, without the skills and attitudes conducive to an abandonment of this zone of comfort, facilitation through integration can never be achieved. Third, from a methodological perspective, a partagogical approach to early childhood development requires that young children and the significant adults in their lives be given the opportunity to construct their own knowledge in social settings. In short, it is not only young children for whom a socio-constructivist approach to growth and development is essential.

The adults or older siblings who care for them must also have the opportunity to develop metacognitive skills that facilitate the solution of novel problems and the transfer of knowledge to new settings and situations. The implications of this assertion are far reaching since they suggest a whole new set of training requirements for teachers and other paid child development workers. Such professionals need to understand not only how children learn best, but also how to communicate the essentials of child development in ways that are partagogically sound for adults. Thus, for example, the oft-delivered talk on nutrition or child development would fall by the wayside to be replaced by problem- and discussion-oriented outreach to caregivers.

Small-group work would become a feature of many interactions among peers, regardless of whether the peers are adults or children. In other words, the socio-constructivist orientation deemed desirable in promoting child development would also constitute the framework for promoting caregiver development. Thus, modeling, coaching and scaffolding, the core skills of cognitive apprenticeships, would be the techniques of choice for helping caregivers acquire an integrated set of child development skills. Similarly, guided practice and reflection would be suitable techniques for enabling adults and older siblings to make productive observations about the young children for whom they care.

Then, on the basis of these observations, learners might select from among alternative strategies those actions most conducive to supporting a young child's healthy growth and development. Exploration, another approach to learning associated with the cognitive apprenticeship model, could also be used to develop a caregiver's ability not only to solve child development problems that are externally identified, but also to gain self-confidence in formulating the problems to be solved. The advantage of such methodological consistency (using similar techniques with both caregivers and "care receivers") is twofold. Caregivers become more motivated to use the approach when they themselves experience the growth and learning it engenders. The method also enhances the learner's self-confidence and ability to successfully confront new child development challenges.

A fourth conclusion to emerge from this analysis is that the specific content of a partagogically-oriented curriculum geared to caregivers must be drawn from multiple domains. Included in such a curriculum would be broad problem-solving skills related to maternal nutrition; child nutrition; prenatal care; prevention of unwanted pregnancy; and techniques for promoting the sensory, cognitive, and emotional development of young children. Explicit instruction on why, when and how to access local services that promote child development would also be extended. In this manner, adults would develop the necessary self-confidence to avail themselves of these resources (and participation opportunities) in a timely and appropriate fashion.

A partagogical curriculum might also seek to improve a mother's basic literacy and numeracy skills when deficits in these areas are significant. Throughout the curriculum, both domain-specific knowledge and metacognitive skills would be explicitly developed with an eye toward creating strategies that promote the transfer of knowledge to new settings. A fifth conclusion arising from the present discussion is that a child's transition to primary school involves two important processes: readying the child for school and readying school for the child. For the child, readiness is a product not only of cognitive, social, and emotional development, but also a reflection of health and nutritional status.

For the school, readiness involves the capacity to incorporate and build upon a child's previous experience. Since new knowledge is constructed in social settings from existing knowledge (the essence of socio-constructivism), a partogogical approach to working with children would call for moving from the known to the unknown in terms of language, patterns of relationships, abilities and knowledge. In many developing countries this recommendation would translate into greater use of the vernacular, a modified mirroring of traditional practices for teaching children new skills, and greater reliance on folklore (in particular, songs, games, stories and local cultural festivities).

Similarly, there would be an increased concern with the erection of bridges between abstract, theoretical thought, on the one hand, and activities that are part of a child's daily life, on the other. Heightened attention would be paid to getting the school ready for the child by systematically building on the knowledge, relationships, traditions, and practices which comprise the fabric of each school entrant's life. Early childhood development initiatives would be viewed as valid in their own right, as important investments in human capacity development rather than frilly initiatives designed only to prepare the child for primary school. The final conclusion that can be drawn from this discussion of the link between early childhood development and partagogy is that no single service delivery model or approach is definitively best under all circumstances.

Rather, there is a broad range of acceptable options depending on costs, needs, and preferences. One program model is the direct delivery of services to children through home day care, integrated child development centers (in or out of the workplace), preschools, and the downward extension of primary school. Another alternative is to improve the skills of caregivers whether parents, siblings, members of the extended family, or adults outside the kinship group. Home visits, parental education, mass media, and child-to-child outreach have all been successfully employed in low-income countries to reach caregivers. Activities that improve the quality of home-to-school transition, whether home- or center-based, would be essential in light of the importance that has been attached in this discussion to the creation of settings that enable children to use what they already know to construct new knowledge.

The value of any such program, regardless of type or venue, must be viewed as a function of the degree to which it promotes a child's Active Learning Capacity as defined earlier. The essential requirement for all programs concerned with home-to-school transition is that they offer young children structured opportunities to engage in problem-solving and active, inquiry-based learning. Such opportunities should be combined with attention to the health and nutrition status of children as well as their level of short-term hunger. This mix of concerns can be responded to in conventional day care centers as well as in home-based programs. The promotion of good parenting skills may also make it possible for these requirements to be met in any child's home environment.

Training and social promotion directed toward caregivers may be highly effective in helping young children acquire the necessary foundation for lifelong participation in activities related to promoting family development, earning a living, protecting the environment and contributing to civic life. Such training, however, should allow for face-to-face contact in group settings, in keeping with the constructivist underpinnings of partagogy. Mediated communication (radio, pamphlets or photo-comics) can complement, extend and reinforce such highly interpersonal encounters.

INDEX

American Association of Higher Education (AAHE) 100
Andragogy 279
Associationism 21

Bottom-up strategic processing 213

Campell Interest and Skill Survey (CISS) 28
Choreographed differentiation 125
Class brainstorming 46
Cognitive apprenticeship 273
Collaborative instructional contexts 193
Common Essential Learning 35
Computer technology 75
Cortex 203
Curriculum knowledge 39

Design experiments 200
Developmental readiness 193

Egalitarian setting 260
Environmental stewardship 278
English as a Second Language (ESL) 5

Fundamentals quizzes 110
Hand-held calculator 56
HCI methods 196
Home base seats 138
Homogeneous classrooms 121
Human geography 261
Human technology 72

Ill-defined problems 269
Improvisational differentiation 125
Independent learning 90
Individual differences 194
Information-driven society 249
Inquiry-based learning 293
Intellectual disabilities 193
Inter-denominational schools 260
Intonation 16

K-12 classrooms, 199
K-12 curricula 40
K-12 learners 200
Kindergarten 46
Knowledge-skill-attitude 201

Language modes-listening 40
Leapfrogging" 248
Learner-centered design or LCD 199
Longstanding economic barriers 251

Malnourished children 288
Maternal malnutrition 283
Modules 205
Moral reasoning 87

Multiple livelihood activities 251
Myers-Briggs Type Indicator (MBTI) 28

Native Culture 7
Non-adult education 275
Norman' model 199
Numeracy 50

Partagogy 278
Positive learning climates 194
Problem-solving strategies 273
Protein-energy malnutrition (PEM) 281

Radical Behaviorism 20
Reading boxes 125
Rising-falling intonation 16

Saskatchewan's 37
Scaffolding 273
Sensory feedback 213
Socio-constructivism 300
Socio-constructivist theories 275
Strategic thinking 190
Superiority effect 207

Task cards 131
Taylor's principles 256
Teacher-prepared discussion guide 43
Technological Literacy 33, 69
Toddlerhood 282
Top-Down Processing 216
Traditional curricula 209
Two-way communications 193

Village-level economies 250
Virtual groupings 248
Vygotsky's theories 273

Wireless" technology 248